# ENGAGING INFANTS

# ENGAGING INFANTS

## Embodied Communication in Short-term Infant–Parent Therapy

*Frances Thomson-Salo*

LONDON AND NEW YORK

First published 2018 by Karnac Books Ltd.

Published 2018 by Routledge
2 Park Square, Milton Park, Abingdon, Oxon OX14 4RN
711 Third Avenue, New York, NY 10017, USA

*Routledge is an imprint of the Taylor & Francis Group, an informa business*

Copyright © 2018 to Frances Thomson-Salo

The right of Frances Thomson-Salo to be identified as the author of this work has been asserted in accordance with §§77 and 78 of the Copyright Design and Patents Act 1988.

All rights reserved. No part of this book may be reprinted or reproduced or utilised in any form or by any electronic, mechanical, or other means, now known or hereafter invented, including photocopying and recording, or in any information storage or retrieval system, without permission in writing from the publishers.

Notice:
Product or corporate names may be trademarks or registered trademarks, and are used only for identification and explanation without intent to infringe.

British Library Cataloguing in Publication Data

A C.I.P. for this book is available from the British Library

ISBN 9781782205913 (pbk)

Edited, designed and produced by The Studio Publishing Services Ltd
www.publishingservicesuk.co.uk
email: studio@publishingservicesuk.co.uk

# CONTENTS

*ACKNOWLEDGEMENTS*   vii

*ABOUT THE AUTHOR*   ix

*INTRODUCTION*   xi

### PART I
### ENGAGING THE INFANT IN INFANT–PARENT THERAPY

CHAPTER ONE
Recognising the infant as subject   3

CHAPTER TWO
What an infant brings   25

### PART II
### ENGAGING INFANTS IN PERINATAL SETTINGS

CHAPTER THREE
Infants and their parents in the perinatal period   41

## CHAPTER FOUR
Infants with young parents　　　　　　　　　　　　　　　67

## CHAPTER FIVE
Infants and their parents in neonatal intensive care units　　81

## PART III
### ENGAGING INFANTS IN PAEDIATRIC SETTINGS

## CHAPTER SIX
Infants and their parents in paediatric settings　　　　　105

## CHAPTER SEVEN
Infants and their parents in therapy groups　　　　　　127

## CHAPTER EIGHT
Relating to infant and parent in the context　　　　　　149
of family violence

## PART IV
### TOWARDS UNDERSTANDING SUCCESSFUL OUTCOMES

## CHAPTER NINE
Countertransference in infant–parent therapy　　　　　161

## CHAPTER TEN
The therapeutic alliance, the presence of the　　　　　181
therapist, and transformational moments

## CHAPTER ELEVEN
Responding to infants and interpreting transference　　193

## CHAPTER TWELVE
Revisiting mechanisms of change in infant–parent therapy　207

*AFTERWORD*　　　　　　　　　　　　　　　　　215

*REFERENCES*　　　　　　　　　　　　　　　　　217

*INDEX*　　　　　　　　　　　　　　　　　　　227

# ACKNOWLEDGEMENTS

I especially acknowledge Campbell Paul, long term colleague who has unstintingly shared many insights. I also thank others who have shared their experience including Dilys Daws, Juliet Hopkins, Brigid Jordan, Sarah Jones, Ann Morgan, Sue Morse, Michele Meehan, Meredith Banks, and Bev O'Sullivan.

I am grateful to those families I have known who have enabled other families to be helped; all have been de-identified or composite vignettes given, with as little background as possible. I hope that if any one recognises themselves they will feel they have been described in a respectful way.

I thank the following publishers for kind permission to draw on previously published papers:

Chapters One, Three, and Six draw in part on Thomson Salo (2007). Recognizing the infant as subject in infant–parent psychotherapy. *International Journal of Psychoanalysis, 88*: 961–979.

Chapter 1 also draws in part on Thomson-Salo & Paul (2015). Looking forward, look back: hospital-based infant–parent therapy with Chinese families living in Australia. *Australasian Journal of Psychotherapy, 33*: 35–52.

Chapters One and Two draw in part on the paper Thomson-Salo et al. (1999). "Free to be playful": direct therapeutic work with infants.

*Infant Observation Journal. The International Journal of Infant Observation and Its Applications, 3*: 47–62.

Chapter Two draws in part on Thomson-Salo & Paul (2010). Being there: the "something more" that the baby brings to the therapeutic process. *Australian Association for Infant Mental Health Newsletter, 23*: 1–4.

Chapter Two includes some ideas from an earlier paper, Thomson-Salo & Paul (2011). Reconsidering parental sexuality, and infantile sensual excitement and greed: what is lost in infant mental health without these concepts? *The Signal, 19*: 7–12; a fuller version has been published in 2017: Understanding the sexuality of infants within caregiving relationships in the first year. *Psychoanalytic Dialogues, 27*: 320–327.

Chapters Two and Ten also draw in part on Thomson-Salo & Paul (2015). Why do infants laugh? A transformational moment in the therapeutic encounter. *Australian Association for Infant Mental Health Newsletter, 28*: 2–4.

Chapter Four draws in part on Thomson-Salo (2014a). A preventive attachment intervention with adolescent mothers: elaboration of the intervention. In: R. Emde & M. Leuzinger-Bohleber. (Eds.), *Early Parenting and the Prevention of Disorder: Psychoanalytic Research at Interdisciplinary Frontiers* (pp. 343–357). London: Karnac.

Chapter Five draws in part on the chapter, Thomson-Salo (2014c). Care of the long-stay infant and parents. In: R. J. Martin, A. A. Fanaroff, & M. C. Walsh (Eds.), *Neonatal–Perinatal Medicine, Volume 1*, (10th edn) (pp. 642–646). Philadelphia, PA: Elsevier.

Chapter Six draws in part on Thomson-Salo & Paul (2014). Levels of feedback, levels of interaction. *The Australian Association of Infant Mental Health Newsletter, 27*: 6–7.

Chapter Seven draws on a 1994 talk I gave at the Sydney Institute for Psychoanalysis, *Therapeutic Interventions in Postnatal Depression: Groupwork,* and on the 1997 paper co-authored with C. Paul, Infant-led innovations in a mother baby therapy group. *Journal of Child Psychotherapy, 23*: 219–244.

Chapter Eight draws in part on Thomson-Salo & Paul. (Eds.) (2008). *The Baby as Subject.* Melbourne: Stonnington Press.

Chapter Eleven draws in part on Thomson-Salo (2015). Interpreting in the infant transference. *Australian Association for Infant Mental Health Newsletter, 28*: 2–5.

## ABOUT THE AUTHOR

**Frances Thomson-Salo**, Associate Professor, trained in the UK as an adult and child psychoanalyst and is a member of the British Psychoanalytical Society and of the Australian Psychoanalytical Society, of which she is a past president. She is a training analyst, and was overall chair of the Committee on Women and Psychoanalysis for the International Psychoanalytical Association from 2009–2015. She is Series Editor for Karnac's "Psychoanalysis and Women" series and a member of the Editorial Board of the *International Journal of Psychoanalysis*.

(I)n some way or other (babies) look around for other ways of getting something of themselves back from the environment.

Winnicott, 1971, p. 112

# INTRODUCTION

The concept of the infant as subject arose from engaging with infants in paediatric settings, in-patient and out-patient. The book's title, *Engaging Infants*, encapsulates this approach: the *Embodied Communication* of the subtitle refers to therapists intuitively using embodied communication to understand infant and parent to bring about change in each and in their relationship (Shai & Belsky, 2011; Trevarthen, 1998; Tronick et al., 1998). The book's focus is mainly on infants in the first year to convey an effective way-of-being with infant and parent, and the transformations for infant and parents do not rely only on verbal processes, which may not fully capture interactive reflective and communicative processes.

This approach views an infant as entitled to an intervention in their own right within the infant–parent relationship, in the family setting if possible. It has extended to a baby-led care approach in a maternity hospital; with some infants spending many months in a neonatal intensive care unit (NICU) they may benefit from infant mental health input.

This book, primarily a clinical one, shares ways of engaging infants and their parents, what a therapist might say, do, and reflect on. As I note in Chapter Seven on the mother–infant therapy group from the early 1990s, we had found our way to embodied communication in advance of much of the literature, and before that time it was being used in work in a paediatric hospital (Chapter Six). The role and efficacy of embodied communication as an integral part of the process in intervening with the infant–parent relationship, not just with parent or infant, is a point that is increasingly made (Zeanah et al., 2005). In recent years, with increased time pressures I am continually aware of how little may need to be done to shift the developmental trajectory of an infant; a brief relational intervention may often produce clinically significant change. The principles and clinical notions described are relevant for those working in settings where most interventions are likely to be short term, while recognising the limits of what may be possible in brief interventions. These also show the importance from an early age of infant–infant interaction and the infant as therapist, as well as other clinical notions. I cover a broad sweep of presentations. I hope these principles and concepts generalise to a map of the field.

\* \* \*

In Part I, Chapter One sets out aspects of a psychodynamic approach, followed in Chapter Two by outlining several factors that infants bring to an intervention, including their sexuality. In Parts II and III, several chapters cover specialised settings in which intervention takes place. In Part II, *Engaging Infants in Perinatal Settings*, Chapter Three, I describe brief interventions in a maternity hospital engaging infants and their parents, including high risk populations such as those with anxiety and depression, and those who have experienced trauma and lived borderline experience or that of mental illness. In Chapter Four, I describe engaging young parents and their infants, and in Chapter Five discuss how most the parents in a NICU feel traumatised, which impacts on the emotional relationship with their infants, and there is often a need for psychodynamic exploration before these difficulties can be modulated. Infant–parent therapy in paediatric contexts is considered in Part III, such as in hospital settings (Chapter Six). I then discuss engaging infants in long-term and short-term groups, in particular in a slow open mother–infant therapy group where what an infant may contribute to other infants and their mothers as well as to their own mother, emerged into view (Chapter Seven). In Chapter Eight I discuss relating to infant and parents in the context of family violence. In Part IV, *Towards Understanding Successful Outcomes*, I touch on cases where I felt something was missed or felt I failed (Chapter Nine), to think about how a therapist listens to countertransference to guide in intervening. In Chapter Ten, I discuss the importance of what therapist factors such as authenticity and playfulness in the therapist–patient relationship contribute to the *therapeutic alliance*, including the alliance an infant has with a therapist, and briefly consider *transformational moments*.

While vignettes throughout illustrate this way of intervening as well as some change factors, Chapter Eleven focuses on the transference that infants develop to a therapist and in a fuller vignette how a therapist might respond to an infant and interpret the relationship they make. In the final chapter, "Revisiting mechanisms of change in infant–parent therapy", I review some factors I see as contributing to this approach being effective.

# PART I

# ENGAGING THE INFANT IN INFANT–PARENT THERAPY

CHAPTER ONE

# Recognising the infant as subject

This book describes a therapeutic approach with a focus on interventions that are infant-led. Engaging infants engages the change processes. The therapeutic interventions I describe are mostly short-term when infant and parent are referred in the perinatal period and the first three years. The infant is viewed as a person in his or her own right and is involved in the intervention, in an approach that upholds the rights of infants. In recognising an infant's intentional self from birth (Stern, 1985), this interactive approach with awareness of the infant's theory of mind is likely to contribute to developing the infant's sense of self even if in a small way. An early sense of self crystallises around an infant being treated as a psychological being who possesses a mind so that the infant develops a sense of self and identity through interactions with an adult carer who reflects on his or her mind. Even a single meeting with a therapist can contribute to this.

When describing the interventions, I try to convey the transformational nature of a therapist's embodied communication (Shai & Belsky, 2011) with an infant. In the infants becoming meaningful to the therapist, they usually become more meaningful to their parents; parents often need to first see change in their infants before they can become more reflective. (Reflectiveness is here used as a thoughtful and open way to appreciate feelings and intentions in others as well as in oneself.) Seeing an infant responding to a therapist often triggers a reflective moment for the parent. This way of interacting with an infant can also be successful on those occasions when a therapist needs to intervene with an infant alone, when a parent is not available (see Dee, Chapter Six). What also has the possibility of being transformational are certain aspects of therapist engagement, such as at times accepting being used as needed (Chapter Nine), or at times trying to find a sense of acceptance for parents (in the face of evoked hateful feelings in the therapist), and may be particularly needed in longer term work arising out of evoked childhood hurts that a parent has experienced.

This approach can engage even very young infants with emotional and psychological difficulties. As the clinical interventions described take place mainly in maternity and paediatric settings the intervention is likely to be brief rather than long-term, and the transference to the therapist mainly positive. In the perinatal period, most difficulties are around bonding: the emotional relationships between infants and parents, the parents' relationships with the infant as a separate person, and their relationship with their own mothers. A therapist would try to explore the painful feelings that parents experience that despite their trying to cope with this in the best way they could, they still did not feel bonded to their infant. For frightened and ambivalent parents, experiences in hospital and immediately afterwards may complicate the relationship with their infant, and intervention can change that trajectory.

## Infant–parent therapy

An infant needs to be in a relationship, even a temporary one. Any experience offered by a therapist could give an infant an experience of positive intersubjective relating. The interventions may be very subtle, holding an infant in mind, so he can see himselves in the therapist's eyes. "Being with"—attuned to—the infant as well as with the parents is a core principle of intervention (Thomson-Salo & Paul, 2001), as therapists begin an exploration of "not-knowing" the infant whom they meet for the first time. In parental embodied mentalization (Shai

& Belsky, 2011), the parents have a sense of their infant's communication from "reading" their movement, and therapists do this as well. While the quality of gaze and voice is powerful, a therapist may go beyond that and use touch, in embodied communication. In the intersubjectivity between infant and therapist, infants can understand that a therapist understands.

Understanding the infant becomes a communicative interaction and the process of understanding the infant–parent relationship is an intervention. Therapists observe closely, to try to know the infant in a similar way to how a parent does, to understand the relationship and the problem while trying to look beyond the presenting symptoms or developmental delay to see the whole person of the infant.

A central therapeutic mechanism is trying to understand an infant's experience from her perspective, and conveying to parents and infant something of this understanding that the infant has a mind of her own, and her own experience. The relationship a therapist forms with her is an intervention and putting it into words can act as a powerful change mechanism. Parents generally welcome this intervention, which is likely to increase their reflectiveness as well as the infant's. Responding to the infant as a person can shift the view of an infant as an object, to be fed and cleaned, towards that of an infant as intentional and relationship-seeking.

I have used the word "parents", while aware of an increasing number of kinds of families. Where I have referred to the mother as the primary carer, the father is included in the intervention as often as possible. While many couple relationships function satisfactorily despite temporary stress, many face long term stress. When parents have major long-standing difficulties, they may also need their own therapy or couple therapy so as not to continue to project their difficulties on to an infant whose development is shaped by this.

In engaging with an infant, a therapist usually relates to infant *and* parents in the presence of frightening emotions and fantasies to try and understand them. Close observation of infants underpins this approach (Bick, 1963). As a therapist responds to an infant, this has an impact on the infant's representations, so that the sense of self and agency consolidate more. The parents can see how the therapist recognises their infant and understands the infant's experience, and the infant takes the changes back into the relationship with the parents. The interaction with the infant is a non-verbal communication to parents about their infant's experience, which the therapist may put into a verbal communication.

This approach can be effective with many symptom presentations and most of the vignettes illustrate only the central point I am making. In the interests of space, I only refer briefly to the work of other colleagues in this field apart from the identification of those parental projections that Fraiberg (1975) termed "ghosts in the nursery", by which parents unconsciously contribute to their infant's symptoms, and that are likely to need containment and interpretation. An infant may remind parents of unresolved traumatic experiences of abuse, or a disavowed part of the self, or an unmourned infant who has died, or the infant's illness or disability may increase their ambivalence. A therapist tries to understand how parents' experiences shape their feelings about and behaviour towards their infant, with the infant contributing to interactional difficulties through physical or temperamental characteristics that have a particular meaning for the parents. It needs clinical judgment to decide which collection of projections could remain problematic if not absorbed in an enriching way. (One mother who, when her baby was very little, was reminded of birds attacking an upturned turtle's belly, and at nine months had become a most loving mother.) A therapist, in becoming a container for the projections directed to an infant, aims to disconfirm pathogenic beliefs, withdraw negative and unhelpful projections, and change the parents' representations, to free the infant from the effect of distorting projections. As intrusive projective identification lessens and parents' sensitivity increases, an infant's behaviour changes. Even when an infant appears to be despairing, a single session with a therapist may be enough to reverse this. The vignette that follows is an intervention with a baby who seemed to be on the point of giving up.

### Aimee

Aimee, a six-week-old whose parents thought she was blind, deaf, and autistic, was admitted to hospital. She lay in her cot, her hands very passively on the blanket, her eyes closed, sucking on a dummy, very unresponsive to everyone, her parents silently watching. When the therapist met her, she talked in a whisper to her, and the infant stopped sucking immediately. The therapist then held her hand and stroked it while she talked to her. Aimee began to stroke the therapist's finger and then her own finger and kept stroking them. The therapist was certain the infant heard her, and was aware of her but also was making the other aware of her as separate and thoughtful. After this Aimee became less withdrawn, and her parents no longer related to her as damaged. A home movie of Aimee being bathed showed the water lapping near her face as though her parents had difficulty "seeing" her, whereas the therapist's intervention broke through the effect of the projective cycle. Through the therapist's embodied communication, the parents could see their baby was object-related and processing her experience.

A mother's sadness about her own mother's unavailability may, for example, be evident without being too distressing for her infant. While an infant can perk up within a week of the mother's episode of depression, or serious mental illness easing, or if she responds more contingently, that may not be enough, and an infant is likely to need further input (Zeanah et al., 2005). One-year-old infants of depressed mothers are significantly more likely to be insecurely than securely attached. There is increasing recognition that when parents and infants experience difficulties it is important to treat not only the parents' difficulties; to ensure optimal outcomes the infant and the infant–parent relationship need therapeutic input in addition. But when a parent rejects an infant support is urgently needed to reduce this ambivalence, to lessen the likelihood of infant withdrawal (Guedeney, 1997) from an episode of parental depression.

## *Theoretical framework*

In this approach, each intervention is uniquely shaped for each infant and family but underpinned by the following theoretical framework. This includes knowledge of developmental factors, including attachment, and of interventions that are developmentally appropriate depending on whether an infant is a few weeks or months old. Therapists view an infant as having from birth a mind and an intentional self, who very early recognises his or her own body and feelings as different from those of others, and has a capacity for empathy (understanding and sharing another's feelings). The framework includes a therapist's experience of an infant's subjectivity and capacity for, or difficulties in, self-regulation. It also includes knowledge of the reality factors in the infant's life, and awareness of how trauma in the infant's or parents' history may dysregulate their functioning. It would include awareness of differential parental response to constitutional gender differences. And to more fully understand the meaning of a symptom to infant and parents the approach draws on the analytic cornerstones of awareness of transference–countertransference and unconscious factors (such as projective identification, defences, and ambivalence).

## A psychodynamic approach

In a psychodynamic approach in which a key mechanism is increase in self-understanding, a therapist:

1. is mindful, in finding a port of entry, of the infant's experience and contribution
2. aims to reflect on *countertransference, transference, unconscious factors,* and *on interpreting*
3. has a firm internal setting in his or her mind (Parsons, 2007)
4. and recognises the ubiquity of ambivalence and at times hate in relationships.

## Transference and countertransference

*Transference* is used in the sense of the process by which an infant or parent displaces feelings and ideas on to his or her therapist, which derive from other figures in his or her life, and it is used loosely as his or her emotional attitude towards the therapist. An infant makes a relationship directly with a therapist, who tries to engage with this and to communicate what the infant is feeling and thinking. Even a young infant will engage with a therapist. A therapist, interpreting transference directly or otherwise, works with an infant's positive or negative transferences to him. But when communicating with an infant—especially in the first year—because it is not phrased as an interpretation for an adult, it may not look like working with the transference, although it is an interpretation in the sense of bringing to the fore feelings and thoughts of which infant and parent may not have been previously aware.

*Countertransference*, viewed as the emotional reactions evoked in a therapist, can be used as an important source of information about the internal world of infant and parent, the transference, and the therapeutic relationship, to understand infant and parent. This capacity to be in touch with the feelings of others is likely to include the action of mirror neurons in parents, infant, and therapist, and to be online from birth and to facilitate an infant responding to a therapist's empathy and pleasure in the encounter. Triggered by the processes underpinned by the mirror neuron system, unconscious processes of identification occur with understanding. Transference and countertransference in a therapeutic encounter resonate with unconscious processes in the therapist, when the therapist needs to face taking a parent's pain, sorrow, and hostility into a transformational space that can return to parents a new way of experiencing themselves and being experienced by others (Malone & Dayton, 2015).

A therapist's ability to be involved in this process requires ongoing internal reflection on his own history and experience, and can be a source of anxiety (Chapter Nine). While to wait for change in some parents may take too long for the infant, it is sometimes difficult to get the balance right between attuning to the despair of parents and infant, and intervening.

A therapist offers the setting, holding, continuity, listening, interpretation, and his own subjectivity and otherness towards the therapy progressing. The stance becomes the intervention.

## *Ambivalence when intervening with an infant in the parents' presence*

If a therapist offers an infant an experience, responding when appropriate or when invited by the infant, the parents might feel that the therapist had taken over from them as someone who could parent, or play with, their infant better than they could. They usually, however, describe it as helpful that the therapist tries to understand the infant's experience. It usually gives the parents hope that the infant whom they have at some level hated is less damaged than they thought and may be able to be understood. The therapist responds to the infant differently than the parents, which reframes the infant as less difficult or abnormal.

Occasionally concern is expressed about whether a parent's guilt would be increased if a therapist interacted, say, with the depressed infant of a depressed mother, and the infant livened up quickly. Therapists, while aware of possible resentment and jealousy in parents and mindful not to injure self-esteem, would aim to find ways to engage with a parent's guilt or envy. Assisting a parent to understand the infant's experience usually includes trying to integrate ambivalent projections. If these have resulted in a fixed identification of an infant with an internal object, a parent may feel there is no gap for her to think her own thoughts so that the infant has continually to be on the breast, or a mother dare not contemplate she might partly be relieved if her sick infant died. Every link an infant makes creates a space between parent and infant for thought. By interacting, the therapist does not accept the parents wiping out the infant but implicitly tolerates her hateful feelings. The tightrope that therapists walk with some ill parents is that if he is experienced as taking the infant's side too quickly, he risks losing the parents. But most parents, however ill, know when their infant is at risk and feel guilty if the infant is unprotected and are grateful if, by law, a therapist must report if violence is disclosed, while also trying to intervene therapeutically.

If parents feel a therapist has taken over from them, this can usually be verbalised. If a parent were to ask, for example, "Why does my infant talk to you and not to me?" or say, "You're good with my baby" this could potentially start a dialogue about *why* the infant does this. While parents may sometimes feel envious of the therapist interacting with their infant, it is usually possible to engage with this negative transference and often essential to try. This is implicit in the following vignette.

### Ben and his mother

Twelve-month-old Ben was referred by his nephrologist as he was growing at a slower rate which was thought to be due to his renal problems. His mother had had a deprived childhood and parenting her small sick boy seemed to make her feel special. She pressured the therapist for help in playing with him and eventually the therapist suggested she allocate ten minutes a day. "That sounds pathetic; I should be able to do much more than that." The following week the mother said it was a complete disaster. "What sort of mother am I that I couldn't do this?" The therapist felt she had made a mistake and left the area of play. Later there was an attack on her playing with Ben. He brought a difficult jigsaw puzzle over to her, and she said, "Sometimes it's hard and sometimes you can't get the right piece," and because the therapist was not anxious about his achievement they could play with quiet pleasure. It took three minutes in all. His mother with a touch of concealed anger asked the therapist, "Have *you* got children?" and when the therapist gently queried why she was asking she said, "I can't bear the way you play with my child. I can't play at all." The therapist said that perhaps she was asking because it seemed as if the therapist could do something she could not. Being able to express her anger and having it accepted was enormously relieving and Ben's mother was subsequently able to play with some pleasure.

## The presence of fathers

Father-inclusive practice widens the point of entry for intervention and fathers are, if possible, included. With transition to parenthood, which has been described as a second chance, a father is changed irrevocably and his identity reorganised. Recognising fathers as parents usually contributes in them becoming the fathers whom they want to be. Fathers frequently attend sessions after their infant's birth but less often in the longer term with their return to work. A father's recognition of his infant's sense of self agency is a powerful support in his infant's ongoing development. Infants may feel more helped with separation issues in their father's presence. Involving a father may sustain hope with his infant feeling supported by his involvement.

A therapist intervenes mainly with the *father's and mother's transference to the infant* rather than to the therapist, unless their response to the therapist is negative, when it usually needs to be approached directly. When a father is less involved than the mother, whether he presents as healthier or is more avoidant, the therapist's curiosity about the reasons for him withdrawing can contribute to keeping him involved if possible. Exploring therapy for a father or couple therapy may also be needed.

When the father of an extremely ill infant or one who is dying can confide to a therapist that the stress of seeing his severely ill infant baby has at times led him to wish that his baby could die to be spared further suffering, intervention needs to compassionately recognise the pain and guilt behind this wish.

By keeping the father in mind, and if possible present, a therapist does not collude with his being wiped out and keeps a space open, if possible protecting his infant's development, particularly when his role seems marginal, as when he is a separated parent. This could include fathers with a psychiatric disorder or a father who despite past family violence may be able to be carefully involved.

## The contribution of both parents

As parents begin *observing* their infant's emotional response rather than scrutinising the time slept or milk drunk, they usually start thinking about how the infant makes links between feelings of distress and this being attended to. When an infant's crying sounds persecutory, it is often possible in observing this crying with parents for them to hear the meaning of the different cadences as it moves from grumbling, to a request to do something different, to exhausted sobbing.

Parents see the therapist looking at their infant with the same gaze that the therapist gives them that recognises their subjectivity. They see the therapist responding to their infant as an individual, not as someone who is acting in a reflex way or inexplicably, with development only to be charted, or as "out to get them" (or evil). The parents' view can then change to seeing their infant's behaviour as having meaning. Many parents express relief, indicating that they already see their infant as a person, not a collection of systems. When appropriate a therapist might recognise that an infant has a temperament that needs to be understood and the infant helped with it, but without locating all the difficulty in the infant, which may leave the parents feeling that they have no contribution to make. Mothers may misunderstand infants who are very sensitive and dysregulate easily or more highly self-organised infants as rejecting.

If an infant's mood or behaviour changes with a therapist's intervention, most mothers feel they are a potentially good mother and connect again with an internal good object. If a mother has her own separation difficulties, and her infant develops a contact that is separate from her, she often feels relieved that she is not entirely responsible for her infant. One therapist working with a very frightened, young first-time mother and her three-month-old daughter who had been in a special care unit, reported that it was extremely helpful to focus on the infant and her understandable defences and "to see this horrifyingly floppy, unfocusing infant tone up in interaction with me, as her mother's fears were metabolised, and in seeing this her mother realised she had an infant who *could do it* providing she wasn't looking into a frightened or anxious face" (Jones, 2005).

## Meeting an infant for the first time

In meeting an infant, a therapist tries to attune to his state, if he is anxious or sad, while an appropriately attuned smile signals that a therapist is open and available, and speaks to the pleasure the infant hopes to receive from the parents. A therapist might say "Can I say hello?", which greets the infant in his own right, and a playful interaction conveys, "I'm ready to meet you". If a therapist playfully offers something that even a young infant can hold, then gently pulls back, the infant has a sense of someone who recognises his agency, which he can begin to sense for himself, so that he has the possibility to explore and influence his world. Attuning to an infant's affects if he is despairing or angry immediately conveys, "I know what you feel because I feel it too" and an infant often responds immediately. Attuned play may involve very little action. It may be an animated facial expression or expressive vocalisation, tapping out a rhythm, interacting with a physical connection between therapist and infant, or with a few toys. Infants lead and are the driver of considerable interaction; video analysis suggests that playful interaction with the infant is more likely to be a return to the infant's serve than initiated by the therapist. If a therapist thinks a very young infant may, for example, have sight and/or hearing difficulties the therapist might talk in slightly longer phrases to see if she can catch the infant's attention.

Therapists have in the course of an infant observation described how early infants can convey an awareness of a different mental space in the observer's mind (Thomson-Salo, 2014b). In a therapeutic encounter, an infant senses another mind trying to understand his. An infant responds to the gaze of the therapist who is trying to feel her way into his mind as a parent does. Non-verbal, non-conscious ways of relating contribute to the infant sensing the safety in the setting.

When an infant feels emotionally held, the infant senses the therapist's mind is available to contain his feelings. Often in the first session infants are different from usual, as though they have tentatively connected to the therapist. Gazing responsively at an infant may give the infant this sense of being known and therefore knowing oneself, especially if his mother has at times looked at the infant with ashamed, critical, or empty eyes.

A therapist addresses an infant directly, in baby expressive language, and with non-verbal communication, through toys, play, and gentle appropriate, communicative touch.

### Engaging with an infant as a person: containing and emotional holding

What a therapist contributes can be conceptualised as threefold (Thomson Salo, 2007). An infant has a basic need to feel safe, physically and emotionally "held" and kept in mind, so that the eyes she looks into are in touch with hers, not anxious, angry, sad, shaming, or "absent". From birth onwards infants are responsive to the tone in which words are spoken, as well as the intensity of feeling conveyed.

### Being available for pleasurable playfulness

When infants feel enjoyed by their parents this may be the most significant factor in developing an internal good object. Seeing enjoyment on the other's face creates a similar state in the self. Infants want to matter to those who look after them and above all to be enthusiastically enjoyed from birth (Trevarthen, 2001). While the first language is the psychosomatic one, playfulness is another early "language".

Play "has the effect of drawing the child's attention to communication itself" (Bruner, 1975, p. 10). When an adult engages in communicative play, an infant knows that this response is intentionally created by someone who enjoys him, which may kick-start development. When a therapist relates to him this conveys a potential for playfulness, which can ease painful or despairing feelings. A therapist's willingness to follow where an infant leads indicates that the therapist hears meaning in the activity.

Playful interactions with a therapist who is containing may offer an alternative way of relating or trying out states of the self. This is important in underpinning relationships, self-esteem, and brain development. By "pleasure" in the play is meant a genuine enjoyment of an infant's capacities, independence, and personhood. Reflective, imitative play develops an infant's sense of self and joy as imitation is part of dialogue and an infant actively initiates imitation to make a connection.

A therapist interacts purposefully with an infant in a thoughtful way, to understand his relationships using his own self and body in engagement. This includes a simple recognising acknowledgement, playfulness, developing games, and turn taking, which foster the development of intersubjectivity.

### Communicating understanding with an infant as a person in her own right

From birth infants have a capacity for primary intersubjectivity (Trevarthen, 1998), born with a fascination for faces, and recognising other people and communicating. It is powerful for infants to capture another's gaze. They use gaze, searching others' face, pulling them into relating. The mirror neuron system for matching expressive states between people becomes active, providing a neurobiological basis for intersubjectivity or empathy from the beginning (Tzourio-Mazoyer et al., 2002). Infants have a sense of what another person *intends* as well as the accompanying feelings, including that the other person is trying to understand. These capacities propel her to engage with a therapist. When a parent fails to respond meaningfully to a young infant, the infant feels sad and ashamed.

What infants need for optimal development are other minds trying to understand what they are feeling, thinking, and communicating, minds that can cope with experiencing strong emotions, and able to process them. With younger infants, a therapist works at making a connection with gaze, gestural communication, and vocalisation. Therapists use a range of interventions with infants and parents; with an infant, these may seem to consist of little more than facial or hand gestures, talking and following her play in an approach to understanding the infant's experience through interactive dialogue between therapist and infant, and sharing this with the parents. When trusting his intuition to understand an infant's communication he can respond in a way uniquely fitted for the infant, sometimes in ways that he could not have predicted, such as attuning to an infant's anger (see Blaze, Chapter Six). With an older infant, a therapist's communication in verbal interventions is clear. "Each child's self actively grows by sharing meaning in relationships" (Trevarthen, 2011, p. 1).

## Cultural factors

Culture as a system of beliefs, attitudes, values, and practices that bring alive shared meaning is transmitted transgenerationally; an infant's mind is shaped by culture in how he is interacted with. Yet however much parents may try to do the best they can for their children, they may struggle with an internal legacy of their own parents' difficulties.

Therapists, aware of resonances of otherness and alienness in a family's mind and in their own mind, need to find effective culturally appropriate interventions. Even the term "infant–parent therapy" may reflect a Western approach of seeming to privilege the infant. Parents in a country with different cultural beliefs will face stresses that might impact parenting, views of infant development, and understanding the lived experience of mental illness.

For first generation immigrants, infant difficulties indicate the stresses of parenting against a backdrop of memories coloured by sadness when separated from the land associated with their own mothers. Unresolved loss and sadness may haunt immigrant parents and contribute to their infant's symptoms. Linked with a family's sadness about losing the motherland, "not seeing" an infant may be more marked in migrant families because family and infant feel to some extent that they are neither "seen and known" in their culture or the new one, as they feel at times mirrored non-contingently. Questions to elicit relationships with external and internal maternal grandmother, and about naming the infant, may open the door to cultural resonances.

In some cultural models, parents may assume that illness or disability has occurred because they have done something wrong and they show courage in accepting an infant mental health referral when they are aware that the approach may be different culturally, with less prohibition on expressions of sexuality or protest. In culturally sensitive practice a therapist might listen from a stance of "informed ignorance" to lessen the possibility of misreading parental behaviour.

Aware of different cultural perspectives, I acknowledge how much as a therapist I am "within" my culture as well as the difficulty of being fully aware of and doing justice to the customs and ethnicities of another country. However, despite sometimes broad differences in cultural beliefs about parenting, development, and mental illness, and despite occasionally needing to use interpreters, I draw on psychodynamic principles for infant–parent therapy. Infants can "read" a therapist's attempts to engage them with playfulness.

Whatever the cultural differences in views about infants are, ideas about the importance of sensitive parenting and attachment seem to have universal applicability. While infants prefer to look at faces of their own ethnic background (Kelly et al., 2005), a therapist can to a greater or lesser extent read the language of the eyes and gestures of infants from other cultures, as there is some universality of affect expression. A therapist tries to engage an infant's internal self and that of the parents', mindful of bias in concepts about the individual self as opposed to the we-self, which is more evident in cultures when infants are shared by parenting figures.

In considering the appropriateness of transference interpretations, a therapist needs not to lose the lens of culture. As therapists of the "majority" culture intervening with "minority patient-dyads" (Tang & Gardner, 1999), clues about the transference are present in how parents try to deal with cultural differences between themselves and a therapist. Interpreting the parents' transference to a therapist adds layers of complexity, with parents' relationships with their mother linked to their relationship to language and culture, and needs careful, reflective restraint in a therapist's approach (Eisold, 2012). Parents' critical feelings towards their therapist may be difficult to acknowledge.

When working with *interpreters* or cultural mediators (Berg, 2012), a therapist trusts that their sensitivity is evoked, particularly if the therapist uses parentese. Sometimes parents want to talk without an interpreter, particularly if a mother feels that the therapist would in the countertransference intuitively understand or she would feel ashamed in her small community. Use of Facetime to link a mother with her family of origin overseas could in time be more commonly implemented. In the following vignette the engagement with the toddler and mother was done entirely through an interpreter.

### Candie and Colin

Thirty-year-old Candie, who spoke no English, was referred twenty-one weeks pregnant for difficulty in feeling close to her unborn infant; she said that she did not like the foetal movements and conveyed that she might give the infant up for adoption. Five years previously she had moved from Asia with her husband who had a record of being violent; she had a five-year-old daughter and a two-year-old son, and said she had not wanted any of the unplanned pregnancies. It seemed Candie might be depressed and her son, Colin, was anxious and unable to separate from her, and was electively mute and biting his nails. That Candie had internalised something good from her mother was seen in her looking forward to her mother visiting and she readily accepted infant–parent therapy. The therapist drew pictures with Colin and said, "If we talk about worries and thoughts, that helps". Within two sessions he became less anxious as his mother's mood became warmer and she began playing with him. At the end of a session he spontaneously and unexpectedly cheekily mimicked the way the therapist said goodbye. Here the therapist unconsciously stood for the absent grandmother, external and internal, and conveyed acceptance of Candie's mothering, as well as hopefulness.

When a therapist finds certain cultural beliefs challenging, a path of action is clearer if such beliefs are enacted in behaviour that is against the rights of the infant.

### Therapeutic action: promoting reflectiveness

A therapist aims to engage an infant as equal therapeutic partner. The infant makes a relationship directly with the therapist, who "interprets" what she thinks the infant is feeling and thinking and tries to intervene as close to the infant's own language as she can. This approach of engaging the infant with the parents comes from the view that change results from understanding the infant through interactive dialogue shared with the parents, affecting representations, and implicit memories.

The serial nature of some infant–parent therapy may indicate that the parents had major unresolved long-standing difficulties in their own right and to effect change in their internal objects they need parent or couple therapy. Otherwise, they may unconsciously continue to project difficulties on to the infant, even though infants do experience difficulties their own difficulties, for example, new developmental stages may lead to sleeping difficulties (Daws, 1989).

An intervention may provide a space in which the ambivalence towards the infant can be acknowledged at the same time as offering hope. As relational *knowing* starts developing, the parents not knowing how to be with their infant is dissolved (Lyons-Ruth, 2003).

Infant–parent therapy I see as: first, therapists try to *understand the infant's experience*, to enter the infant's world rather than primarily through the parents' representations. They do this in the way that attuned parents would, mindful of how fragile an infant's state may be, and then they communicate that understanding. Engaging with infants usually seems to bring about a change in their thinking, feelings, and behaviour, and in their parents as well. Understanding others as intentional agents who are like the self can have cascade effects (Tomasello, 2000).

Second, therapists convey *their understanding to the parents* to reflect with them on what their infant could be feeling and thinking, not as an object whose behaviour needs to be fixed. As the therapist makes links between the infant's behaviour and emotional experience, the parents' perception usually changes; starting to feel that they understand their infant's experience indicates changes in their representations. This approach with parents may include exploring with them to make more sense of their own life and early history. Containment of their feelings, being able to bear at times regression and primitive states at a deep level, as well as the heat of the transference, is often followed by an easing of projections and may at times be as important as interpretation.

This starts the following spiral of interconnecting developments and I would conceptualise infant–parent therapy as comprising four changes whose interconnection magnifies the outcome.

First, *changing infant representations and behaviour*. When infants experience their mind as existing in the therapist's mind, and being responded to in a new way, this offers them the possibility of responding differently. Being with a therapist who is interested in understanding the meaning of their experience, open to experiencing this in mind and body, is mirrored back to the infant in a way that he or she can feel bodily, with changes in behaviour and representations. (An infant feels, "I am now different".)

Second, *changing parental representation* through verbal exploring and making links, concurrent with seeing their infant differently in the therapist–infant interaction. This re-presents the infant to the parents who have the possibility of seeing the infant as less damaged than feared, whom they had at some level hated for not being perfect and having made them feel "bad" parents. (A parent feels "I see my baby as different and feel different myself".)

Third, *changing infant–parent interaction* with the infant taking the changed way-of-being into the relationship with the parents, increasing their sense of having regained their infant. ("We do things differently".)

Fourth, *changing parental ways-of-being with the infant*. When the therapist interacts with the infant from a position of finding the infant intentional, understandable, and potentially enjoyable, the parents are likely to have mirrored in themselves a similar experience. ("We feel differently together".)

As Stern (2004) wrote,

> the visual information we receive when we watch another act gets mapped onto the equivalent motor representation in our own brain by the activity of these mirror neurons. . . . We experience the other *as if* we were executing the same action, feeling the same emotion, making the same vocalization or being touched as they are being touched (p. 79).

When parents see the therapist intervene and their neuronal pathways are activated as if they were carrying out the same intentional acts with the same emotional tone, they are offered the possibility of a different way of being a parent alongside what is laid down in implicit memory. This means a potential for repair. The therapist–infant interaction can shape the parents' representations and implicit memories of relational behaviours. These are more accessible with the processes of childbirth and early child-rearing and in the relational encounter with the infant could be modified faster than at other times. Neuroscience data supports the idea that therapeutic action may begin non-verbally, at an implicit level, providing a setting of trust and safety, and in the next phase the therapeutic action may consist of the therapist providing a new way of relating that parents and infants could take into relationships (Pally, 2005).

Interacting with an infant in the parents' presence may do more to rework implicit relational knowing than only working with the parents. Significant change takes place as the therapist interacts with the infant when the parents had not been able to see the infant accurately. Seeing a therapist relate meaningfully to their infant may act as a "moment of meeting" (Stern, 2004), a strong feeling of connection, that brings about change when parents feel "heard" by the therapist responding. Parents and infants have an awareness that what they fear is known at some level by the therapist. When the infant responds to the therapist with pleasure, and his despair and anxiety eases, the parents usually look at their infant with theirs eased, too. When the infant looks in the parent's eyes and sees someone reaching out instead of someone whom he finds frightening, a new interactive bridge can form. Not including the infant in the intervention may mean that something that is not faced in the parents may be repeated with the infant. This multi-directional intervention can impact on the parents' implicit memory system to bring about change. Reflectiveness often begins to develop relatively more quickly in infant–parent therapy than in adult therapy.

Often while a therapist is assessing, infant and parent start changing from the first session. If the situation is urgent for infant and parent, therapists need to assess quickly and sometimes intuitively how to angle a psychodynamic intervention.

Infants connect with others from birth, and experience sadness and shame if they do not feel they are important to someone or feel lonely. An infant makes his own contribution to the therapeutic process, mirroring the therapist's engagement with him; a therapist "marks" the infant's experience and the infant learns about his own and others' minds in interaction with his. Research has shown that at least from two months onwards visual interactions between mother and infant release endogenous opiates for the infant. When therapists tap into this, it has the potential to get things moving. Creative play brings freedom from fear and evokes hope to move forward. A therapist's interaction with an infant offers a new experience, with meaning. With infants, communication is embedded in body language. I try early on to find some meaning in behaviour so as not to leave the parents feeling that nothing has meaning and everything needs to be on hold in a void. I may not be right in the understanding I offer but I would rather have a go so that the parents see the baby as potentially being meaningful. Sometimes hope that it will pass feels like all I can offer and it is important to remain hopeful. With infants in vulnerable families, it would be therapeutic if the parents' capacity to think reflectively about their infant's mind could increase, even fractionally, as an infant can respond so well to even small changes.

## Criteria for ending

Reflecting on when therapeutic aims in a short-term intervention are achieved, and the importance of a thoughtful ending, it is likely that when increased reflectiveness has been achieved, the intervention has lessened symptom distress and an ending can be planned. Internalisation and identification enable a therapist to remain part of a parent's internal world (see Helen and Hugh, Chapter Three).

Parents end their involvement in different ways: with some it is planned, while a few fade away somewhat as a transitional object does. If possible, parents make the decision how to reduce and terminate. In families where an infant's development is on track, parent and infant are eager to get on with their life together, while sad to say goodbye to the therapist who may become like the left-behind teddy transitional object, and if I feel it is not an avoidance I may not take up transference over-vigorously. Letting parents go in this way may facilitate their having a "whole" experience with a therapist, there to be left if they have felt deeply understood. Occasionally even with a very positive transference, a family fade away before an outwardly adequate termination process takes place and this may be a way of coping with early abandonment feelings. Some continue to "touch base" from time to time over several years.

Occasionally it is clear why a therapist has lost a family, for example, in trying to refer on too quickly without being fully in touch with the parents' dependency needs, and their defensiveness or envy is missed. Through processing inevitable countertransference enactments, a therapist may regain a position where therapy can continue.

## Conclusion

Therapist and infant begin an exploration of not-knowing, with the therapist aiming to make a connection with the infant, so that the infant recognises that the therapist recognises him, and is available to make a connection. The therapist tries to understand the infant's experience in an interaction that feels safe and potentially playful.

When the focus is on intervening with parents who have trouble with parenthood, to include the infant and respond in this way is more likely to *promote a greater degree of reflectiveness in infant and parent*. Nothing would be more convincing to a parent that her infant has a mind that reflects and can be reflected on than a therapist doing this with her infant. In this approach a central therapeutic mechanism lies in understanding with the parents their infant's experience from the infant's perspective and in doing so, modulating representations of infant and parents. As the therapist becomes important, infant and parent extrapolate the implicit relational knowing in this relationship, and modify it towards more secure relationships. An infant catalyses help for the parents, their presence often chasing away the ghosts. The therapeutic relationship powerfully provides a safe space in which infant, parent, and therapist change. Research has found a cascade effect of change lasting longer after psychotherapy than other modes of intervention, stemming from increased reflectiveness (Shedler, 2010).

Many interventions with infants and parents, individual and group, short- and long-term, are effective and the task is to become clearer about the process of change. Sometimes because of pressure of time an intervention may be no more than a relational encounter informed by psychodynamic thinking (such as containment of feelings and thoughts at a time when unconscious meanings distort a parent's relationship with her infant). Therapists may face a dilemma of doing just enough to get parents and infant moving when they know how much better the family would be with more intervention.

CHAPTER TWO

# What an infant brings

Here I describe the active contribution that even young infants make to the therapeutic encounter and their therapeutic alliance. I take for granted their expectable endowment of their capacity to communicate from birth, including triadic intersubjective communication, and their resilience. I highlight some emotions (Thomson-Salo & Paul, 2009), while aware that these concepts may not apply in all cultural contexts, beginning with a sense of immediacy, with both positive and negative emotions, and potential for playfulness and humour. An infant's moral capacities emerge quite early, along with the wish to know and be known in a truthful experience. Infants bring a willingness to enter the therapeutic process and often take a risk to do so. They look at the therapist so attentively that they seem to have an awareness of being in an emotionally meaningful encounter, gazing at the therapist to find out how available for interaction they are. They also bring a wish to be creative, free, integrated, and "alive", and a capacity to pace their engagement. Even infants with an insecure attachment seem prepared to take this risk in the therapeutic process.

An infant tries to make sense of the person trying to understand her; the therapist aims to co-create a space for a deeper dialogue and relationship. Infants know if they are listened to and respected. From the moment of birth, newborns have a sense of their own existence (Hart, 2008). They explore their environment to figure out how it works; within twenty minutes of birth they move their hands to express their emotions. One newborn, a "very chilled" baby, and her mother gazed at each other for three hours virtually non-stop on the first day—the baby was getting to know someone whom she had already known for a long time. Even an extremely premature newborn just before being connected to the monitors seems to look for a response from others.

What is often overlooked is a delight in their sexuality; restoring their sense of being in control of pleasure in their own body is, for example, crucial with infants who have had so many oral traumas that their autonomy is restricted to food refusal.

## *Immediacy and positive emotions*

An infant may respond without too much filtering and defensiveness and expects a response from the therapist, bringing a sense of immediacy to the encounter. A doctor described her sense that it really mattered even for six-week-old infants present in a consultation how she responded to their mother's emotions. A six-month-old girl, who had looked intently at a therapist as she talked, nodded her head after the therapist spoke. The father of a seven-month-old boy would, as the therapist was talking, look at his son and ask, "Are you listening?" and sometimes the infant took his dummy out as if to listen better.

Newborns imitate facial expressions conveying affect, including smiling and surprise. In the first hour after birth, before attaching to the breast a baby looks at the mother's face searching for a smile that helps the social communicative system between them both kick in (Porges, 2011). Babies seek to engage with others from birth, seeking the new as a positive nutrient. For infants to be curious is on the way towards thinking and reflecting. This shapes what they bring to the therapeutic encounter, including enjoyment and humour. When they feel enjoyed, they feel understood, meaningful, and valued. Infants try to make sense of faces and find it both exciting and soothing to be gazed at by someone who delights in them. They search for the enjoyment of interaction—including joking and teasing—and when they achieve it, they feel safe and happy; the world takes on more meaning, and they feel some hope. A two-week old can have a "conversation" with another, adult or infant, and actively engage with them. He or she finds it joyful to be the focus of another's attention. Infants bring the wish for fun with another and as their sense of self increases, their anxiety decreases; with safe fun, their cognition develops. When play gets going, development gets going too (Trevarthen, 1996). When things go well, they have "confidence in the generosity of life" (Parsons, 2016).

A fifteen-month-old boy with poor feeding was falling away on the growth percentile and appeared depressed with no desire to eat or be independent. A therapist's playful intervention led to an enlivening of his desire and when he gave her a kiss his mother felt hopeful again and his eating improved.

### Infant humour

When infants are amused and find something funny, they are likely to feel more themselves. Infants intuitively know when *humour* is an authentic communication, intended just for them. Parents seeing their infant's humour can usually invest in his or her ongoing existence and with this may come a shift leading to a moment of meeting.

Imitation may be the beginning of humour (Greenacre, 2015). Play, imitation, and humour are closely linked in development and therapeutic engagement. Infants seek the joy of surprise, and may from birth onwards seek humorous engagement because it is playful and hopeful. With the mirror neurons in play, when a parent smiles with amusement at her infant, the infant may feel the amusement, and begin to see the humorous side of things. This smile may open the door to pleasure and humour. A smile may be a common pathway between humour and feeling safe and happy, and an infant may very early act in a humorous way to evoke a smile, and delight. Within an hour of birth an infant initiates tongue-protrusion: a two-day-old put his tongue out at me several times and I laughed; his father had done it so often that the infant now did it to evoke an interaction with me, which suggests that he was seeking to make me laugh. (The vocal pattern of human laughter appears in rudimentary form at least by two months (Panksepp & Burgdorf, 2003).)

Humour links with trust. Being humorously amused may open a transitional space of safety, relief from stress, and hope. Sharing something funny creates intimacy. Playful *teasing* builds an infant's sense of enjoyment. Infants know the "rules" and vary them on their own initiative to get a rise out of the other. When they join in teasing with the therapist, their parents may see a completely different infant. A sick infant girl in hospital, when offered her bottle, would only open her mouth the fourth time it was offered—refusing the bottle was her way of being alive and interacting (see also Chapter Ten).

Infants might find any rebelliousness on their therapist's part enlivening and humorous, if it impinges on them in a way that nevertheless respects their right to disagree.

## An infant's negative emotions

Gaze aversion may be an expression of negative emotion. A therapist respects when an infant turns away but nevertheless may gently "pursue" if she senses that at some level the infant wants to be found. The capacity to protest that something does not feel right is important and means that an infant has not given up hope. It is striking how often an infant's protest evokes a supportive smile from the therapist—and the infant reads and feels buoyed up by this response when the environment may until then have seemed largely negative.

Infants can show anger at one month with an expression of anger and facial flushing and behaviour indicating frustration. They do not hide their rage and destructiveness, unless they have learnt to do so self-protectively. From six months onwards, if there is fleeting pleasure that it does hurt if they pinch and hurt their mother's face this would be a *sadistic* aspect of infants in their pleasure in hurting another.

## An infant's moral capacities and wish to know and be known in an experience that feels truthful

The development of moral feelings starts quite early: infants know within the first year how to make moral choices between right and wrong, between the good guy and the bad guy (Bloom, 2009). An infant can show reciprocity early and is sometimes generous and quite caring in offering food to parents or therapist. The infant's capacity to forgive may be seen in his moving forward when he has felt hurt or saddened by the parents' withdrawal or sarcasm, from at least ten weeks, which can be viewed as a generousness.

An infant wishes to know, and be known, in a truthful experience. When an infant senses he is in the presence of a therapist who is trying to understand his experience, it usually brings considerable relief. He brings out an honest response in himself and looks for a response from the therapist in such an attentive way, with a heightened intersubjective alertness, that he can only be described as having an awareness that an emotionally meaningful experience is taking place. He is at some level aware of the resonances in the therapist's mind, even when very young. When infants gaze for a long time they are seeking to know whether the other is available for interaction (see seven-month-old Eric, Chapter Seven). When a therapist said to the parents of a fifteen-month-old infant, "You're doing this and the infant says no", at one point the infant echoed the "no". A two-year-old boy pointed at pictures in a book, and when the therapist asked him, "Who is there?", tapped himself on the chest to show the therapist that he was there, a useful communication to himself and his very anxious mother.

Infants are born able to sense authenticity in another's communication (Siegel, 1999). When a therapist pretends, for example, to eat food, infants know from at least the second year, perhaps earlier, that the therapist is not being straight with them.

### *An infant's willingness to enter the therapeutic process, and capacity to pace engagement*

Most infants thrive on experiencing what is new. Extending this to the therapeutic situation, the first time an infant meets a therapist, there is often a sense of him being courageous and open to the possibility that something might emerge from the experience. This links with Winnicott's (1971) statement that when things are not going well for infants, they look around for what they might be able to take in. If a depressed and withdrawn infant can feel someone trying to engage with him hope is usually rekindled.

Sometimes, as if to allow the parent the chance to have some time with the therapist, an infant seems to become less demanding. The infant seems to understand the intentionality of a therapist trying to engage and help.

### *Dario*

Many of the points above are illustrated in this vignette. Two-month-old Dario and his mother were referred for his severe failure to thrive and he responded to the therapist talking to him and providing an emotional holding that the family had not been able to. In the first session, he cried as his mother and grandmother said that he was not feeding. When the therapist commented, "Another anxious week", Dario looked at him wide-eyed (with immediacy). As his mother talked about the failure of breastfeeding Dario fell back against his mother, crying and refused the bottle (with urgency and negativity). The therapist said, "Sometimes it's easy to work out what he wants, sometimes too hard". His mother conveyed she was tired and frustrated. The therapist, noticing Dario had calmed, said, "He's looking about in a thoughtful way". His mother said, "He's thinking he's making a fool of me". As she relaxed when she did not feel shamed by the therapist, Dario turned to the therapist and stared intently for fifteen seconds, smiled, then continued staring almost unblinking for another thirty seconds (seeking a thoughtful, truthful, containing object). The therapist commented, "A big stare", smiled and asked, "Do you think I could say hello?"

He held Dario so that he could see his mother and said, "That's your mother. That's a big smile", as Dario smiled at his mother for the first time. (As she smiled forgivingly at him he might feel this was the first time he brought her joy.) His mother told a saga of woes, including the car being stolen. The therapist murmured to Dario, "You've lost your car", and to his mother, "It feels like a bad cloud over you". She clicked her fingers very loudly at Dario. The therapist observed that Dario was looking at her and she replied, "He doesn't see too much". The therapist gently said, "I think he could see very well, although sometimes he stares off into the distance". Dario wriggled, and the therapist commented to him, "You're a bit of a wriggler", and Dario moved, as if in confirmation. As the therapist observed that

Dario was tense, his mother waved a rattle at him. The therapist commented that sometimes Dario looked a bit sad and asked if she thought Dario knew that she had worries. (An important verbalisation as his mother could not bear his sadness and waved a rattle instead of offering her receptive face and he disconnected further.) When the therapist gave him back to his mother she asked, "Good boy, where've you been?" Dario vocalised vigorously, she smiled and talked tenderly, and instead of being floppy he sat up, as if sensing a change in his mother's feelings. The therapist talked about how sometimes it is hard for infants to say what they are worried about. When he said that the tests had revealed nothing organic, Dario's eyes moved back to him, as if aware something important was unfolding.

The therapist continued, "Maybe he gets distress in his body when he's really wound up and gets more distressed and feels unsure about things, and things go from bad to worse". His mother looked directly at the therapist, and when she moved Dario away from the therapist's direction, he turned his head round to look directly at the therapist. The therapist continued, "It seems he's a bright boy but he seems sad and worried and tense as if he doesn't quite know how to work himself out. If he gets a pain he gets very frightened and panicky". Gradually with his mother taken care of, Dario went to sleep against her (pacing his engagement), and she could then use the time for herself.

She told the therapist that when Dario was little he had stopped breathing and she had screamed, "My baby's dying". The grandmother told of the unresolved mourning for his uncle, who had died at birth thirty years previously. When his mother no longer identified Dario with his dead uncle she could trust that he might live and immediately stopped brusquely patting him as if to resuscitate him. Dario began to thrive and won two competitions as the most attractive infant.

## Discussion

What might the therapist's physical and emotional holding and interacting, verbal exploration, and communication provide? When a therapist "holds" an infant this seems likely to ease feelings of catastrophic anxiety, instantly providing safety. Here, the therapist was receptive to Dario's fear and communicated safety to him psychosomatically, emotionally as well as physically. He ascribed affect as well as thinking to the infant in a combination of direct dialogue with him and understanding comments to the adults. It was playful interaction, particularly when the therapist commented, "A big stare", smiled and asked, "Do you think I could say hello?", and holding Dario so that he could see his mother commented as Dario smiled at his mother for the first time, "That's your mother. That's a big smile". This was followed in a triangulation with him on hearing about the loss of the car, with appropriate affect, murmuring simply to him, "You've lost your car". This play scaffolds the infant to have "a conversation". When he gives Dario back to his mother who asks where he has been, Dario vocalises vigorously, telling her with feeling, bringing the experience with the therapist in which he had changed, into the relationship. The therapist shares the formulation as appropriate with the mother and grandmother, particularly why they are presenting at that time and who this infant is for them. Nor is the infant only responding to the therapist's containment of mother and infant, but is responding from a position of being in the presence of another person who uses embodied mentalization to communicate an understanding of his predicament. Touch may be most important in communicating safety, enjoyment, and understanding (cancelling out a mother's fearfulness that communicates unsafety and dysregulation, disorganising attachment). When a therapist engages with an infant his thoughtful actions convey reflectiveness. The therapist also uses the word "big" twice to Dario—he helps him manage his "big" feelings (and those of his mother and grandmother).

### *An infant's sexuality in the first year*

An infant's innate joyful excitement in sexuality in the first year is not often reported in clinical interventions. Infant sexual excitement refers to the biological and psychic response system that leads an infant to seek and initiate behaviours, to experience sexual and erotic feelings from early on, as different from the importance of feeling "gendered". An infant is capable of intense autoerotic gratification at the same time as experiencing erotic ties with external objects, and early oral satisfactions lead to the psychic internalisation of a "good breast" and a good relationship with the external mother. What follows is a developmental perspective that pays close attention to an infant's body with observational data about bodily sexual excitement. Therapists, with greater awareness of an infant's body as sexual, could in their countertransference (with a reverberation of their own sexuality) become more aware of the experiences of infant and parent, with a potentially fuller understanding of their experience.

Cuddly infants may have many encounters that are directly physical, fondling, and potentially erotically stimulating, and by their actions actively seek erotic stimulation and response (Martinson, 1973). A two-week-old infant can be extremely snuggly and squirm sensually with delight in the mother's gaze. From about two months onwards, as parent and infant gaze at each other, opioids become active, making gaze one of the most powerful experiences and this basis in sexual excitement can be so intense. When a four-month-old infant locked eyes on to his mother, he began a lover's look (intimate, for someone special), compared with the social smile he gave others. No one looks as long into the other's eyes as mothers and infants, and lovers, do.

The essential sexuality of an infant is part of the pleasure of feeding: the sensuality of skin and genitals are part of enjoyable sexuality and his or her sense of self and self-esteem. The connection between mother and infant can at times be very erotic for them both and is needed to start the infant off well as a person (Fonagy & Target, 2007). A mother's sexuality may be expressed towards her infant in her pleasure in breastfeeding, and can be highly exciting for them both:

> When there is a real connection between the mother and the infant, it is highly sexual—the dilemma is that the baby needs it, but . . . (s)he needs to . . . withdraw what is exciting, without upsetting her baby's pleasure and mastery in the feeding and relationship to their body. . . . What is important is the separation of the child from the mother has to be from a sexual base—it excites them together, it's the connection with, and the joy in the body and the nipple in the mouth which is climactic, and both have to give it up. (Morgan, 2007)

Infant research and clinical experience also point to infants reaching out early with gesture to include the third person, which could ameliorate later feelings of wanting to exclude the other parent from a special relationship, and modify views of infant oedipal jealousy and hostility. Evidence about the connectedness of infants from birth, having their own constitutional endowment for responding, beginning life already neuronally endowed for multi-person interactions suggests they bring this into interaction rather than only being evoked by parental sexual responses.

By six months of age infants often exhibit a different quality of sensual excitement with which they respond to male and female therapists: male observers report four-month-old girl infants acting flirtatiously with them, indicating how important countertransference reactions are in assessing whether behaviours are joyfully sensual or anxiety-driven. Although Fonagy (2008) suggested that mothers do not mirror sexual excitement, unlike how they mark other emotions, some infant therapists would disagree, having observed mothers able to look on at an infant's lusty adoration.

Infants love being stroked and a mother's sensual stimulation of her baby's body in caring particularly for the erogenous zone of the skin, the body's largest organ, increases her baby's sexuality and erotic desire, and brings deep sensual pleasure. This can be seen in infant erections during massage.

## Breastfeeding

The major potentially erotic encounter involving infant and mother is the sucking relationship. This is not to devalue bottle-feeding, as infants can suck just as lustily at the bottle but to trace a line of bodily sensuality. An infant enjoying his body and breastfeeding is a good basis for sense of identity, self-esteem, and sexuality. An infant's satisfaction is likely to increase the desire to suckle frequently. The total body may show rhythmic motions of hands, fingers, feet, and toes occurring with the rhythm of sucking, with the infant soon looking ecstatic. After feeding, an infant's dreamy relaxation is like that characteristic of a satisfactory sexual response (Newton & Newton, 1967), interpreted by fathers as dreaming of the breast. From an early age babies love stroking the skin of their mother's breasts, continuing to want to touch the breast even after breastfeeding has ceased (Barnett, 1989).

A sucking infant may reciprocate by putting his fingers into the mother's mouth; she responds by moving her lips on her infant's fingers. The infant moves his fingers; she responds with a smile and the infant studies her face with rapt attention (Spitz & Wolf, 1949). In time, infants pat the mother's breast while sucking, pat her face, turn a cheek to be kissed, clasp her around the neck, and lay their cheek on hers, hug, and may bite. Vigorous sucking by active boy infants may be accompanied by penile erection that may last for several minutes after the breast is removed (Newton & Newton, 1967).

A six-week-old boy held his mouth open around the breast and touched it gently a few times with his lips as though playing with the nipple. He sucked in a slow rhythmic way, gazing in a focused way at his mother, holding the breast almost as though he were caressing it, and his loving feelings for his mother were clear. By fourteen weeks he held himself more erect and his hands touched the breast almost as though he was holding it. When her mother offered him the other breast, he touched her skin around the nipple. When she tried to remove her nipple, he held on so tightly the nipple stretched, as if he felt that the breast was his possession and he wanted to keep it until he was ready to give it up. At seven months, his mother said, "He just wants to sit and play with my nipple now. Look how he touches my body all over." He breastfed as though he was controlling the feed, sat up satisfied immediately after it, and looked at the observer as though saying, "This is where I want to be."

A five and a half-month-old infant was described as "into his mother as if it was sexual, trying to mouth her face", and by six months he would clearly flirt with her and the observer. Another infant who fed with lusty almost ecstatic sucking, her eyes half-closed, became a sensual, wriggly toddler. An eight-month-old infant who was weaned would slip his hand under his mother's clothes and hold on to the breast as if indicating, "This is mine". One father thought his four-month-old son might be jealous of his parents "being intimate" when he lay on the bed beside them: he cried loudly whenever his father touched the mother's breasts (McWilliams, 2013). Infants also stare at the breasts of other mothers.

### Genital play and masturbation

In the first year, infants are responsive to stimulation of parts of the body other than the mouth, including the genitals. On ultrasounds, male foetuses have erections while infant girls also display signs of involuntary arousal. In a survey all the mothers reported erections in their sons from birth onwards and eighty per cent of the girls' mothers reported genital excitement in their daughters from three months onwards (Fonagy, 2008). Fathers describe with pride even their very premature baby's pleasure in touching his penis.

An observer noted that six-month-old infants enjoy being massaged around the scrotum in a way that was different from being massaged elsewhere (Flynn, 2007). Girls or boys may discover the body's sensualness in the groin region by pressing, thrusting, touching, or rubbing. Pelvic thrust movements in eight to ten-month-old male and female infants appear to be an expression of affection and evidence of pleasure in which the infant holds on to the parent, nuzzles them, and rapidly thrusts and rotates the pelvis for a few seconds (Kagan & Lewis, 1965). Kleeman (1971) described five infant girls and one infant boy fingering their genitals during the first year with erotic pleasure. Examples from infant observation or clinical work include a six-month-old infant grabbing his penis as his diaper was removed and making an "ooooh" sound of pleasure; his mother told him he was too young to make that noise and covered him up quickly. A mother reported her twelve-month-old son, while enjoying playing with her nipple, would often delightedly fondle his genitals. Another one-year old boy would masturbate against the strap of his pushchair and in bed going to sleep.

## *Countertransference*

A therapist aware of her own bodily countertransference to infant sexuality contributes a more nuanced view of the parents' and infant's experience and development. She might be in touch in a fuller way with all aspects of an infant's experience in breastfeeding, as she may be when physically holding an infant and being aware of the infant's erotic pleasure in being held without needing to anxiously distance herself.

A therapist who had sexual thoughts about a five-day-old infant who did not want to feed and was losing weight used these to frame an interpretation that touched the mother affectively and her infant recovered (Acquarone, 2004). Some male observers reported becoming sexually excited watching an infant breastfeed, perhaps mirroring the infant's excitement. One observer, a medical practitioner, did not want to think about a mother who while cleaning her ten-month-old daughter's genitals gained pleasure while absent-mindedly rubbing them. This may indicate her difficulties with sexuality and perhaps his mirroring her difficulties.

### *Intervening in difficulties in the path of infant sexuality*

From the viewpoint of an infant as joyfully sensual, therapists might see the driven nature of symptoms such as excessive thumb sucking or other self-stimulation as defensive or a failure of defence. Parents' difficulties with sexuality may on impact their infant, influencing the way that their infant understands his own body and integrates his sense of self and identity. An infant will be aware when parents feel shame about his sexuality, as well as their own. A mother did not like breastfeeding her infant because he was such a long baby that she found it hard to think of him as a baby and not a sexual boy. Many psychosexual disorders and delays start with the parents' inability to have a healthy enjoyment of a sexual investment in their infant's body.

### *Conclusion*

How an infant is introduced to his body has consequences for him in terms of relationships and sexuality. A therapist needs to be able to reflect on the issue of sexuality in a way that is helpful to that infant and parent and have it available in her mind whether or not she decides to overt it with them. Sometimes facilitating an infant's excitement or liveliness in the presence of the parent can be transformative. Being more aware in the countertransference of the interplay of infant sexual excitement and parental sexuality could extend a therapist's understanding, initiating intervention in ways that might be experienced as more empathically in touch with the whole person of the infant and his parents.

# PART II
# ENGAGING INFANTS IN PERINATAL SETTINGS

## CHAPTER THREE

# Infants and their parents in the perinatal period

Many women struggle with transition to parenthood for several reasons, and with the conflicting feelings roused by love and regression. They may have considerable ambivalence about pregnancy, birth, and child rearing, such as child abuse, or difficulty facing the dependence of a needy infant, or trauma (from any point in her life including a difficult pregnancy). Anxiety symptoms are one of the commonest complications of pregnancy, and include a reactivation of past trauma, particularly the stress of lack of partner support, and the lived experience of mental illness in one, or both, of the partners. Parents may be caught up in old conflicts with their own parents, and childhood experiences of deprivation are triggered in looking after their baby. Some mothers find the changes to their body during pregnancy, birth, and breastfeeding frightening, disgusting, or traumatic and feel the need to take their body/privacy back. A mother may feel that if her infant is "bad", she is bad. Infants in the first year can show difficulties in every physical and emotional domain including post-traumatic stress disorders. The mental health needs in vulnerable women with borderline personality difficulties or with symptoms of anxiety and depression, substance use, intimate partner violence, and/or psychotic disorders, unstable accommodation, and contact with protective services, multiply difficulties for them and their infants, and rapid discharge from hospital may exacerbate bonding difficulties.

I describe an infant mental health approach in a tertiary maternity hospital, when the pregnancy, birth, and/or the infant is feared or proves traumatic, so that a mother may be referred antenatally, as an inpatient or after discharge. There is an overlap in some presentations and further examples are given in the chapters on infants of adolescent mothers and infants in neonatal intensive care units (NICU). Therapists are called on to maximise the effectiveness of brief therapeutic interventions when experiences around birth are challenging for infant and parent, especially when a traumatic birth lands on a mother with a personality disorder, dysregulating her and potentially disorganising her infant. Usually time constraints do not allow unlimited time for intervention so I may refer on for more long-term intervention or to more specialist services.

Offering a confidential space to explore these feelings in the hope that knowing that another person knows what they feel, without rejection, is usually therapeutic. Often a therapist being able to respond very quickly enables a mother to feel relieved and "heard", as though a "good" mother is available for her.

## Antenatal and perinatal consultations

When pregnant women who are or may experience difficulty, and if possible their partners, are referred to facilitate them responding to the infant with pleasure *in utero* and at birth. A more positive maternal–foetal relationship is linked with mind-mindedness after birth, and women who during pregnancy report stronger prenatal infant attachment and representations such as imagining what the infant looks like, show greater maternal responsiveness after birth (Auhagen-Stephanos, 2013). Distress during pregnancy can affect mother–infant attachment. If a mother is stressed in pregnancy, a high level of cortisol can be passed to the foetus potentially sensitising the stress response before birth.

In engaging with a pregnant woman, while exploring her ambivalence and grief, I try to keep a space for the baby, and who the baby represents. I try to personalise the baby if they are not in the mother's mind. I may ask about awareness of what the baby is like *in utero*, how active they are, what music or times of the day they like, and why their name was chosen (with "Anarckie" or "Delilah", who did the baby represent?). One woman when pregnant spontaneously asked, "Would the baby know I sometimes didn't want him?" To ease a negative projection, I might say that I do not think that infants are out to cause their mother pain but want to be enjoyed, and to help their mothers develop a new fuller identity, and we can do lot to help bonding develop.

As part of a conflictual identification with her mother who was felt to be neglectful, a woman may be determined not to love her baby, and may be totally distanced from the pregnancy without dreaming, unable to believe she would have a baby, convinced the "real parents" would claim the baby. Or in identification with the girl whom she once was, she feels unable to make an infant experience what she experienced (Raphael-Leff, 2014). Women may have experienced anxiety in case they have harmed their baby through substance use or have to manage high levels of distress when diagnosed with cancer, particularly when impacted by treatment for the illness.

When there has been childhood sexual abuse a woman may be very anxious about this being retriggered in childbirth. The more difficulties she faces, the more likely the need to work with a coordinated care system without pushing her to talk about child abuse. With a mother who was fixated in her loss of trust in a pregnancy that did not go well, a therapist might ask, "What do we have to do for you to trust a little?" Guilt and remorse during or after a pregnancy with a *second* baby may be quite strong if there are fewer difficulties with a second baby than with the first.

## *Eva and Erin*

Eva referred herself, anxious that she would succumb to postnatal depression, and we only managed one half hour meeting before her baby was born. She had wanted for a long time to have therapy to come to terms with her immigrant background, her difficult father, and her depressed and unavailable mother who died when she was young. When Eva's baby was born, she became quite upset and asked to see me urgently and I went to the ward on two consecutive days to talk with her. She was the fourth child of fourteen siblings, and a sister who had died had received more attention than Eva had. I spent some time observing her daughter, Erin, and sharing this with Eva, personalising her baby the way a grandmother would do for her daughter, giving meaning to Erin so that Eva changed from having a baby who was not seen as Eva had felt herself to be, to having a baby who was seen and welcomed. With Eva seeming to feel that there was a place for her in my mind, which she had not felt in her own mother's mind, this seemed to be enough at that time for her to feel she was coping. We spoke on the phone subsequently, and she said she was doing fine. When she sent in an evaluation form, she was very enthusiastic about what she had taken from our meetings, seeing me as the benign mother in the transference.

## Newborns and their parents

Sometimes there is little sign that there will be difficulties in the parent–infant relationship until the birth. Fear and pain around childbirth, for example, a traumatic birth with medical complications, may lead to difficulties in bonding, particularly with shame about negative feelings about it, or a previously wanted baby may be rejected. A difficult pregnancy and birth may have traumatising effects on a baby who is born with an unsettled mood and tone, which make the first months harder for both baby and mother. With a traumatic birth, some mothers cannot look at their baby. A therapeutic intervention may be quite brief, from one to five sessions, which allows exploration of feelings about becoming a mother, sometimes with a woman who had an identity as a successful adult professional woman and then feels unprepared for a baby's dependency needs, particularly if she does not have much familiarity with babies. Sometimes even in the face of a mother's rejection of her baby the countertransference may paradoxically not appear troublesome, perhaps if a therapist intuits her wish to be reconciled with her baby. In the countertransference, a feeling of a motherless girl may suggest the need for longer term intervention.

I try to explore with the baby present why a mother was ambivalent about the birth or found it traumatic, and to engage with the baby, however young. If a mother finds it hard to look at her baby from birth we may be able to use that as a starting point to explore the relationship difficulties, for example, if she cannot look because she is trying to hide sadness or anger (or guilt about "failing" breastfeeding). But the birth may have highlighted other deep-seated anxieties that had until then been pushed away. Parents may see one twin or a triplet as hateful or "bad seed", especially if a multiple birth was unexpected.

## Early intervention: Fred

A mother and her newborn, Fred, were referred at the end of the working week as his mother had rejected him, saying that she had no feelings for "it". She said that she would look after "it", but she had two high-needs children by a former partner who needed her and she felt very connected to them and did not feel needed by her new baby. I first observed Fred sleeping, and then feeding peacefully and I shared this with her. I talked with her that he needed her as much as his brother and sister, but that he was different from them. She confided to me that she had in effect felt forced to have this baby to keep his father as her partner. Her partner eventually joined us and seemed to be claiming his son and I shared my observations with him of Fred as an easy-going baby to include his father in our talking. Offering Fred's mother a chance to explore her anxious and sad feelings brought a quick change, immediately seeming to alleviate the projections and when I returned on Monday, she said she felt differently about Fred now. I had responded quickly to her need and given her an hour where she could tell me what she needed to, about the "ghosts".

## Some clinical guidelines for single sessions

I try to receive the referral early, antenatally if possible, and to include a mother's partner if I can, unless there is no ongoing relationship. Sometimes a therapist needs to respond immediately: one midwife rang an hour after a birth to refer a mother because she thought there was something unusual in the way she looked at her baby. Sometimes all I can arrange is one session before discharge so it needs to count even though I may not know much background history. I also include her mother if she wants that. Unless it seems contraindicated I feel that, for example, if the mother wants to have older children there, to find a way to include them in what we talk about, will benefit them as well as their mother and the family.

I aim to explore two main issues, first, the meaning the baby has for the mother and her partner—and second, what the mother's supports are, including external mother figures and the mother "inside". I am mindful of the likelihood of being the recipient of a good mother/grandmother transference to rework the representation of object relations. I reflect on what the anxiety is, whether I need to explore why the baby is "not there", or a mother's neediness, or whether she is rejecting of the baby. If appropriate I offer sessions, weekly if possible, to explore and contain anxieties and negative feelings, and to see if they can be integrated rather than disowned.

I try to hang in there with containment and persistence. I try not to be pushed away if the mother's response early on that is everything all right, and if she suggests we finish a session early. If there is internal and external family chaos I try to accommodate that into my schedule; a mother may be able to use me for even half an hour.

I am also mindful of the likelihood of trauma—it would be rare in referrals if there was not some trauma, childhood abuse, or disorganised attachment. If mothers have struggled with their first infant I try to accompany them until they have had the next one or to refer on so that they can get further help.

## *Clinical guidelines for a five session intervention*

### *Beginning session*

Setting up the intervention, exploring the meanings and feelings around the presenting difficulties, and an initial aim of beginning to build a therapeutic alliance in a setting that feels safe, for example, outlining that both parent(s) if possible, infant, and therapist will meet weekly for about five weeks. This would include engaging the infant.

### *Middle sessions*

These sessions usually consist of containment, verbalising affect, linking, reframing the projections and attributions around anger, shame, and loss, and interpretation and working through the negative transference to the infant (and the therapist if appropriate).

## Ending sessions

These sessions would be working towards ending. The therapist may be aware of a low-key atmosphere and the affects of sadness, consolidating the idea that distressing affects and experiences can be faced and talked about.

## *What I do and say: containment and relational experience*

Primarily I offer containment in a relational experience, which usually seems to make the most difference for mothers exploring difficult feelings with infants and modifies their internal objects, at least in the short term. A mother may be viewing the therapist as the mother she never had (Stern, 1995), looking at her baby in the way that she wished her own mother could have looked at her and her baby. Many of the mothers feel that their own mothers, internal and external, are not loving and sensitively available, and are so often seen as unhelpful. Containing powerful, often distressing, feelings that become known in the countertransference through projective identification is therapeutic; containment may convey many silent interpretations. As the hospital setting is unpredictable, while I work with a stable internal frame, my approach is flexible: a combination of analytic thinking, and what I have learned about infants informed by clinical experience and infant research. And while how I engage with an infant and his family is shaped by the setting, I try to create a confidential space with a relatively unstructured approach. I observe and engage with an infant to get a sense of his personality and feelings.

I try to convey a sense of enough time in my mind for a mother to tell her story in her own way. I need to balance that with knowing that, most likely I will intervene actively in the first—and sometimes only—session, which surprisingly often may be enough. Often, trying to feel my way into the experience of an infant and mother helps her feel that her infant is more resilient than she had thought, and at the same time containment can lead to some development of reflectiveness.

Mothers may identify with my way-of-being, and through a positive transference, severe self-critical tendencies may soften slightly, and a degree of more playfulness and reflectiveness develop. I try to accompany a mother past her internal self-criticism to see her baby as a person. I try to help her have the courage to look at and interact with her baby and to find moments of enjoyment. A therapist's spontaneity at times in the relational experience is likely to be very important. A mother seeing how early her baby is ready for social interaction is an important early intervention that can lessen her anxiety. Seeing her baby has a capacity to respond, and that the therapist enjoys her baby, is usually relieving. If a mother has questions about her infant's emotional development I answer briefly if appropriate.

## Interpretive comments

I usually make some links and interpretations in a generally explorative approach, sometimes commenting on things more quickly than I might otherwise. I involve fathers if possible, and explore partner intimacy and sex if appropriate, which often opens up difficult issues. In taking up the projection that a baby is rejecting his mother, I might point out that babies do not reject their mother, but want her to be happy and I might point out the baby's contribution in wanting to attach and bring pleasure. I mainly intervene in a parent's transference to her infant, trying to disconnect it from projections from the past, as with the mother whose three-month-old baby son breastfed peacefully but in a projective identification she exclaimed that he was like an adult man fighting her. I asked about her background and it emerged that she saw her baby as like her father and brother who had suffered episodes of schizophrenia and were at times abusive. It was easy to hear a projection of this experience on to her baby and I pointed out I did not see him as she did, that I observed a baby who was feeding peacefully and with a different history, and personality, and genetics, and a different father from her brother.

For some parents, it may be helpful to take up their projections with observation of a very sensitive baby responding to the birth and needing extra input to help settle. I might point out that from birth, the infant brain processes the image of the face of their parents (an infant will search for gaze when struggling parents often loom in too closely to kiss and cuddle).

The most relieving interventions are around a mother's guilt and hateful feelings. A negative transference to me I usually interpret quickly. Some reasons for quick change are a revival of memories of which mothers were previously not aware, of being taken care of, and finding a good mother figure for nurture for themselves.

### A five-session intervention: Helen and Hugh

Helen, a thirty-two-year-old married professional woman with a supportive husband and extended family, was referred for feeling distant and detached from her three-week-old infant, Hugh. The pregnancy was planned and trouble free: "too easy, I could do everything I wanted". She said she had felt excited and attached to the baby during the pregnancy. But she had felt overwhelmed and increasingly anxious about him since the birth and felt pushed out of hospital after forty-eight hours insufficiently prepared to care for him. The feelings were exacerbated the previous day by her husband, Hudson, returning to work after two weeks of paternity leave. She referred to Hugh only as "him" and "that" and she openly described how she felt it was a burden to care for him; however, he *was* cared for and fully breast fed, which she described as "nice". She had an episode of fleeting, intrusive ideation of "running over the baby", which she emphatically denied she would ever do, and one of self-harm ideation where she thought that if she broke her leg by falling downstairs she would no longer have to care for him. She described wanting "an older baby", able to respond to her rather than just lie there. She said that she had no formal mental health history and said that the risk of harming herself or her baby was very low and she was insightful about her feelings.

I saw them to discuss Helen's hatred of Hugh's screaming at night and she found it hard to explain why she felt very ragged hearing it. She had felt completely panicked at having to care for a baby when left all alone with him the first two nights. She conveyed a sense of not doing it right and shock at becoming a mother although she said that her mother was supportive. Hudson seemed very quick to offer to take Hugh out of her arms, perhaps afraid she would hurt him although both concurred that she would not. She was beginning to warm towards him; he did seem a slightly irritable infant and I worked with them about not changing too rapidly what they offered him as that could increase his anxiety. When I offered her an appointment the following week she was keen to accept. The following week they said that seeing me had been helpful for several days and she had then crashed. I tried an interpretation about her not getting on with her younger brother who had been ill and took a lot of their mother's attention but this seemed ineffective.

The following week she said she had felt fantastic and her husband concurred, and they said Hugh had made considerable progress, including vocalising and sleeping through the night. She told me quite quickly she had asked her mother if she had minded her younger brother crying, so that the interpretation I thought was too experience-distant had been taken up immediately. (Helen asking her mother allowed some expression of her feelings to the primary object and perhaps also brought some healing. I wondered about a sad, terrified child with the defences covered over until they blew in hospital.) But she was very clear she did not want a second child because she found the crying so terrible. However, she did seem quite loving in the way that she touched him at times. When I said lightly to her that she needed to be careful if she was falling in love with her son, intuiting her difficulties tolerating closeness, her husband's face was radiant that I was hinting at this. I queried whether I had missed her depression but they did not feel that I had.

The following week she felt even better and Hugh was more alert, holding his gaze when he was not crying, and I pointed out he was a strong-willed infant with an interesting personality. His father referred to things I had said previously, commenting that they made sense. Hugh although not very hungry fed with gusto and sensuality. His mother was very loving at times and talked in motherese. The following week he had slept through the previous night, stretched his feeds out by another half hour and was crying less. Helen had improved but still had difficulty tolerating closeness as she seemed slightly sarcastic in asking me about myself and mimicking horror at me being away for three weeks as though I was to assume that she could not care less but I think she was concerned. At the final appointment a month later, they continued to do very well. She found her son enjoyable and fascinating and was much more looking forward to having a second child, which suggested that the ghosts were less frightening. When she became pregnant three years later she told the obstetrician that at the time of Hugh's birth I had been very helpful.

## *Infants and parents with anxiety and depression*

I turn now to infants whose parents experience some mental health issues that involve varying degrees of risk for some infants. Postnatal depressive feelings may be in response to a difficult birth and subsequent difficulties in feeding, feeling worthless, and compounding misery, but usually a revival of a mother's lived experience as the infant daughter of her own mother (and probably a transgenerational connection with the great-grandmother as well). Infants of a mother who was depressed in pregnancy exhibit less optimal behaviours shortly after birth (more irritability, unavailability, lethargy, and stress, and less motor tone and activity (Abrams et al., 1995). For every depressed mother and father, there is an infant at risk of depression unless an intervention is received; mother and infant do not feel close and the infant detecting the averted, empty gaze of a parent, and the shame in how the parent handles his or her body, turns away. Infants may misinterpret an adult's worried face as angry. A three-week-old infant may have a compliant smile; in the same way, when a mother is ill with, for example, cancer, we may find a "sparkle plenty" infant (Stern, 1995). By two months or earlier a mother's depressive feelings can be reflected in her baby before she has expressed them; if a two-month-old baby does not expect pleasure with his mother, and feels self-conscious and ashamed without joyful mirroring, his feelings are dampened down, in a self-fulfilling way that there is no pleasure. By four months of age infants can discriminate when an adult "looks through" them. A depressed mother's gaze and handling of her infant show transmission of the trauma in a body-to-body way and without intervention this can be at the core of an ongoing depression. Intervening in the infant–mother relationship is likely to be needed to explore and reduce anxiety and depressive feelings, and enliven the infant in interaction.

Boys, with every difficulty that a mother shows, are more fragile so that their mothers may find them more difficult. When boys have depressed mothers, they feel more angry and deprived (Tronick, 2007). Mothers with high depressive symptoms showed significantly more negative affect to their boys who needed more scaffolding, and with escalating difficulties this is likely to generate even more negative affect and regulatory problems. Interactions of depressed mothers and sons have longer and more chronic failures of repair, although

Tronick did, however, wonder about a mother's sadness about her daughter's distance

When a mother can be accompanied by a therapist until after her next child, this may, in the therapist's "knowing" of her, lessen the likelihood of a recurrence of a severe postnatal depression.

## *Ilene and Iliana*

When a therapist is most open to feeling desperate and despairing, parents and infant usually feel that they are not alone. Immigrant parents and their four-month-old infant, Iliana, who was failing to thrive, were referred to a therapist. Ilene, her mother, whose English was very limited, was extremely depressed and the family were angry that the psychiatric services had not helped more. Ilene who was blank and distant could not look at Iliana. When she cried, Ilene rocked her in a way that the therapist found horrific, and then forcefully bottle-fed her, pinned to the rocker, until she vomited. The therapist felt incredibly lonely, hopeless, and deskilled; she thought the mother felt unheard. However, she thought that there was a tiny breakthrough when she asked the mother how it was for her and she replied, "How can I tell my family?" When the therapist said, "You can tell me", the mother said, "My life is over—I have no life". She asked, as if she saw no point in living, "How can I look after her when I can't look after me?" The therapist felt that she could not do much with Iliana, because Iliana was very distressed, and she was worried that the mother would suicide. But the following week Ilene was less depressed and intrusive, and Iliana had begun to feed.

The therapist had "lost the baby", as her mother had done as it was only in supervision that she remembered that she had achieved an interaction with Iliana. She had talked to Iliana about how hard it was, wiggled her fingers, and got Iliana to hold a finger. The therapist had looked deeply into her eyes and was struck by how blue they were, gently stroked her head, and asked her mother for a rattle. Her mother had tears streaming down her face as if seeing Iliana for the first time. The gaze and interaction between therapist and infant allowed Iliana to view herself reflected in a different way. The therapist, after containing her own painful anxieties about being useless, had brought Iliana to life in her mother's mind, lessened her anxiety, and given her an experience of pleasure. Iliana and her mother continued to do well over subsequent months.

### Infants of parents with a lived experience of serious mental illness

Infants of parents with a lived experience of serious mental illness are particularly vulnerable to emotional and developmental difficulties: when parents struggle with profound disturbances in mood, thinking, and relationship capacity, they can find it hard to keep in mind the relationship that their infant urgently needs. They need to be viewed as having the *potential* to be capable parents. The father of an infant with a lived experience of mental illness may be totally absent or of unknown identity, he may live apart or may be the effective primary carer. When an infant's parents have a lived experience of mental illness, they may, when unwell, become scared of their infant and locate their issues in the infant or seem devoid of their feelings for the infant.

After a parent has begun to function better, the infant does not always recover fully. If a mother with a lived experience of psychosis might be put too much in touch with her depression about, for example, not receiving from her own mother what people might expect her to give to her baby, this needs to be managed with enough support that her depressive feelings do not become unbearable. With a mother recovering from a psychotic episode a therapist might try not to contribute to her feeling persecuted by commenting too closely on what was noticeable about her infant; with a mother who hates her infant crying, asking who "heard" her when she cried as an infant. The following two vignettes continue the theme of the need for continual processing in the countertransference.

Being caught up in a projective identification of despair to show the therapist how bad it is, it may be very difficult to think and it may only be *afterwards* that the therapist can make use of the parallels it can illuminate. With a psychotic mother, a registrar had tried to think about the baby who was draped over his mother's legs, and ignored. When the registrar offered to help, his mother gave her the baby and did not take him back so that he was still ignored and she permitted the older siblings to draw on the walls. When able to think in supervision, the registrar said she found the mother's sense of entitlement difficult, and felt guilty and ashamed of her internal criticism, and her own despair could not be acknowledged until it was named in supervision. (A therapist might explain a mother's illness to a two-year-old as "mummy is so sad".)

## *Jane and Jack*

Jane and her six-month-old son, Jack, were referred for difficulties in bonding and both seemed to need the holding of my gaze. I saw them about six times. Jane's severe bipolar disorder was controlled with high doses of medication and Jack had an air of acceptance of the stillness imposed on him to lie flat in his pushchair, like an inanimate object. When I engaged with him, he would give me a wide gummy smile at the same time often giving a quick checking-back look at her face. When his mother said that she had not known it would be so boring so much of the time with an infant, I felt in my countertransference very sad, shocked, and a little angry, perhaps reflecting whether I could tolerate her being so shut-down. She was extremely anxious about going out with him in case he cried yet he was so interactive and good. She avoided my gaze or seemed to look slightly sullenly bored, but when I turned back to face her after I had talked with Jack, I would catch her looking at me with pleasure.

The following session, I found it difficult in the countertransference to sustain my interest and wanted to finish early, perhaps feeling hurt by her lack of interest in Jack. Yet she was lovely holding and talking to him, and called him "darling". (In a way, he had not changed so much before she changed; it was the meaning I attributed to him and their relationship, underpinned by my countertransference processing, which I think she found helpful. Perhaps she needed to see him change from "boring" to being animated with me.) She now said she was bored when he slept. She said he was very interactive and at a clinic developmental check up reported with pride that she had many more than the bare minimum of two conversations a day with him. She told me that while she sometimes felt bored she realised that she was not depressed, although she was worried that she would pass on to him a depression that would be even worse than her severe bipolar depression, and in exploring this vigorously I hoped to lessen the projection of these extreme fears.

Six months later her clinic nurse told me that she was doing well, and seemed less mechanical and her psychiatrist had reduced her medication, a good outcome considering the risk of relapse in the postnatal period. (See Chapter Nine for further discussion of countertransference.)

### Infants and parents with experiences of trauma including family violence

Many women facing birth and pregnancy find the doors to their traumatic past painfully opened. They may find that as they transition to parenthood they face a greater vulnerability to family violence. A therapist may find it hard to stay in touch with some parents who have experienced trauma and felt hated in their childhood. The parents may feel overwhelming for the infant and close to being negligent, or having an accident, or hurting the infant; they may not feed the infant enough or be aggressive even if indirectly, or extremely narcissistic. They may present in an intellectual way so that it is hard affectively to be in touch (as with Mariah, later in this chapter). An infant may be so despairing that a therapist may wonder whether the infant has given up. (See also "Boundary issues and families with multiple risk factors", Chapter Five.) While one fifth of women experience intimate partner violence, as with depression, abuse is infrequently disclosed to health professionals.

### Kaye and Kobie

A mother with a history of relational trauma may communicate with shocks in the countertransference. Kaye, a young mother, was referred with her infant son, Kobie; she initially locked me out of my room, leaving me feeling left and helpless as she probably had from childhood onwards and in the following session started to roll a cigarette, testing me out, and throughout she was extremely loud. It was very important for her to see how I recovered my emotional balance. She had experienced violence in her childhood, had begun sex working early, and the infant's father who had pimped her for several years was violent to her when he felt neglected. She needed me to have the experience of the continual shocks that she had experienced. Her six-month-old infant would cover his ears with his hands so as not to hear her outpourings about his father's violence. When she met me outside the hospital cafe and spilled out that the father was not violent in front of the baby I emphatically took up that therefore he *could* manage his violence and control himself when he was alone with her, and I asked whether she was safe. Her baby did not cover his ears for this conversation despite his mother's dysregulated state, I think because he felt my concern. Respecting a woman's need for safety can empower her: within a month Kaye had barred the father from her home, although fully disengaging from traumatising relationships was a longer process. Her second baby died shortly after birth. She wondered if the older infant was affected by the death and if I could help him. She may partly have kept having babies to keep in touch with hospital staff, verbalising that contact with the hospital was the first time she was treated with respect.

Research suggests that parents with a history of child abuse/neglect do better in psychotherapy than on medication alone. Those with the experience of complex cumulative trauma seek a respectful connection as can also be seen in the following vignette.

### Lou and Len

Lou, an older mother, from New York, was referred for extreme anxiety during an unplanned pregnancy. She had a history of childhood abuse, and had decided she would never have children. I saw both parents for a few sessions during pregnancy to mitigate their anxiety, associated particularly with Lou's adverse childhood experiences (and I also suggested couple therapy). She became a loving, sensitive mother. After nearly three years of therapeutic contact there was a rupture in therapy when she quickly ended a session, hurt and seeing me in a negative transference as an absent mother. Without knowing fully what I had said or done I had somehow unconsciously acted out the role of the initial traumatising object and I think she felt it was beyond words, coming from a time beyond words. But in my wish to repair, it was repaired. Ruptures between parent and therapist offer opportunities to be heard and repair. Awareness of countertransference is essential in salvaging a therapeutic rupture and the working through of these ruptures is now conceived of as an essential part of how therapy is successful.

Working through the rupture was therapeutic. She could then bring how her son's eyes reminded her of his violent father (possibly of all abusing eyes): having not felt safe with me these feelings threatened to entrap her loving relationship with her son. A few weeks later she got a good job and felt she had joined an exciting world so that a substantial degree of healing had taken place. Her son, Len, said that he now knew that monsters were "just pretend". I appealed to the hospital so I could continue seeing them, to not continue the cycle of abandonment and loss, and to allow enough time for her to resolve the experience of hateful feelings towards me.

## *Infants and mothers with lived borderline experiences*

Women with lived borderline experiences are likely to experience post-traumatic states, the effects of which are passed from one generation to another, and to experience difficulty during the perinatal period because of the increased stress. Parents with an abuse history may not experience the same lighting up of affiliation networks. They may struggle to look at and understand an infant's neutral face or may interpret it as sad or abusive and they have a heightened sensitivity to perceiving potential threat in their infant's face; with difficulties being empathic and reading what the infant is trying to communicate they feel abandoned and it could be important to verbalise this early (Newman, 2015).

A high proportion of parents with borderline experience are likely to have had traumatising experiences in their childhood and to need sessions over at least a year. A mother who feels no connection to her past is likely to repeat this with her infant. The most difficult countertransferences with a mother with borderline experiences are stirred up when resorting to early defences, primarily splitting and projective identification to ward off awareness of disturbing feelings and thoughts. Repeated therapeutic experiences of containment and reflectiveness help to weather the storms involved, resulting in a parent having less need to employ these defences, which in turn lead to increasing personality integration. With a mother who could not bear sharing attention and who might feel jealous if I interact with her infant too early, I try not to increase feelings of deprivation and envy. A parent with borderline difficulties may say, "My baby is happy looking at me but I don't feel that. How do I work out what my baby wants when no one did for me?" and a therapist can acknowledge that it is hard but together mother and therapist can do it. Intervening usually involves connection around a mother's own unresolved trauma issues that are triggered by the infant as both an object of hope and of envy, and who can therefore be hated.

A therapist may feel drained of resources and may need to acknowledge with the mother that what he says does not seem to be helpful. Sometimes what alerts me to this countertransference difficulty is a wish to keep giving advice, and I may have substituted a wish to pass on what I have learnt instead of being emotionally available, and keeping the space open without intruding long enough for the parent to feel it is safe to trust that I might want to hear and not be overwhelmed exploring a relational trauma. We need to find a place of accepting unresentfully being used as needed by parents with borderline experiences or similar presentations (see Chapter Nine). In the countertransference, women with borderline difficulties with psychotic features may evoke responses in the therapist that convey awareness of hidden aggression and if we can accompany a mother to access her own spontaneity and playfulness, her infant may also help the relationship develop.

### Mariah and Mary

Mariah, a young woman who had been diagnosed with a personality disorder, was referred while pregnant as the clinic staff felt that she was very cut off from the experience of being pregnant and found her hard to get on with. She was depressed, anxious, and related in what felt like an inauthentic way. She used a lot of therapist-speak, was cut off from me and I felt cut off from her. Her mother was a health professional, to whom Mariah was initially loyal. Mariah lived with her partner in her mother's house and her mother was better at settling Mary; it only gradually emerged that she could feel disempowering to Mariah. During Mariah's pregnancy, a cancerous tumour had been removed from her neck. The baby's father attended sessions early on until the relationship between the parents deteriorated.

I tried to see her weekly for a year. In her first session with Mary, her one-month-old infant, Mariah had her breasts exposed in a very seductive way; she said she was determined to breastfeed but she did not like breastfeeding, because she could feel her nipples opening and the milk coming through and she sometimes fed the baby with expressed breast milk. I was concerned about Mary who had not gained much weight and about her mother's relationship with her—Mary looked like a starving refugee infant, peculiarly fluffy and huddled over. Mariah tearfully told me about her father's abuse when she was eight years old: he had smashed her head against the table, so that she could not breathe.

Although Mariah sometimes seemed to hold Mary in quite a caring way, at other times I thought that she held her in a way that would feel intrusive and I mostly thought that Mary was not given enough support for her head, a message that a baby reads. She seemed at times to go very quickly to sleep in an avoidant way. Mariah said that she loved Mary, but felt depressed, indicating that she felt trapped. I asked about support and she said that she did not want to go to the young mothers' group, because she was better than the other mothers. When Mary cried a lot, Mariah said that she could not be hungry as she just fed her half an hour ago, and she had taken ninety millilitres. She was invalidating her daughter's experience as hers felt invalidated by her mother. I supported her to try feeding again and Mary took some more and Mariah then said Mary had had enough and had taken another ninety millilitres; I thought Mariah overestimated the amount that she had, and when Mary cried again I suggested she might still be hungry and she took a second top up. Mariah spontaneously said that I could ring her nurse, and tell her anything that I wanted to. (I was the mother in the transference, with the deprivation that Mariah felt contributing to her in effect passing on the experience of depriving her infant.) Mariah kept telling me that her weight gain was satisfactory and I thought I was going mad as Mary looked as though she was starving. I talked to Mary as I ordinarily would, and the following week she looked at me and half smiled. Mariah, probably jealous, faced Mary away from me to look at her, and Mary looked over at me and seemed almost serene. But Mariah seemed interested that I talked so much to her. I sometimes felt desperate in the countertransference and I wonder what the baby saw in my face.

When Mary was three months old, I particularly had to struggle in my countertransference, when she fed Mary who had to cling to the breast like a mountaineer using her hands as crampons, as Mariah only supported her neck not her back, and I gently explored this. But I thought, "This is too hard to see a baby whose needs are being so missed." When Mary struggled at the way the milk was propelled into her mouth from the way Mariah held the breast, Mariah held her tighter, then sat her up and Mary cried immediately. Mariah kept repeating that Mary was doing well, as though in the transference I was someone whom she had to convince and she had a quality of being so unreal this contributed to my feeling that "I can't do this"—until I thought that I *had to find a way* to get through to her. She then told me that when she had said to her mother, "I'm pregnant and if you had to save me or my sister, who would you save?" her mother had said, "Your sister, because you're a loser". (Which I had just repeated in the countertransference. What I did not repeat, however, was the outcome of her mother's hurtful words that she seemed to have experienced as so damaging.) My heart was often in my mouth as I watched the way Mary was treated, sometimes held over Mariah's legs as though she was about to drop her or Mariah stood her up when I thought she was too little to stand. I was very anxious as I thought this infant was not putting on weight but Mariah told me everyone said she was.

Finally, at three months Mariah had told me that Mary had been weighed and was found to have dropped from the thirtieth percentile to the ninth percentile, close to failure to thrive. Mariah was feeling very defensive and when Mary cried, Mariah rushed to say that she could not possibly be hungry. Mariah had developed another possible tumour but was more contained than the previous time, which the medical staff thought was because she was in therapy with me. At four months Mary looked calmly at me *the whole time*, while her mother fed her, continuing to relate to her in a way that seemed slightly manic, inauthentic, and careless. Mary fussed at the breast and for the first time, Mariah got angry with her and openly revealed her revulsion at breastfeeding.

A month later the situation deteriorated when Mariah cried all day and feared murderers coming to the door. She thought she might not have sterilised the bottles properly but nevertheless gave them to Mary and felt that she was a bad mother. I made a gentle link between her feelings that she could do something terrible to her daughter (be like a murderer) and her worries about intrusion. She howled quietly saying that she had not known it would be this hard. She wondered if she needed to increase her medication although this did not feel like her usual depression. I wondered if her partner feared Mariah would hurt Mary or would suicide. I thought Mary looked sad and she took some time to warm up with me. Once as Mariah swooped her past dangerously close to the desk corner I instinctively put my hand out protectively (as if this unconsciously represented the abuse from her father).

When Mary was nine months old Mariah, apologising that the milk would be a little cold almost force fed her a bottle; Mary pushed away but eventually gave up and went to sleep as Mariah wanted. Mariah felt depressed and lonely, and I talked about how with the change of identity we could feel very lonely, not knowing ourselves as we grew into the new identity of being a mother. At the end of the month Mariah came without Mary, and said in a very real way she had been unfaithful to her partner and would like more structured help to work through issues about her being too anxious to eat out, rather than for mother–infant issues, which I accepted. At eighteen months follow up, Mariah said she was doing well, did not cry like she used to, and might go back to school, although I thought Mary looked a little waif-like.

I had mainly provided containment and persistence, a space where they could both feel listened to, and been a more protective person than Mariah had generally experienced, although I could have picked up more quickly the revulsion to breastfeeding and the transgenerational difficulty that linked how Mariah could not feed herself or her baby. These repeated with her baby being the unwanted one as she had felt with her sister, and the borderline disorder experiences may have been more a manifestation of underlying feelings of sadness in her relationship with her mother.

### *Infants whose mother wanted a baby of a different gender*

Sometimes a mother very strongly wants a baby of a different gender and seems likely to be responding to a stubborn hurt in her childhood, aiming to repair it this way, to make herself feel whole again, or to change an abusive past. Some women who are extremely negative in pregnancy become a loving mother if an accepting space is made available for the negative to be integrated and repressed. When parents are desperate for a baby of a different gender, they do not see the baby for who he or she is. An intervention would be shaped by the strength of this fantasy. A therapist may need to carry a projected failure to provide some relief from an impossible maternal or self-introject but it may be harder to alleviate if this is close to delusional. Some parents can come to love their baby whatever the gender, particularly if the baby can help them feel they are a loving mother or father and therefore good.

## Nora and her infants

Nora had been referred as she was unsure that she could bond to her second daughter, as she wanted a boy. The psychiatrist had discharged her, having assessed her as not depressed. The obsession to have a boy was making her so unhappy that she was becoming depressed as she told me that she was extremely unhappy about everything and complained continuously. Her two-year-old daughter accompanied her to sessions and was an easy-going, attractive little girl, but I was concerned about the anger that Nora brought about her, bursting through a couple of time in expressions towards her, including once when Nora imitated an expression in a way that I thought did not have a pretend quality to it (and I needed to raise that her daughter could find it scary). She told me that after she learned that her second baby would be another girl she used to shop during her pregnancy for a rope to hang herself but had not told the psychiatrist. I also learned that there had been an earlier termination of a male foetus and so the longed-for boy baby was to be reparative. Her third baby was a boy but she looked at him at birth in a way that alarmed the midwife enough to refer to me. Presumably at some unconscious level he reproached her for the dead boy and did not make up for him. Although I tried to help her see the baby behind his gender she experienced extreme anxiety after his birth about fear of persecution. I broached referring her on, but lost her, as I probably had not kept seeing her long enough.

## An infant conceived for a dying mother: Oriana and Olena

A woman may decide to have a baby to make her mother happy before she dies, and the mother–baby relationship is shaped by the strength of this fantasy and regret when it does not keep the grandmother alive. Oriana, an older woman, who had never wanted children, decided to become pregnant as her mother was dying. Her mother died before the birth and her difficulties bonding were in the context of a complex grief reaction. Oriana, her daughter, Olena, and her partner were referred when she felt suicidal about being a mother for the rest of her life. She found it helpful that early on when I held Olena, her eyes skittered over me, and I could not catch her gaze. Her husband attended all the weekly appointments for the first eighteen months.

Olena was a beautiful princess, and the second infant, a son, was avoidant of me. With her second infant, Oriana wanted another girl, perhaps to be like herself, perhaps to keep the tie with her mother, as a more symbiotic fusion. Gradually she was more able to have some joy in her children and often seemed caring with them although she could also withdraw from or yell at them during anniversary reactions. Later she told me about what she said were little cruelties towards them, facing her son away and giving him nothing of herself, or yanking an arm a little roughly, and said she silently rejoiced if they hurt themselves. I usually felt I had not helped her to change, as if occupying a place of deadness in my mind was linked with her dead mother, the infants were dead objects for her, and her husband was also dead for her despite the support he tried to be. Once she texted me that there was no point going on and I tried very hard but unsuccessfully to contact her that day, very concerned about the possibility of suicide. I think I had to experience how desperate she was although the countertransference feeling of having little traction could signal that an ambivalent attachment could develop (see Chapter Nine). After two years of keeping in touch with her, she seemed a little sadder and softer.

## *Infants whose parents use substances*

As women who use alcohol and drugs on the background of mental illness often find it difficult to "be" with their infant, they are at risk for maladaptive parenting; up to fifty per cent may lose care of their infants with six months after birth. If the infant is frightened, triggering a mother's past trauma, for example when she is trying to nurture the infant who is distressed, this elicits earlier fears in her and she often withdraws or becomes aggressive with the infant. If a mother connects with her infant at birth this gives a window of opportunity to intervene.

## *Paulette and Pattie*

Paulette, a forty-year-old single mother, with a long history of cannabis use and living in deprived circumstances was referred for help with her relationship with her baby. Paulette had unexpectedly become pregnant and thought about doing the abortion herself but felt unable to abort her baby. The baby, Pattie, was thought to have died at birth and had to cope with many difficulties of prematurity. Paulette while caring fiercely for her seemed at times overwhelmed. Initially she would bring Pattie to a half hour session about every two weeks. She said she did not love her and asked if it would be better for her if she was adopted (Paulette did not feel she had anything good in herself and was also recreating her experience of feeling she had not been invested in an infant). I said no and said that what mattered most was that she conveyed to Pattie that she would always protect her. I was therefore not asking her to do something she could not do. It took about two years before Paulette could say that she loved her. Pattie, who for a long time had a very negative transference to me as potentially coming between them, was so connected with her mother who became less overwhelming and so loving and accepting of the intimacy, mirroring and affirming Pattie in a way she never felt she had received from her parents. Even when Pattie went into child care they still attended. Paulette gave me a first card and a present of some chocolate and thanked me for my "love"; when Pattie was four years old, Paulette wished me a "magical Xmas".

Paulette's reflectiveness had collapsed around the childhood trauma of her brother's sexual abuse, which had been denied by her father, and had burdened her transition to parenthood. I think my persistence contributed to this mother forming a close relationship with her own infant. She had dared to become tender and known to her, as she had dared to become known to us and trusted us. Her daughter began achieving unbelievably well cognitively. By four years Paulette would keep in touch with me about every two months as a secure base. She was working in her own therapy to being softer to her parents and trying to understand it from her father's perspective and was at this point ready to seek more formal psychotherapeutic input to try to give up substances.

## *Conclusion*

A few sessions of post-birth intervention around maternity are sufficient for many mothers to allow themselves to come close to their baby, aiding the neuroplasticity of a mother's (and father's) brain that is changed in part by her baby's neurons contributing to regulate hers. A greater number of sessions for parents with lived borderline experiences is usually needed, and for women who postpone motherhood out of anxiety about whether they want it or would succeed in it. A parent's own childhood emotional neglect is a strong predictor for number of sessions needed. It takes longer to intervene on behalf of mother, father, and infant when a parent experiences extreme states of mind, as the infant also has the experience of traumatic states that may mean that a therapist is doing something more like child psychotherapy in the presence of the parents. It is essential for this intervention to include the infant for the infant–parent relationship to more fully recover.

CHAPTER FOUR

# Infants with young parents

While many adolescent mothers use their pregnancy as a catalyst for positive change, about half may struggle as this population carries disproportionate risks, presenting considerable developmental challenge for many infants and their mothers. The risks include generations of poverty, mental illness, and sometimes a history of neglect and abuse, depression, substance use, and coercive partner relationships. For the infants, there is a risk of developmental delay and later of conduct disorder and depression. Targeting the relationship that the mothers have with their infants is a window of opportunity for intervention in that the infants are less likely to be securely attached at one year of age. A young mother is negotiating herself through the adolescent process as well as the new experience of becoming a mother. She needs support so that she can participate in some teenage life, with professionals seeing some health in rebellious behaviour, mindful that an adolescent mother may hardly be cognitively ready to be a parent. She may use less mind-related comments in interaction with her infant. She may find it hard to empathise with her infant, as she may be hardly out of childhood herself, and may at times be rough. When her infant cries, the helplessness and terror may remind her of her own helplessness and if she feels very persecuted, she may walk away abruptly, increasing her infant's anxiety and anger.

The availability of fathers is important not only for the infant but also for the mother, and I include the father or partner if possible. For many young mothers their relationship with their own mother had its difficulties, for example, not feeling they were enjoyed when they were nurtured and they feel deprived in a way that makes it hard to be reflective: when, as a new mother, she turns to an internalised mother for understanding, she may feel this cannot sustain the self at a time of crisis, and this is the space into which a therapist steps. I describe both a young mother and an intervention I designed to help parents connect better with their infant.

## *Saphire and Sara:*
## *a young mother having difficulty bonding*

Sometimes a therapist's feeling he has nothing to offer protects against the anxiety of being rejected as offering nothing of value. This was partly the case with a sixteen-year-old adolescent, Saphire, who had been in the child protection system since she was a young child and was currently living in a refuge. She appeared extremely cut off and was referred late in pregnancy for difficulty in feeling bonded to her unborn infant. She was diagnosed as having an antisocial personality disorder and her use of marijuana, ice, or cocaine had increased in pregnancy.

For the first visit with me with her three-week-old infant, Saphire arrived two hours late, with a friend, both talking volubly on the phone. She was said to be mechanical and to not look at her infant, Sara. She was a bit flat and negative about her and said that she was not in love with her, and asked me if that was normal. I said it sometimes took time. Later when I asked to hold Sara and talked to her to see if she would open her eyes and interact with me, she did so and gave a few smiles and I had a sense that Saphire was interested and amazed at what I was doing. I talked about Sara's crying as a strength in wanting to be close to her mother. Overall Saphire was angry but cut off; she had felt cut off from her mother and in turn she distanced herself from Sara and me. I was despairing and I did not think I would be able to help and wondered whether I should suggest anger management instead, perhaps a countertransference enactment. I may have been in projective identification with Saphire's unconscious feelings of uselessness and inadequacy that led me to question my own capacities. My countertransference feelings might signal that a disorganised attachment could develop, with a higher risk of borderline features for the baby, if there was no input.

Next session Saphire was only a quarter of an hour late and was more forthcoming. I commented that Sara looked different and curious, and she asked how and then told me she had got her first smile from Sara but said she interacted very little with her because she needed to do housework. She told me Sara was a good feeder and I tried exploring possible pleasure for Saphire in breastfeeding to help this become not just a functional relationship but a fuller one, open to the infant's sensuality and her own. Saphire said that when she fed her daughter, she looked away because her neck hurt. I said, to convey I was serious about trying to be effective, we could get that fixed in the hospital. This brought out a transgenerational trauma: Saphire's mother had not able to breastfeed her because of a horrific injury to her own breasts. Saphire said she was getting irritated with her partner, Sara was unsettled and I said she was picking up her feelings but I was not sure how much Saphire took in. She very readily became angry in the outside world. She felt people reported on her (and I wondered to myself whether I was included in this transference and whether she perhaps did not want to keep her baby) and she said she might lose Sara (and again I wondered to myself whether she wanted to keep her). She cancelled the next session, just before my break, so I was surprised to hear from the support worker that Saphire could look more at her daughter since the visit to me.

Formulating at this point, I thought that what was unconscious transgenerationally from her early years were terrifying feelings. Her resistances of lateness and blankness were self-protective. My countertransference was hard to bear—feeling helplessly frustrated, as she perhaps did. At that point I was so *immersed in* the countertransference that I doubted that I would be able to offer anything through my usual ways of intervening. In my telling myself that I could not give up despite feeling I had no point of contact, that is, my processing something, perhaps allowed her to feel she could return to engage with me. I got little sense of Sara—was she already shut down because of the experience of partner violence *in utero* and during her first month? But also in the countertransference I was standing up for Saphire's right to breastfeed with pleasure. Motherhood for most adolescents is a point of acute crisis (Lemma, 2012) and for many the earliest relationship with their mother is in some ways disturbed; if the core anxiety is about fragmentation of the self and psychic survival, the envy may be more destructive. When an adolescent mother feels herself to be a rival with her baby, she may feel her baby is robbing her of adolescent freedom and opportunities and may relate to her own breast as a sexual breast as a symbol of her desire to develop a separate identity and may complain that her baby gets in the way of her having a life. (We could see this with Mariah although less so with Saphire.)

A month later, Saphire fed Sara who got extremely distressed with wind and fixed on the light switch. Saphire insisted she could not be looking at a white wall and out of my mouth came the statement that Sara might be discriminating textures, like Eskimos with white snow. (I had just read *Miss Smilla's Feeling for Snow* (Hoeg, 1993)). My unconscious was implying she was not just turning away from her mother. Perhaps because I had looked for meaning Saphire then turned Sara round so that I could talk to her (and perhaps make more meaning) and as I did so, Sara started to smile and interact vocally with me, responding and initiating. When I said, "You *are* clever", she smiled and vocalised more. I said to Saphire that I thought Sara was doing well and that she would have got that from Saphire. When I talked to Sara, Saphire looked interested, but then told me she did not have a clue what was going on in Sara's mind. Then jealous of my involvement, she put Sara on the floor on the other side of the pram, tightened her fingers round a hard rattle and to my amazement Sara kept looking in my direction fixing on my eyes. I found it very hard leaving her there but felt I needed to, otherwise I thought her mother might not come back. I asked Saphire about life being hard for her and there was a torrent about how she was "effing furious" about "effing" workers who were "effing" stupid, she could do nothing, nor go anywhere—the transference was obvious but it seemed sufficient at this point to work with it but not in it. I tried to *feel* what her experience would be—it was still so hard to find the pain—and she brought her despair that she had lost her passion for graphic design, which was her intended career.

Next session Saphire was on time. (It took her two hours travel each way to see me—she had to walk, take a bus, a train, and a tram—and of the thirteen workers initially involved with her, I was one of only two whom she had not sacked—presumably she felt I had something to offer that she needed.) Three-month-old Sara worked so hard to connect with me, smiling at me in her pram, coming on like a light bulb. To my amazement, Saphire immediately unselfconsciously began talking motherese very easily to Sara, so we had reached some good implicit memories. When I talked about Sara's responsiveness with Saphire, she said "OK" several times as though she was open to the ideas, interested and accepting of the positive. She told me that she had got her first laugh from Sara and had rung her own mother to share this, reconnecting with her own mother after a long break in their relationship. She echoed a phrase I had once used about Sara, "She'll do it again" as though being able to be reflective about ongoing development. Then also to my amazement, and for the first time, Saphire talked freely. She said she had an awful week, had been in a fight with a foreigner who said she was corrupt and disgusting being a teenage mother, that is, invalidating her, and she was accused of possessing a knife. But she also told me about another infant who had empathically understood Sara's crying and I wondered about a beginning empathic state of mind in Saphire (oscillating with the more out-of-touch one I had seen at the beginning; I think this was an awareness of the infant's theory of mind—that infants do think about the minds of others). She sat back to talk to me: she had not been able to go back to design but had lost weight.

There were many things I did not initially take up, feeling that I walked a tightrope. In the first four hours of intervention initially I did not think I had touched her addiction or personality disorder, but the mother–infant relating was better. I thought that Sara's responsiveness and the intervention had helped with the depression and I question whether what was diagnosed as borderline personality disorder was really underlying depression. Sara did her bit, trying so hard to respond to me, and then allowing her mother time with me. Saphire was clean of drugs. She seemed to feel that I could help with something that she wanted help with and she did seem to be thinking her infant might have a mind that she could be curious about. She wore make-up and new clothes on the fourth visit. Sara continued to be responsive at home. We met together for about nine months, she was always on time, and was very bonded to Sara. Something of Saphire's mother was rekindled or she found something new with me. She once brought her mother to a later session.

## A two-session intervention with young mothers

As intervening when a mother already has postnatal depression is not ideal practice (Murray et al., 2003), I designed an intervention to assist pregnant adolescents to be more emotionally available and respond more sensitively to their newborns, which was carried out with a PhD student, Susan Nicolson. The intervention has been semi-manualised. The aim was whether a brief, perinatal attachment intervention, offered to pregnant adolescents in the third trimester to fit with routine maternity care, would be associated with a better quality of infant–mother relationship when the infant was four months old. It consisted of a discussion antenatally of DVD clips of the amazing capacities of infants and I then visited the mothers and infants at birth to try to help them see their infant as a person, and their importance to their infant. When the infant was four months old, the interaction of all mothers with their infants was videotaped at home; and the seventy-three videos were blind rated using a validated coding system for different qualities of mother and infant behaviour, the Emotional Availability Scales (Biringen & Robinson 2008).

This was to my knowledge the first brief, evidence-based programme for adolescent mothers that fitted with routine maternity care and tried to influence their relationship with their infant from the beginning.

The intervention was designed to be replicable and to overcome some of the barriers to care. We hypothesised that an attachment intervention offered to pregnant adolescents would be acceptable to them, that the intervention would be associated with enhanced maternal sensitivity, as assessed by infant–mother interaction at four months of age, and with a reduction in negative maternal perceptions of their infant. The mothers in the control group were recruited before the intervention group as the young mothers used the same waiting room and often developed social relationships.

Its two components, antenatal and postnatal, focused on helping the mothers to see their infant as a person, the infant's social capacity, their importance to their infant, and the potential for mutual delight from the beginning, to support bonding. All mothers completed a questionnaire at the end of the study to provide information on symptoms of depression, self-esteem, and their infant's temperament. Emotional availability is predictive of infant attachment at one year and the six scales provide a dyadic assessment of the relationship, via expressed emotions as well as behaviours in mother and infant.

## *The antenatal session*

The antenatal component was a forty-five to sixty minute group session for the adolescents from thirty weeks' gestation. This was informed by an account of a group for pregnant adolescents with conduct disorders in a research programme in Toronto, whose infants were significantly more securely attached following a group session discussing a DVD on comforting crying infants (Zoccolillo, 2003).

I designed the session for two to six young women before or after an antenatal check-up. Accompanying partners, friends, parents, or other support persons were welcomed in the sessions and it could be provided individually. I set up the session not as a classroom experience but to be enjoyable and developmentally appropriate. We showed five brief video clips (of a total of ten minutes duration) along the lines of the following DVDs: *Your Social Baby* (Murray & Andrews, 2002), *Getting to Know You* (Blick & Warren, 2003), The Circle of Security *Shark Music* (Circle of Security, 2002), and *The Simple Gift of Comfort* (Benoit &Goldberg, 1998). The other clip was an extract from an interview with a teen mother, with her permission, when her infant was four months old who shared how surprised she was at how interactive her infant was from the beginning. The clips conveyed the social capacities of newborn infants and their urge to connect, the importance of comforting a crying infant, and the negative feelings that may arise with a crying infant, as well as parents' varied experiences of bonding. The clips were chosen for their relevance to the aim of the intervention, and their acceptability to a group of culturally diverse, adolescent women.

After showing the clips I invited discussion. This provided an opportunity to talk about surprises, fears, and dilemmas such as what to do when they felt under pressure, when their "buttons" were pressed. I aimed to convey two key messages: the amazing capacities of an infant as a person, and second, the importance of comforting a crying infant, that crying is a communication and how important it was for infants to feel that someone was there with them trying to understand and comfort them so that they did not feel alone. The Circle of Security clip that shows how the music accompanying a beautiful scene changes to the menacing music from the film *Jaws* conveys graphically how a mother might sometimes feel that it was too hard—still the same infant but the music had changed. Before playing this clip, I described it and said their infants might be affected hearing the music. We could use this to talk about what steps they could take when they felt this happening, and how to "chill out". Mothers who were likely to be "good enough" used the session as reinforcement of these tendencies, while mothers who were anxious or negative needed the neonatal intervention as well. Many mothers who already had an infant accepted the intervention yet were often negative in the group discussion but I think they hoped that the attachment process would go better with their second or third infant. The reason I aimed to do this intervention some time before their infant was due was to enable enough time for the young women to process it.

## The neonatal session

The neonatal component was a thirty to sixty minute individual session that built on the antenatal session, through exploring their *own* baby's social capacities and urges to connect with them through their seeing this. I visited the mother on the postnatal ward ideally on day two and said something like, "I've come to meet you and your baby". Generally, I carried out the neonatal session with whoever was visiting, whether it was father, grandmother, friends, or children. There might be little privacy if it was a two-bed ward, highlighting the need for a secure internal setting in my mind. If the infant was in NICU, I did the session there when it was appropriate. During the session, I engaged mothers in a conversation about their perception of their newborn as a person (and before birth), what they saw of their infant's personality, and likes and dislikes. I tried to engage in a discussion about "reading" their infant's behaviour in terms of the internal states that might contribute to it, that is mind-mindedness (Meins et al.,

2002). If a mother needed some prompting, I might ask questions such as, "What's your baby like?" or "How do you see her personality?", or looking at the infant, enquire whether she thought that her infant was active, calm, curious, alert, or sleepy; "What does he seem to enjoy and dislike? What was she like before she was born?" I aimed to encourage mothers to wonder about their infant's experience, based on experience that an infant can be "knowable", to increase a mother seeing her infant for who he or she was, as trying to communicate, rather than what they can do.

Many mothers seemed to envisage a full relationship with their infant and said that they looked at their infant "all the time", commenting that their infant "only wants me". One mother gave five descriptors of her son: "bright, determined, sensitive to my presence and wants me and to sleep with me". When I asked her how she knew, she said that he cried loudly if she went to the toilet and he stopped when she picked him up. If there are any parent–infant relationship difficulties that are linked to parental emotional unavailability due to trauma, this approach may be a circuit breaker in which parent and infant become more attuned, in the hope of influencing parental representations of the infant.

If the infant cried, I would wonder with the mother what her infant was experiencing and see how the infant could be consoled. I might ask mothers how their recollections of the antenatal video clips related to their experience so far of their own infant. I reframed negative attributions to an infant's behaviour, for example, "He's so lazy, he sleeps all the time," as what a newborn infant did in the early days or that an early smile was not "wind".

I interacted with the infants, often holding them, to understand their experience and communicate this back as well as explore it with the parent, to shape the parent's and infant's representations. I would try to ensure that a mother could see the interaction and point out if the infant was looking at her when with me. If an infant gave a smile of pleasure in response to interaction and this went unnoticed or if an infant held his mother's gaze, I used it as an opportunity to wonder together about the infant's experience, to facilitate mothers getting to know their newborn and to promote a sense of connection and mutual enjoyment. Some mothers found it quite dramatic, when they saw how their infant could follow with their eyes. If a mother did not seem able to claim her infant and seemed initially passive in the presence of her partner, or particularly if a maternal grandparent seemed to monopolise the infant, I would try gently to bring her to the centre by passing her infant to her to hold.

## Some findings

The group was very multicultural and quite a high proportion had mental health issues. Acceptability of the project was very good. Eighty-seven per cent were having their first infant. Despite most of them having a partner, they were dependent on their family and government benefits. A high proportion was homeless at some point while pregnant and there was a high rate of psychosocial vulnerability: twenty-three per cent said that their main mother figure was not the birth mother. Forty-five per cent had a family mental health history. Depression reduced dramatically post-birth. Significant differences were found between the intervention and control groups, measured when the infants were four months old. The intervention group scored significantly better in two of the subscales for maternal non-hostility and maternal non-intrusiveness when a twenty-minute episode of play alone was observed and coded for emotional availability. When a twenty-five minute episode of play-plus-brief-separation–reunion was observed and coded, the intervention group scored significantly better in three of the subscales (maternal sensitivity included). The intervention was therefore associated with a better-quality infant–mother relationship.

## Theory of the approach

I tried antenatally and neonatally to increase a mother's observation and thinking about her infant's mind, to change beliefs about her infant and confidence in her capacity to read her infant, and particularly at birth to help her delight in her infant. I tried to convey support, understanding, and affirmation, techniques related to higher therapeutic alliance: "a more active, engaged, motivating, yet open-ended stance by the therapist was important in a positive therapeutic relationship" (Hilsenroth et al., 2012, p. 375). I tried to enhance the mothers' self-representation, and regulation of affective states (Karlsson, 2011). Most of the women had a positive relationship with me.

In the context of the brief therapeutic window of a maternity hospital stay, this approach supported a mother to be attuned to her infant, to enable mutual enjoyment. It seemed to influence representations of the infant, particularly reflectiveness. I tried to connect with the infant in his or her own right, and—for a mother who felt that she did not know her infant—to connect him or her to the mother. It would be evident I found it potentially enjoyable when I was with them.

It seems likely that the effectiveness of the intervention stemmed in large part from a good mother/grandmother transference—following up at the momentous time of birth, affirming that the mothers either already "knew" their infant or showing them that they could know their infant in a way that could be internalised at a procedural level. As Schechter (2012) pointed out, many adolescent mothers who may have gone "off the trail" hope to reconnect with their mothers and the intervention offered a potential bridge. The intervention was welcomed in assisting mothers to be relationship-focused.

I tried to reframe projections on to the infant, although trying to move a negative projection towards a positive one in a short session in a busy hospital often within hours of birth is working under pressure. In countertransference processing I may have taken on some of their emptiness, despair, and terror of having an infant. However, being able to intervene around the first day or two of birth offers therapeutic advantages as it is such a momentous time, in a mother's becoming aware that what was inside is now outside.

## Impact of the approach

In addition to some of the results above, a high proportion of mothers were still breastfeeding at four months. (One mother, who had not breastfed her previous infant so as not to spoil the shape of her breasts, breastfed her newborn as she thought that it was better for the infant.) Those mothers who already had children and were initially negative in the group discussion became warmer in the neonatal intervention. The qualitative feedback was positive: most of the mothers at four months felt that the intervention helped them be more confident and above all to enjoy their infant in a way most of them had previously thought unimaginable. One mother said, "At a time when everything was frightening, it was helpful". Involving the fathers non-judgmentally empowered them: many fathers were involved with their infant. One DVD clip (Murray & Andrews, 2002) showed a newborn copying his father sticking out his tongue; most mothers were intrigued, as were their partners and most fathers had tried this. One infant when I first met him spontaneously put his tongue out at me two to three times and his parents said that they had done this so much with him that it was now part of his repertoire.

To reduce maternal intrusiveness, which is usually highly stable from the first day of life, is a very positive result. The intervention may have been effective because it functioned to boost oxytocin (Feldman, 2012). This is important in the physiology of early attachment in the experience of safety and the development of trust and empathy, with this contact being offered at a critical period.

Overall, the intervention worked for several reasons: I tried to increase observation and thinking about their infant's mind, increase confidence in their capacity to read their infant, and help them delight in their infant. I aimed for collaborative communication between them and myself, and mother with her infant. I supported parental attunement and mutual enjoyment, influencing parental representations, particularly reflectiveness.

## Ms T and her infant

In Ms T's antenatal group session, I was not able to facilitate any discussion; she seemed truculently negative and as though she felt "captured" for the intervention. The neonatal session initially seemed the hardest of all the sessions; she looked at me blankly, and was very negatively resistant. She answered my questions by saying, "I can't help you, the baby has no personality, I haven't noticed anything, she has vomited a lot, and is causing jealousy for the older girl". Ms T had fed her infant and said that she would now go to sleep and there was no way that she would wake up. I resigned myself to that. She said the infant had not smiled much. I tried exploring the usual topics such as who was there for support for her and what her partner thought of the infant and Ms T's replies seemed robotic. In the transference, I seemed to be an authority figure: she wanted to know what I wanted to know and what I was looking for. The infant already seemed rather shut down as the recipient of the projections on to her. I took a risk and asked if I could hold her infant, anxious not to receive more from the infant than her mother had, but thinking that it might be helpful if I could wake the infant up psychologically, which I was able to do. I then turned her round saying that I was doing this so that her mother could see and she was quite smiling and chatty, which I reinforced. When I gave her back, her mother smiled warmly for the first time and welcomed her infant back, I think seeing her as an infant and not as an older child with the intent to spoil things. From a stance of "knowing it all" Ms T moved to a position where she seemed softer towards her infant and to acknowledge a richer life within her infant and in the relationship between them.

## How do we understand the intervention's results?

Confidence about mothering skills while reduced in the intervention group was associated with improved infant–mother interaction four months later and most of the mothers enjoyed their infants. The intervention encouraged reflection, and increased reflection on the infant's experience may affect a mother's self-esteem: "(I)t may be that the mothers who expressed concerns about their confidence/ambivalence about being a mother in the current study were more reflective about their feelings and wishes for their children" (Murphy et al., 2011). Other therapy studies rating outcomes suggest that some appear to worsen after review—and that patients were possibly more in touch with difficulties. As also noted in evaluation theory literature, participants in a programme may not only gain knowledge, heightened interest, and motivation but also increased anxiety (Weiss, 1997).

While attributions to an infant may change after a single session because the plasticity in this period pushes development forward, other internal systems may be more fixed and need more psychological intervention targeted at specific difficulties (Schechter, 2012). The mothers' self-esteem may not have improved because they became less defensive than the control group, more in touch by projective identification with their infant's anxiety, and open about distress because they knew that it would be heard non-judgmentally. Four months may be early to assess that the mothers felt that they knew their infant well enough to feel good about their knowing. But the rate of improvement in depression was better in the intervention group over time.

## Conclusion

Showing and discussing the clips and meeting the infant at birth was associated with increased quality of the infant–mother relationship. Many only needed the antenatal intervention and others needed the neonatal intervention as well. Any early change in the first four months is beneficial; one effect of the intervention may make it easier for mothers to seek therapeutic input later. With Saphire and Sara, I provided a space where they could feel listened to and be calm, and dare to think they could know something of the other's mind and begin to start thinking reflectively.

CHAPTER FIVE

# Infants and their parents in neonatal intensive care units

Working as an infant therapist in a NICU could be subtitled, "Finding the baby whom parents do not feel able to interact with". Parents with an infant in NICU face many stresses—the total experience and their anxiety about their infant's physical and emotional struggle to survive contribute to most parents suffering symptoms of post-traumatic stress. Many parents are terrified to attach to their baby in case he or she dies. I try to suggest meaning in how their baby is and in his or her behaviour. Some parents need to care for a surviving infant when they are simultaneously grieving the loss of a dead twin. Parents may want to talk about unbearable and unmentionable feelings of rejection for a baby with a disability, or previously undisclosed family violence.

With advances in medical and neurodevelopmental care, premature or seriously medically ill babies may have admissions of many months' duration and there is increased awareness that the quality of social interactions between parents and babies in NICU can lessen adverse effects of preterm birth and guides therapeutic interventions. A multidisciplinary team works in partnership with families to understand the complexity of the needs of baby and family, to increase sensitivity and bonding, and decrease parental stress, and an infant therapist particularly contributes an infant perspective: I may do a consultation with a baby, for example, whose parents are not able to visit or engage in therapeutic interventions with infants and parents in the parent–infant relationship, and families of a long stay infant may need specialised help. While much work is with the staff, and it is often helpful to be around for staff to talk with in an informal way, I have focused here more on direct interventions with babies and their parents. Many parents and staff attribute intentionality and a thinking mind to babies from the first day so that babies may from the beginning have a sense that their experiences are thought about by others interested in them.

## Family stress

Parental anxiety may remain high for months because of concerns about health, and parenting challenges: anxiety often lies behind forgetting information, avoidance, and aggressive behaviour. Parents bond in different ways and need to be supported in this; parents of very preterm babies may need support in sensitively sharing eye contact and smiling to promote optimal outcomes for their baby, reinforcing that the baby prefers the parents to the nurses. Parents who are unable to hold or touch their baby over long periods face greater difficulties in feeling connected and maintaining hope. Parents find it helpful to be reassured that they retain the capacity to positively influence their baby's development. Parents can be bonded with their baby without holding them or doing skin-to skin care (Bergman, 2010).

There is increased recognition of the importance of presence of the *father* or other parent, both to support them and in developing those bonds—infants move differently in response to a father's voice. Fathers want to be viewed as important to their infant while different from the mother. Fathers' early involvement positively influences the attachment process and supports the mother. When fathers are helped to care for their infant they relax more beside the cot in opportunities for "meaningful fathering moments" (Johnson, 2008), contributing to increased paternal nurturing behaviours. Involving fathers in developmental care reduces neonatal stress and its neurobiological sequelae, and is likely to promote better infant outcomes.

Siblings may experience adjustment reactions of jealousy and anger and feel neglected; reading relevant story books can help them process this.

Having an infant in NICU is a stress on the couple relationship; relationships already in difficulty often do not survive this stress and parents often separate within a couple of years. Parents who may not be able to accept support during the admission sometimes re-contact and engage later. One mother contacted me when her second son, an ex-NICU infant, was nine months old and continued to see me until her third son was about a year old; and then contacted me again when her son was four years old as she and her partner were experiencing difficulties in their relationship.

Assisted reproductive procedures in the conception may increase stress, for example, if a mother is grieving her loss of reproductive possibilities; or between mother and donor over having received a donor egg if the baby's mother is having difficulty bonding. IVF parents may see themselves as high risk and their baby as high risk too. When a mother said that her baby was not of her genes I said that the baby *was* her child, *related* through love, a new perspective for her.

## *Supporting bonding*

A baby usually feels stressed if the mother is not there to hold and feed him and this may have the quality of a trauma. With very young babies, interventions may be more about helping parents to overcome trauma and deepen their bonding with their baby; what parents usually want is knowledge of what their baby likes and needs. They want to know what would make their baby happy, such as talking to their baby, holding, and skin-to-skin care; stroking and gentle touching, seeing if they can catch their baby's eyes with "soft" eyes. Parents helping their babies find pleasure in their body is likely to increase resilience, as is being able to explore novel experiences. Books such as Alcorn's (2008) *To Be Delighted In!* can help parents find joy in their baby. A therapist can stress the importance of recognising the baby as having agency.

Babies can have tears at twenty-eight weeks and clearly can feel pain. Helping soothe and comfort their baby with gentle touch, stroking their hands, or giving them a finger to hold helps to develop the capacity to self-regulate. Even a very low birth-weight infant from twenty-three weeks onwards may grasp a parent's finger. A therapist can help parents be mindful of their baby's state particularly in response to high levels of sensory input. When parents cannot touch their infant because the skin is too fragile, they may be able to cradle his head. When they can do little to interact, a therapist can suggest they observe closely for a short while to see what the baby might be feeling.

Babies need voices and melody: an interesting intonation and parents keeping their voice soft, humming or singing. A therapist can suggest holding a mirror so they can see their baby's face when they do skin-to-skin care or when the baby interacts, trying to imitate sounds and movements. What a baby needs is a specificity of care, a parent who is there as much as possible *for* the baby. Babies cared for by their parents for up to eight hours a day put on more weight, have less infection, and are discharged home sooner (O'Brien et al., 2013). Babies respond best when parents are with them as much as possible and interact with them, with positive reciprocity and contingency without overwhelming them. This has positive results for cognitive and psychomotor development, and parents who feel supported knowing that their sensitivity, when they interact, optimises brain development, can support interactions with volunteer "cuddlers", when the parents cannot visit. Parents report increased intimacy when they read stories to them; fathers may prefer books such as ones written by Dr Seuss. Babies respond positively to a mutually supportive relationship between parents. Parents who can closely observe their baby and become curious about the meaning of behaviour, such as playing with the dummy, responding to imitation, being alert to the parent's feelings, and fighting sleep can begin to think about the baby's mind as intentional. Encourage family members whom the baby recognises to be there longer if possible. Even with very little skin-to-skin care, cognitive and emotional development increases.

Interventions to *minimise a baby's distress* aim to reduce stress and integrate the parents in their daily routine. Coming to know their baby's "stop" signs is part of hearing what the baby is saying; as a parent said, "He has his own language, his own way of telling me." A therapist can point out that negative affect expresses intention, and when parents view this as being active and can share it in a social exchange, infant competence increases.

If a parent is preoccupied with anxiety or loss that usually needs to be explored first in a quiet space, although conversely sometimes helping parents feel bonded helps anxiety lessen.

If I am beside the cot I talk to a baby, as if I'm thinking aloud, about what I see and feel, sharing with the baby emerging thoughts, about what I think he is feeling—"You look happy, you're listening to what we're saying . . . you didn't like that". I also speak for the baby with the staff, for example, with a fragile month-old baby withdrawing from substances rather than encourage the baby to go to sleep in his cot without being held, I would think it would be less traumatic for the baby to be held until falling asleep. Babies who cry less in the first six months cry less in the next six months.

Babies long for feeding as part of the infant–mother relationship to be an enjoyable experience in which they feel that their cues are recognised. A mother's love for her baby is shown in the experience of feeding, and where there are feeding difficulties the fate of the baby's erotism is crucial. Supporting breastfeeding promotes bonding, pleasure, and autonomy for the infant as he learns the intricacies of feeding. A mother may be anxious about whether she has enough milk or may feel more valued for her milk than her presence. She may delay breastfeeding out of ambivalence, may feel a failure if her baby is slow to suck or feel confused between her breasts being used for nutrition or sexual intimacy. A baby's sensual excitement is often affected as the handling he has received may distort healthy investment in his body. Very premature babies who experience many painful, traumatic oral interventions may show little excitement when expected to breastfeed, which often results in difficulty in feeding. Babies who become exhausted feeding, or experience painful oral interventions, or are fed forcibly may develop an oral aversion. They may become distressed sucking if they do not feel securely bonded emotionally and feeding difficulties in turn contribute to insecure parent–infant attachment. A focus might be on finding excitement in their mouth (opportunities to suck, lick, nuzzle, then still and smell), as much as on technique.

If a baby is comfortable with eye-to-eye contact, positioning the baby so that he can see his parent's face, trying to catch the baby's attention, speaking in short phrases including the baby's name. A baby reaching new developmental stages may be overwhelmed or bored in a long admission and his developmental stage and behavioural cues need to be recognised.

Some parents need a space to bring the negative that may not be easily brought to other staff or dispel the ghosts, for example, the death of a baby prior to this birth. Personalising a very sick baby as a person may be particularly important for a terminally ill baby (see later this chapter) so that he feels accompanied by a parent.

## Brief interventions

### Ursula and Urwin

Unanticipated stress for a mother may delay her welcoming a wanted infant. Ursula, aged forty-five, a single mother from Shanghai, and her infant were referred at the last minute by the special care nursery nurses, as they thought that she had difficulty bonding to Urwin, her first infant, who was conceived by artificial insemination with donor sperm. The nurses thought a consultation might help her to observe and relate to him differently, as they thought that she was over-anxious and unable to recognise that her baby was no longer a sick premature baby and that his irritability might stem from reflux. When I sat beside his cot with Ursula I could communicate despite her limited English that I observed her baby who seemed to me to be peaceful, and his experience of being with his mother was a peaceful one. Ursula used this time to talk for the first time about some of the negative experiences of her life, such as feeling defrauded of money and love. Prior trauma exposure had sensitised her to the stress of a premature birth, and having a baby in NICU, and she may have been more likely to misinterpret her infant as ill and therefore vulnerable. The loss of the possibility of a natural conception and birth would also have to be grieved. I had found a space for this mother to feel that I was "alongside" her in a supportive way, so that the "ghosts" did not need to have a major effect. It became clear that Ursula bonded well with Urwin and she could then use the support of her sister.

### Rosalie and Roxana

Feeling that as a therapist we have been useless may be a projective identification we need to bear. I was asked to see a mother of a baby with the worst brain bleed the neonatologist had seen who was too terrified to attach. I went to see her immediately with some books to read to her baby and as she was frightened to do skin-to-skin care I took a book on its benefits but I did not think I had been helpful. Rosalie however contacted me a year later with some books for other babies because the ones I lent her had been "so special". Roxana was so bonded to her mother who also seemed so happy and so bonded with her (she would say she was "adorable") and Roxana was related, social, agile, bright, alert, and trying to work out what she saw going on around her and over the ninetieth percentile for cognitive and physical development. Rosalie said she appreciated that the care team had let them know in the first week they were split about how best to proceed in the light of the likely outcome and had taken the time to think about it; she also said of all the things in the first week the infant mental health intervention had been most helpful. (Going with my books signalled that I thought the baby was worth reading to.) She had not returned to work to give Roxana the best chance and was delaying having more children for the same reason. They had not celebrated her birth or taking her home but they had had a big first birthday party. This bore out the research that infants with loving, sensitively contingent care despite severe neurological difficulties can do so well compared with others with less severe ones.

*Parents soldiering on: Vee and Vicky*

Often, although it is hard to predict who a single session works for, it can be enough. Sometimes a mother wants to debrief unexpected complications of birth that have interfered with bonding. After Vee's daughter had been in NICU for several weeks, she came to talk about the traumatic events leading up to the delivery of her daughter, Vicky, and her admission to NICU. She was soon in tears and talked about how she had been dissociated with anxiety about the birth until then. She had always wanted to be a mother and felt that the birth of her baby would be the happiest day of her life. Instead her experience was that it was the worst day, and she felt a failure and thought she would never be able to talk to her daughter about it. I talked with her about how she would be able to find words to describe to her daughter what happened, that sometimes birth does not go the way it is planned but that had no effect on how much Vee loved her. Vicky said that it was helpful to have words around it and felt relieved and less guilty; this meant that she no longer had to see her daughter as split off from a nightmare trauma of guilt and anger that might overwhelm them both. A week later they were in a totally different space. Vee said that the first time that Vicky tasted breast milk she paused, looked around with her eyes happy, pleased, curious, wondering, and interested, decided it was an extremely good experience and started sucking like the "best milking machine ever seen". Vee looked terrific and said that she felt terrific. Vicky had obviously responded immediately to the surge in her mother's mood. Without the intervention, there could have been such an enormous weight of unresolved sadness and shame behind how Vee presented as a "lovely" mother that it was possible that her baby could have become disorganised.

### Babies with disabilities

Many parents of infants with potential disabilities face extreme anxiety about their future and providing a safe space to explore these is therapeutic. A mother of a newborn baby with Down's syndrome in NICU experienced enormous distress and felt completely unbonded to him. She could not "see" him because she could only see disability in his features and said that he could not focus. (Some parents feel that their good infant has died, leaving them with one with a disability.) I searched for something to help her see him as a person in his own right, to whom his condition was normal. I tried to understand his distractibility so that I could point out that I thought perhaps he was still getting himself together and getting the connecting to her sorted out rather than because he could not focus. This seemed to help lessen a little the feeling of damage and distance between them.

### Dads' group

A dedicated fathers' group in recognition of the stress fathers feel helps them feel more secure and connected with their baby (Kuschel, 2014); the baby wishes her father to continue the relationship he had with her before birth. The group is open to all fathers, run weekly in the evening with a male neonatologist and myself, as an embedded psychologist and infant mental health clinician, for a couple of hours. The group can help fathers feel for the first time that they are a father. I sometimes ask about fathers feeling connected to their infants(s) and a major theme is how they see their infant as a person from very early, at times on the first day even with extremely premature babies.

The fathers usually do not know one another, yet when invited to tell their story launch into an account of how traumatic they found the birth and how unprepared they were. Sadness, anxiety, anger, laughs, and tears make it a powerful experience with the fathers reassuring those who are distressed. One father talked about his wife's and his anxiety, sadness, and distress about their son who had had a brain bleed, and their concern he might be very disabled and they would feel unable to look after him; another shared how one twin son was in a nearby hospital and they had been told it was cruel to keep him alive but they wanted him to "declare himself". When one father cried in the group for the first time, he said he had needed to cry and needed the support of the group as only other fathers really understood what he was going through.

A main theme is the trauma of the pregnancy, the birth, and the baby's care, including separation, and watching traumatic interventions. Fathers often do skin-to-skin care on the first day, if their baby can manage it. They are very vocal about enjoying this sensuous experience, which they had not anticipated would give them so much pleasure and they feel so quickly connected with their babies; they encourage other fathers who may be anxious about holding a fragile baby. They feel that they can contribute to their babies equally with the mothers. Most fathers see the baby as a person "from the beginning", with descriptions like chilled, feisty, or angry. They often see twins as different, so that a daughter may, for example, be "laid back" and a son viewed as having a temper, and in turn fathers begin trying to make sense of their baby's experience. Many fathers see intentionality from very early: one father said his son pressed down hard on his finger when he put it near him. Fathers report that older babies may be very still when nursed by a nurse whom they do not like; they may be more active in setting off the alarms when they want the attention of a nurse whom they like, or if the ward is quiet they may move to set off the alarm to get the other babies to join in.

Fathers often feel sad their parenting is in the public domain: one father described movingly how when his daughter had her first bath several nurses had to be present to keep her safe, and the family could never regain what should have been a precious private moment. The parents also describe how thin the curtain is around the cots, separating them from the trauma and tragedy they feel may be happening to other neonates.

Mothers often think it would be helpful for their partner to go to the group before he does, recognising the unrelieved stress on him, and although some fathers attend up to six times, occasionally for months, the majority often come only once for a trauma debrief. Fathers hope to be viewed as important to their baby while different from the mother; they are equally needed and wanted by their babies, and some verbalised that the group did help them feel more connected, which is likely to improve the quality of their engagement with their baby and their behaviour. Fathers say that it is very helpful to hear how their infant can be interactive with them and would love hearing them read to them. For some fathers, having the opportunity to give up a distancing approach and being encouraged to focus on their baby as a person in her own right is helpful: a father who had been traumatised by the birth and was avoidant of visiting, became more relaxed and was very interactive with his daughter; he had not expected this engagement until her second year.

The fathers who only attend the group after their baby has been in the ward for some time are likely to have just held themselves together, whereas those who attend early are more open to support. Most fathers were very positive about the group being helpful and felt they should have come earlier and more than once. "It is good having a dedicated space . . . it show(s) us that the fathers were cared about, and made a big difference to me. I guess there's always a little bit of apprehension, in sharing feelings. To see the daunted look on other father's faces, to hear about everyone's experience, and to realise that others were going through a similar thing, was really helpful and I felt a lot better afterwards. It helped me to feel less stressed out. I think it helped the new fathers on the ward to gain some hope". One father touched his very premature daughter's hand feeling it was not respectful to touch her face and found it unbelievable she immediately reached out to touch back. "That made me feel more secure."

## Consultations with infants

### An infant becoming depressed: Xander

Xander, born at twenty-three-weeks, was referred for a consultation at thirty-six weeks corrected age; his parents could not advocate for him as they had had to return home with his twin sister two weeks previously. He no longer smiled or cried and was sleeping much of the day. Throughout a play session with me he coughed, could not clear his secretions, and was restless; none of his favourite things—mobile or music—helped. He sat against another staff member, and rested his hand on her leg but was still restless. Six times the moment the staff member held him *en face* he quietened, resting his hand against her arm. Yet when I walked behind to try and catch his eyes, he avoided my eyes and his face had a sad, unhappy, frozen, even terrified look, as if he was beginning to tune out. His state had changed when his twin moved from the cot beside him; his parents could not visit as often—and he continually turned his head to the left where his twin had been. He was on his way to becoming depressed, perhaps feeling that his parents did not delight in him. I recommended the nurses (and volunteer cuddlers) interact more with him, waking to hold if necessary. His nurses changed his developmental trajectory within a day: the following day he had a long interactive session, and gave his primary nurse several smiles.

### Infant–parent therapy

This approach in NICU generally is one of flexibly fitting in, sometimes needing to respond immediately. I bring in knowledge of early development, pointing out while the nurses keep an attachment bridge open (as an infant would benefit from having at least five attachment figures, having several good figures early on contributes to a rich inner mental life), babies need their parents (or substitutes) because the attachment is primarily to them and they feel lonely without their parent; they do not feel abandoned when someone devoted to them is present. When parents find it hard to attach to their infant this sometimes needs to be first explored, and I may talk about the baby's personality to see if that can connect them quickly. One young mother who spoke no English was too fearful to visit as she thought her baby did not like her and preferred the nurses: she had misunderstood the doctors performing a caesarean section because the baby was "not happy" (stressed) and we needed to confirm that her baby was so happy when her mother was there as she was the one she knew, and loved best, and was sad when she was not there. With parents who feel that they need to first ask "permission" to hold their baby I point out that they do not have to ask permission to be a loving parent.

An intervention may take place in different venues: beside the cot, in the interview room, the corridor outside the infection control room, the tea room. I usually try to explore with families how their anxieties and mixed feelings affect their capacity to bond with their babies, particularly if this prevents them from getting help. If possible I offer parents weekly appointments together, then flexibly as needed; but with the rapid discharge of infants there may only be time for a single session. I can offer confidentiality in meeting away from the ward, offering a space for parents to process trauma so it need not have a lasting legacy. Giving a mother a space to talk about her guilt about feeling a bad mother in not holding her infant to term is a common intervention. The following day, I might touch base for five minutes, saying, "I was just wandering by and wondered how you are." I try to be available for as long as possible because of the nature of the traumatic experience of having an infant in NICU or refer for specialised help. With parents who are phobic of entering the unit initially, I explore anxieties and ambivalence and whether, feeling that they are a bad parent, they are also trying to protect their infant out of love.

If parents continue to approach their infants reluctantly this may indicate a prolonged complex reaction, different from a mother's reaction after birth when being close may stir up mixed emotions, including feelings of failure about the preterm birth. When parents cannot hold their baby, they may find it hard to believe the infant is theirs. Mothers of a very low birth weight infant may feel less effective. A mother may stay away from the NICU for many reasons, which is hard for her baby; however, it may be done to protect her infant from her ambivalent feelings, if she feels she is not maternal to have had a baby who does not look like a baby and who may have many problems and in that way, she acts out of love. Because of the appearance of some premature infants it may feel hard to love them. Parents may continue to resist engaging with the infant because of a traumatic birth, shock at the infant's appearance, or a poor prognosis about survival and disability. Parents of a twin who has died may face what seems an impossible task of grieving one baby with another one living. In addressing parents' negative perceptions of their infant and how they perceive the infant's vulnerability, if in this process of infant redefinition (McCue Horwitz et al., 2015) parents no longer view their infant as abnormal or vulnerable, this would positively affect parental behaviours and child development.

## Long-stay infants

With a long-stay infant, parents may increasingly value a confidential space to process feelings about the NICU experience, the grief and anger about having a preterm infant, or anxiety about the effects on a couple's intimate and sexual relationship, and shame about what the baby is not and the baby who is "lost". I would talk about the birth and the NICU journey as much as the parents wish, and see if I can make links with the past or what they feel in the present. One mother of twins felt guilty that she had contributed to her sons' premature birth and birth damage by not listening in enough detail to what was being said during pregnancy or reading enough. With parents with severe anxiety who are either hypervigilant or detached and have difficulty identifying with their infant, I provide an opportunity for them to express distress and resentment about the difficulties, and to think about their baby's experience, their baby's mind as intentional, and how to feel connected to their baby.

### Wendy and Wilson

Wilson was a very much wanted infant in the context of years of difficulty in becoming pregnant for his mother, Wendy. A brain injury meant that he was a vulnerable baby and she had enormous separation anxiety and was unable to leave him for more than three minutes, and was very needy yet pushing support away and underneath was angry. I would share how I found him very aware of his mother's attachment to him. She was angry that her husband did not hold Wilson and being able to express this to me, her husband was immediately able to hold him, and she could also explain to someone outside the family for the first time some of what had happened with her son. When Wendy said that she felt very guilty, I talked lightly about guilt as a wasted emotion (in this context), which she liked so much she put in her mobile to remind her. Wilson subsequently became seriously ill and on the point of dying, and I accepted being dismissed by her with quiet anger, "Nothing you say would make a difference at the moment". However, she liked my view that she could never lose Wilson's love. She decided to try my idea of acknowledging the intrusive thoughts instead of trying to block them. She then urgently asked to see me about something she was absolutely terrified of, and slowly worked up to say it just before the ward round doctors entered her curtained-off space, saying that she had a traumatic memory that a consultant had told another doctor that her son had a brain injury and she thought at first this meant that he was not worth saving, then that there may be something worse that she had not been told. It had taken her three days to work up to the retriggered traumatic memories. When Wilson began to develop an oral aversion, sending her on a rollercoaster of emotions that I normalised, she would repeat what I had suggested about one breath at a time. Several years later, Wilson had the most expressive language for his age.

## Families with multiple risk factors and boundary issues

Parents may present with complex needs, such as anger management difficulties, serious mental illness, substance use, intellectual or physical disability, disadvantaged life circumstances, a history of abuse or neglect of other infants, or are very young adolescent parents. Significant numbers of parents with a psychotic illness have contact with babies in the perinatal period, with symptoms and medication side effects impacting on interactions and the parent–child relationship. When a parent has anger management problems, these need to be addressed in a non-shaming way: that anger is unacceptable as babies can respond to a parent's tone of voice, and should not be frightened, and it might be possible to build on parents' interest in neurological and cognitive development that this might affect brain development. In not losing sight of the anxiety behind the violence if it feels safe to do so, a father may to some extent feel understood and not demonised, and be relieved to not need to swagger, easing his interaction with his baby.

A parent's right to be treated as a parent should be recognised whenever possible; parents whose behaviour the staff find challenging may inwardly feel despairing or ashamed, with staff having to work at finding compassion and ways to help, such as a mother with an acquired brain injury, a history of violent partners, who cared deeply about her children (a premature baby and a three-year-old child who had tortured an animal). Staff may consult when they feel stuck, for example, I was asked to assess a baby's mental health and the mother–baby relationship but the wider context was that the staff felt stymied when his mother refused to permit drug screens as part of a total assessment about whether she could take home a baby to whom she seemed very loving. (Some dynamics soon emerged in that I was criticised by her of being the one who did not know my stuff, in a kind of not owning her responsibility.)

An unlikely context does not prevent the possibility of a window of opportunity as the following three vignettes show.

### Zepha

Zepha used substances, had a history of violence, having previously cut a nurse's face with a knife, and presented in a dissociated way when referred. I first saw her with her support therapist, and a security guard outside the room. Her daughter was in NICU for a month withdrawing from drugs and she was likely to lose custody. Seeing it as a small window of opportunity I tried to find some connection between her and her baby to preserve a fragment of mothering, so that she did not immediately start another pregnancy to replace her baby. Observing her give her baby a bottle, I talked about her daughter feeding well and she therefore had something of her mother inside her. Zepha could stay in touch with her for a time.

### Yvette and Yves

Yvette, a young mother with a history of violence and cutting, and her premature infant, Yves, were both withdrawing from methadone when she and her partner were referred for help with bonding. The referral letter started, "Please don't be alarmed by the attached summary." I will omit some details. Yvette had been in care from one year of age, had a history of violence, and a planned monthly admission for treatment of her bipolar disorder. However, as Yves had been in NICU for several weeks and while there have been issues of handling their infant and talking loudly and inappropriately around him, they had not been aggressive and were trying their best. They visited every day and were committed to Yves. The plan was for a psychiatric mother–baby-unit admission when Yves was discharged. Both parents were receptive to input that assisted their skills as parents and to gain better understanding of the needs of an infant. Yvette had attended all appointments at the drug and alcohol service, including regular psychiatric review. The infant was expected to be in NICU for three weeks.

\* \* \*

I met with his parents the following day and Yvette, with the marks of past violence on her body, sat with her eyes closed throughout the session, saying that she was tired, but was perhaps anxious. Yale was a large man with some difficulty reading emotional communication. They said it would be better if we could catch up again the following week. I stayed beside the cot while they gave Yves a bottle and he fed peacefully with his eyes closed. His father had told me a little about his background—conveying that his mother, a professional woman, was unreliable; he said he was mainly looked after by his grandmother until she became senile and he had a criminal history, perhaps downplayed.

When I next saw them, Yvette looked as though she was going to sleep throughout, but when I checked, they said it was "the medication". The nurse said they found it hard to be quiet around the baby. I talked with them about being quiet around their son who dysregulated easily—he had his legs vertically in the air as a kind of stop sign when they talked loudly. Yale suggested that I was a baby whisperer. Immediately after our session, Yvette seemed wide awake. The social worker said Yvette can present in this way but thought that they both took in some information and were happy to see me.

A few days later I saw the parents with their nurse who felt that the one-month-old infant was angry (he was stiff and irritable) as he woke because his parents were so noisy but he always had his eyes shut and was then awake at night as he found it easier with the nurses. I thought that Yves was not a person to his parents but more like a clockwork toy whom they had to be taught how to feed and change. I thought Yves could be angry and had every reason to be depressed.

A few days later the change in Yvette was unbelievable—she was almost radiant, holding Yves so gently, and she asked me for affirmation that she was bonded. Then Yale came and was so out of touch that I leant forward several times unable to stop myself saying, "Gently, he's only a baby". Yvette bathed him beautifully but I heard afterwards that when the nurse had said to Yale to be gentle, he shouted violently at her.

A few days later when I saw Yves in the evening he was so different, focused on crawling and quietly vocalised when I talked to him. When I said to the nurse they had done so well, she said, "You helped". I wrote an email to the senior staff, to acknowledge the "emotional work" the nurses had done had been particularly important in helping this infant do so well.

I heard that Yves was ready to be discharged the following day and there were no beds available in the parenting centre so that he would have to go into foster care. The charge nurse used my email to mediate to prevent further traumatising this vulnerable infant and it would be detrimental for him given the progress he had made and whether he could be kept for the next few days. The hospital kept him. The report was that they did well in the parenting centre.

With the parents, I had affirmed that Yvette was indeed holding Yves lovingly and with Yale, in the transference I was not an unreliable mother. The nurses did the emotional work with minimal input by me: I came when they asked me to and I validated their interventions.

*Some thoughts about countertransference processing*

Early on it seemed possible that Yvette, although well-intentioned, could not take care of him, which is a difficulty in the countertransference: when a mother is not capable of caring for her infant, is it fair to put her in touch and expose her to greater pain or can an intervention help her to accept her baby having another carer.

I wondered if Yvette felt intimidated by Yale. My heart was in my mouth as they fed their infant. Yet, was I the first to listen to Yale and not respond to the projections of him as extremely violent? It is hard to remember that shameful anxiety may lie behind an appearance of intimidation. I spent a considerable amount of time thinking what techniques might best help Yale. It was after this processing, I was able to think that Yale might want to waken his baby because Yves' shut eyes denied his paternity, just as an infant's averted gaze and apparent lack of response denies a mother her motherhood and she feels hurt and looks away as she fears her baby does not miss or need her.

How would I explain Yvette's radiance when I felt I had done so little with her?—that I was a person just for her to help her specifically, like the good mother she had not had, and envy had been behind the violent attacks on people?

## Zoe and Zara

In this vignette, there is an intermingling of minimal infant–parent therapy with input into the unit. Zoe and Zara were referred for help bonding. Zoe said she had fled a violent partner. I had narrow registers within which to work: Zoe saw me for a couple of sessions then said that she did not need me. A few weeks later she asked to see me again in her desperation to keep her baby. She had been discovered to have several assumed names for two babies who had been removed from her care. A history emerged of cutting, externalising behaviours, substance use, criminality, and suicide attempts. While desperate to have a baby, each had been removed from her care when she rejected their neediness. As long as there was a possibility Zara could go home with her mother, the staff needed to work with Zoe.

In the countertransference, it was hard to listen to her blaming, rubbishing any help offered, and mocking, tears, anger, and possibly lies while trying at the same time to understand why she might feel like that. (She was in care several times as a child when splitting tendencies would be reinforced.) She said that the hospital was not supporting her in fighting the likely decision to take Zara away. I said that the hospital could not make the decision about the infant. Despairingly, I said emphatically, "For your daughter's sake, work with us". She said she got no support in the hospital and I said, "I *am* support". I got nowhere and sat there mute, trying to think how to reach her as there felt so little for me to say.

However, the following day, after I let the staff know it could be a difficult day, Zoe was calmer. When I was at the cot I commented on Zara smiling, hearing us talk, and then opening an eye with a lopsided smile; she was quite responsive vocalising with her mother. I needed to accept being sacked and resurrected. But the hospital was more on her side that she realised and when protective services considered taking the infant into care for an unnecessary four days, hospital staff said it would be better for her to stay with her mother and not unnecessarily precipitate a possible feeding refusal in a fully breastfed infant. Noticing and bearing difficulties in my own ability to think or hold in mind led to greater understanding of Zoe's internal world; perhaps the process of arriving at the interpretation through observation of the transference was more important than the interpretation. The court awarded Zara to the father who had not been in the picture from before her birth. I ran several multidisciplinary meetings, as Zara would be transferred to another hospital nursery and the staff wanted advice on how to support her and her father in adjusting to his new role and in understanding the emotions that Zara might be experiencing, for example, going from breastfeeding to bottle feeding, and mother to father. I suggested Zara's world could be turned upside down with bewilderment, upset, anxiety, and possibly irritability but may also be some relief if her mother had sometimes been tense and unpredictable, a little intrusive, and sometimes shouted, and her father was calmer. I suggested Zoe should leave a piece of her clothing and a photo in the cot and the nurses could talk with Zara in her mother's absence so she would not feel alone. When I ran a debriefing meeting for the staff, one nurse shared that she had had a dream (possibly processing feelings for all the staff).

## *Complex trauma reactions and grief*

Most parents find the NICU experience traumatic, which complicates the bonding process if their own trauma history affects their responses. They may be so anxious that they cannot participate in discussions about their baby's care. Deaths of other babies may re-traumatise them. Some parents carry a degree of anxiety that could be quite traumatising for a baby, and a baby whose parents experience post-traumatic stress symptoms is more vulnerable to develop eating and sleeping difficulties in the first year. The complexity of parents' overwhelming experiences that may be traumatic needs acknowledgement.

Part of processing complex grief may include feeling guilty, for example, about reproductive loss, an earlier foetal death, or mourning the unavailability of a mother's mother. Parents may face extreme distress, or guilt, or feel rejecting if their infant is visibly different, or if they feel responsible that the infant was not the one they had hoped for, feel very sad, angry, or disgusted, which are particularly hard feelings to bear. Parents may feel that they face unbearable choices whether their baby survives or not.

Getting to know their baby as a person, who is psychologically alive, creates a memory of becoming the parents of their infant, and is helpful if they face the possibility of the infant's death, aids grieving, and begins to integrate the trauma. If parents feel that they are involved in end-of-life decision-making this is usually associated with lessened grief; mutual confidence and communication encourages freedom and creativity around their baby.

## Redirection of care

Medical and parental views about prolonging life may diverge, particularly when a parent's spiritual and cultural values make it unacceptable to shorten life. A therapist needs to adopt an ethical embracing of difference and recognise when she cannot advise but should maintain a dialogue to help the family work through the decision-making. Parents need to feel supported through the pain of end-of-life issues. Some parents have wanted their very ill infant to have a chance despite medical advice to extubate, which they felt violated the infant's self. When parents can connect with a dying baby, particularly if he or she is their first baby, this makes them a parent; parents have said that if the baby is a person for the therapist despite his prematurity, the baby can become a person for the parents, too.

The parents of a fragile baby may feel it is their decision as parents that he or she not continue to suffer any longer, and if the treating team would prefer to continue with very active treatment, I may be asked to explore the parents' decision. While on the ward parents may intimidate the nurses (perhaps out of anxiety): with me they may be tearful and want to discuss helping their baby die peacefully.

### A loved twin

A twin was born with such a degree of birth injury that she would have such little quality of life that the paediatrician recommended redirection of care. The parents were too distressed to consider this and I was asked to see them for support. We talked widely about the twins, and in the session, I made the comment about whatever decision they made would be done out of love for their baby. Shortly after, the father indicated that they had made the decision in this session to redirect care.

### Anne and her family

Anne was a baby who was too frail to survive and her parents asked for help for her older brother to cope with her impending death. When I went to see the family in a rooming-in room, Anne was lying almost invisible in the middle of the parents' bed. I felt her parents needed support to explain to her brother that his baby sister was dying as she did not have a strong enough body. Before I could engage with him I felt the parents wanted me to acknowledge their daughter as a person with her own dignity, on the point of death amid ongoing sadness. This I did.

Most parents wish for some acknowledgement of their baby's existence and one mother asked me to walk with her and her baby to the nearby park so he could have this experience the day before he died.

## Conclusion

As a team member contributing to integrated care of NICU families this may lessen the pain and trauma that might otherwise stem from enormous unrelieved parental stress at this time: one mother said three years after having a preterm baby that she still did not know what she had done wrong. Yet it is often possible to help quickly even when there are extreme difficulties in bonding, for example, when there are repetitive, irrational, or very painful thoughts.

# PART III

# ENGAGING INFANTS IN PAEDIATRIC SETTINGS

CHAPTER SIX

# Infants and their parents in paediatric settings

The clinical pathway in a paediatric hospital shapes the therapy, out of the need to find interventions for distressed infants who are often in a medical crisis with chronic or severe problems (Paul, 2014). Emotional and psychological difficulties may arise with infants in connection with their own physical health, some of whom are near to dying. Sometimes hospital admission alone is not enough to reverse, for example, when an infant is refusing to eat for no ascertainable reason and with life-threatening symptoms cannot be discharged home. Infant mental health intervention varies according to the specific context of the referral. Many infants in hospital are under three years of age and in the tertiary stages of illness or depression or have experienced a traumatic event with serious psychological consequences. Many parents have significant health or social problems. Infants may be referred when they are in intensive care, or failing to thrive, or need a specific area of expertise such as speech pathology. Depression in infants is often overlooked and seen in medical terms such as sleep problems, feeding difficulties, and irritability and restlessness: further indications are withdrawal from play and family, constant sadness, and loss of interest in everyday activities. Infants are referred for disturbances in their relationship with their parents, or in their relationship to their own mind or body. In hospital referrals, a proportion of the population experiences emotional and physical deprivation and a primarily verbal approach would not soothe a dysregulated or dying infant. There is usually an urgent clinical imperative as infants often do not get better without intervention and this is crucially needed, yet time constraints may mean there is only time for a single session. The intervention is shaped by time constraints—whether an infant is admitted for thirty-six hours or for a week, whether the family lives locally or hours away. Despite the severity of an infant's symptoms, this approach has the potential to quickly begin to ameliorate an infant's representations and those of the parents.

Responding to an infant impacts on their representations, so that the infant's sense of self and agency consolidate more. The parents can see how the therapist recognises their infant; recognising changes minds.

By the time infants are referred, they may fear loss of their self. When a therapist holds a baby, there is a dialogue of feelings in the first "language" of an infant, in which the therapist takes part receptively and containingly. When an infant is angry or despairing, attuning to these feelings usually brings hope. A therapist, in relating to an infant who is dissociating, may begin to repair by emotional holding and being available for communication and could contribute to an infant being less seen as inexplicable, disabled, abusive, or dying, which had reminded the parents of aspects they found hard to tolerate in themselves. Videotaped sessions often demonstrate rapid symptom improvement and in a hospital audit a high proportion of infants maintained good outcomes.

In many of this book's vignettes the infant has some form of feeding difficulties that needs to be understood as this is so critical an aspect of the early mother–infant relationship, suggesting a relational aspect to many of the difficulties. The four vignettes that follow illustrate different aspects of feeding difficulties but the principle emerging generalise to other paediatric presentations. While medical issues may be very important, an infant's motivation to feed is crucial. Very young infants may experience extensive developmental difficulties as a result of their reactions to disturbed relationships and present as if they are autistic. About six infants are referred to throughout the book as having autistic defences (including Cal, this chapter). It is likely that as sensitive infants, they felt overwhelmed at times by the responses they met, as if their mother dropped them from her mind; one mother spontaneously said that a mother's unavailability gives an infant the experience of death. An infant needs to be entrained in personal playful engagement, in a therapeutic space where they can understand the other's intentionality and affects without being overwhelmed and then start making meaning of the world again.

The following guidelines for interventions are as relevant in outpatient as inpatient settings.

## Some guidelines

The therapist usually engages with infant *and* parents in the presence of the feared emotions and fantasies to try and understand their experience.

When the window of opportunity is limited because of the parents' physical or emotional availability, the intervention may have a more pragmatic flavour.

Infant–parent therapy is often brief and I may say something like, "I suggest meeting again (or a few times, depending on the context and urgency of the referral) to see if understanding more about the difficulty would be helpful and then we'll work out if anything else is needed". Parents in this way are given an outline of the intervention, a time frame, and the knowledge that if they need further intervention this will be considered. This could start building a therapeutic alliance with infant and parents, so that they feel they are joining *with* the therapist, which probably gives the clearest indicator of success. Fathers are involved if possible, and any family members whom the parents wish; grandparents may be especially important.

Containment of feelings, reflecting on them and making links, as appropriate, are a main intervention. Infants come to a consultation with expectations about the therapist based on their experience of their parents and what the parents anticipate experiencing in the session. I would expect to engage directly with the infant at some point, with psychological holding and communication in the infant's language of gaze and voice, often with playful gestures. Even a brief engagement can convey to the infants that they are safe and valued. An infant experiences a therapist's engagement and communication as part of learning how his own mind and body are integrated. I see this intervening with the infant's transference to the therapist as understanding an infant's experience, which has the power to "re-present" the infant. If a parent is anxious about the interview, the infant may show a more negative transference than otherwise. In brief therapy a therapist takes up the parents' transference *to* the infant, and the infant to the therapist, rather than the parents' transference to the therapist.

The therapist *assesses* contributing emotional factors to gain relevant information from a situation, including the symptom, the defences, and what is relevant from the parents' history. They would explore what the infant has experienced and what this might mean to him or her; how the parents think this has affected him or her emotionally, and what kind of help to offer. Sometimes the goals may be small. "Life has been really hard and I'm trying to understand what's happened and what can help." The parents may experience the assessment and hearing what they say about themselves and the infant, in the presence of the infant, as therapeutic from the outset. Seeing what the infant does and how he or she responds to the parents' narrative is important.

If there is considerable distress, this needs to be relieved, while trying to move to a position of offering understanding. Containing and psychological holding are often enough to bring about change in brief intervention, particularly if parents feel they have had the time to say what they needed to, in a setting that feels safe. If the intervention is likely to be short term, the therapist is mindful of that so that the ending can be planned. It is not unusual for parents to say that they were helped in a single session, for example, an infant who woke during the night after the mother had returned to work and she thought of cancelling the second session as the infant improved. She said, "I don't know what you said to my baby", although she was present the whole time, having lost the link the therapist made about the infant being awake to spend some time with her.

The therapist offers some understanding of factors contributing to difficulties, whether in the "here and now" or the past—that is most likely to include helping parents see how an infant has "collected" feelings that belonged to others from the past. Sometimes it is clear what are the missing links that could be verbalised, for example, "It seems hard to hear your baby crying—I wonder what it was like for you as a child?", disentangling transference to the infant from the past or asking, "What's it like for you when your baby cries?" It may be appropriate to add that it seems hard to let the partner help and may feel better to be the only one who can comfort the infant. With the infant present, the intervention is focused more on the infant–parent relationship, rather than on the parent or the infant. A nine-month-old infant can play in quite a sustained way, for example, with small toys or torch beams, both communicating information and beginning a working through process. The therapist respects defences while offering understanding to the parents, such as for example, "This may have been the best way you coped when little". With an infant, a therapist might say, "It's important to see you and then there'll be some time when I don't see you and then I'll see you again", or "How hard it is, you want to be with someone and then you're not with them."

Awareness of the contribution of negative aspects of transference and addressing negative projections on to the infant is important. (High levels of affection between mothers and their eight-month infants are associated with fewer symptoms of distress thirty years later among the infants, as compared to those whose mothers showed low levels of affection (Maselko, et al., 2011).) If, however, the transference to the therapist is very negative this would usually be explored quickly to safeguard the intervention.

Sometimes the links are not clear and the therapist may be guided by a predominant affect, for example, of sadness, or if a pattern emerges, for example, of loss, to try to verbalise that. Or if an important, previously undisclosed, fact emerges, seeing how this links. Usually there is a way to say most things, including about guilt and hate. After some symptom improvement, difficulties in the couple relationship may become another focus of intervention.

With parents with serious mental illness or other marked psychological difficulties, intervention draws on similar principles to those outlined above.

### *Countertransference*

A therapist's emotional responses or countertransference can provide invaluable clues. With an infant's distress communicated somatically the therapist's countertransference may be affected in specific ways. The transference may be projected into the therapist's soma or psyche;

therapists describe physical responses, such as feeling panicky or sick as they experience an infant's distress or register a chest pain from a mother's unacknowledged sadness. Faced with an infant who stares back, a therapist listening to how he himself is feeling can help differentiate whether behind the anger the infant is anxious or depressed. As a therapist tries to feel his way into what an infant is feeling this is likely to put him in touch with feelings from his own infancy. In projective identification with the regressed infant, therapists are open to those frightened, confused, and vulnerable feelings. Therapists draw on sensations such as these, as well as images arising in their countertransference to understand.

### *Some feeding difficulties including a post-traumatic feeding disorder*

Here the focus is on one major symptom presentation, which may range from reflux to more extreme symptoms such as forced feeding. It is important to consider what the infant and the feeding difficulties mean to the parents and how this impacts them and their relationship, as intergenerational phenomena affect an infant's psychosomatic presentation when symptoms reflect the qualities of the infant–parent relationship.

When mothers experience shame, disgust, anxiety, rejection, or anger during breastfeeding, one aim would be to help them find some pleasure to meet their baby's erotism. A therapist might convey that breastfeeding could be enjoyable, implicitly holding out hope that this might be possible. When a mother asked why her infant did not drink from the bottle, the therapist replied, "Why would he? He is missing the softness and pleasure of the breast" and his mother replied, "Good boy", patted him and the difficulties eased.

With more serious symptoms, the intervention might centre around playing with the idea of feeding in a therapeutic session that focuses on understanding an infant's emotional life, and dilemmas, and where the anxiety-laden problem is engaged with and played with in a freer space without any pressure. This usually enables infants to move closer to the possibility of enjoyable oral feeding that they feel, importantly, is under their own control. This play enables infant and parents to think about and reflect on their experience. Up to one quarter of babies with reflux may later develop mental health issues within a few years.

The first vignette is an intervention with an eleven-week-old infant, underlining the point that *embodied communication* is key and was an early presentation in a hospital that influenced this approach to infants. Sometimes a therapist is called in urgently when the parents cannot be present as with Dee who had been unable to leave hospital since birth. With young unaccompanied infants, a therapist engages directly and uses interaction as verbal interpretation cannot be used as it is not developmentally effective. This extreme example indicates that therapeutic action does not need to include verbal interpretation in adult mode, which seems unlikely to have achieved the same result as quickly.

### Dee, an unaccompanied eleven-week-old

Dee, a traumatised eleven-week-old, was referred for feeding difficulties; these were said by an extremely experienced paediatrician to be "an absolute nightmare", as she would "freak" out. Her mother could not visit from the country, so there was no parent from whom to take a history. Her case file was several inches thick. The therapist held Dee preparing to feed her; having previously been happy she became sad, refused eye contact, and showed no signs of hunger despite it being several hours since the last feed. She allowed the bottle in her mouth but cried, pleading *sadly* with her eyes, and refused to swallow. Seeing this, the therapist slowly asked her, "What happened to you?" When the therapist again picked up the bottle Dee looked at it, her eyes widening in terror, and the therapist slowly asked, "What would that be like?" The infant pushed the bottle away with her foot. The therapist spent an hour a day playfully interacting with her in ways that helped her feel safe enough to maintain eye contact and interaction. Gradually Dee became more settled and happy, and less hypervigilant. Within two days feeding volumes had improved, and the nursing notes reported "Best feed ever. No crying or fussing".

The trauma that emerged was that when Dee had been oral gavage-fed it took three people to hold the screaming infant down; when she began naso-gastric feeding she screamed, vomited, and became very distressed. Ice cubes had been placed on her cheeks to stimulate her to suck and she had had "suck training" when her mother was told to put on a rubber glove, put her hand in iced water and then put a finger in Dee's mouth to stimulate her to suck.

Playful interactions with Dee helped her regain her autonomy and pleasure in feeding and she purposefully pushed the bottle away with her tongue rather than crying ineffectively. The infant would read some of what the therapist felt, thought, and intended, which was, "I know you feel frightened and I am returning autonomy and pleasure to you". This would be carried through embodied reflectiveness, where the therapist uses her own self and body.

### Blaze and his mother

In this example, eleven-month-old Blaze and his mother were referred for failing to thrive when he refused to feed after being weaned. He was very angry and distressed and his mother was distraught. The therapist had previously talked this through with her, to no effect. When she refused the breast, he yelled and hit her and she put him in his cot. He flung himself back on the pillow yelling. The therapist commented, "He's really angry with you" and empathised with Blaze, "You want the breast, don't you?" He picked up a soft ball, and flung it, yelling, at his mother. The therapist said, "Yes, you're really cross" as she caught the ball and, attuning to the anger, aimed it at the foot of the cot. He was instantly engaged, recognised the communication, smiled and gave her the ball to play a game. While they were tossing the ball and drumming on the cot his mother said, "I hate to upset him like this". The therapist said, "Well, it's reasonable that he's cross with you". As the game became quieter he let his mother join in. At the next feed, he accepted food from her, and with his anger gone, their good relationship returned. His extreme grief and anger had contributed to dysregulating his mother. The therapist, accepting his right to protest, helped reconnect them.

### Cal and his parents

With an older infant, fourteen-month-old Cal, the therapist verbalised her understanding for him and his parents about his complex feeding difficulties. There had been little improvement in his admission for food refusal, longstanding vomiting, possible allergies, inconsolable crying, continual head banging, and autistic symptoms. The moment his mother held him he would arch back, shrieking. Despite several admissions to mother–baby units settling techniques were unsuccessful. The family were referred for an infant mental health consultation, for the day before discharge home three hundred miles away, when there was one free hour on a Friday afternoon. The situation, already urgent, could become more so if his failure to thrive contributed to an insecure attachment. Cal was very miserable and his father, who was very engaged with him, carried him most of the time. He would grizzle to be put down, but once down, would grizzle to be picked up. His mother said that he banged his forehead all day on a tile floor till it was bruised black and blue, and she thought that he must have a pain inside. She had not felt helped by the twelve doctors she had seen. She felt depressed but the therapist did not focus on that, sensing that she might feel blamed and not heard again.

Cal and his father, having left the room, as if to get away from the painful issues there returned from a walk holding a toy dinosaur. Cal had a tantrum because he did not want the door closed. The therapist suggested that when he got frustrated he might not know what he wanted and needed his parents to find out, but had no way of letting them know. She could use his tantrum to start exploring the idea that his emotional difficulties were to do with his not-knowing what was happening inside him. As his mother continued to talk about the difficulties she became very distressed, thinking that it was her fault. Cal, who was in his father's arms, gazed at her silently transfixed by her sadness but his body language was clear that he could not bear to be near his grief-stricken mother. The therapist talked to him saying, "Yes, Mummy's sad but you don't have to fix it." The effect on Cal was very marked. This was the moment that he smiled, and his mood lightened.

The therapist, taking up the parents' difficulties in dealing with his cross feelings, suggested that they needed to be put into words, so that he felt heard, such as saying, "You feel cross" about the door being shut. The therapist picked up the dinosaur and, making it stamp its feet, exclaimed, "Cross! Cross! Cross!" Cal looked at her and she underlined the action, saying, "He's stamping his feet." His parents said, "This makes sense." Later when he was frustrated and started to bang his head the therapist, having previously suggested that in future his parents hold him and say they did not want him to hurt himself, now spoke to him, saying, "You're cross", and communicated that his parents could contain this. At the end of the hour, both parents were rapt and his mother thanked her for listening. The following day Cal could eat dairy food without being sick and continued the dinosaur play with his parents, laughing for the first time in his life. When he bumped himself, he remained upset despite his mother's comforting, and only stopped crying when his father said that the teddy was "Cross!" Two months later the paediatrician wrote to the therapist that his mother had said that he was "fabulous", interactive, playful, and exploring, and was much happier and only had one tantrum a day. He ate a wide range of foods and had put on weight. His parents had been unable to think, and without words, feelings of sadness and anger had contributed to Cal's psychosomatic symptoms—he vomited any goodness he took in and hurt his head to relieve unbearable tension. He may not have understood all that the therapist said, but he felt relieved, understood, and enjoyed. Understanding the meaning of his behaviour and giving him words was followed by rapid developmental change.

### Grace and George

George had had considerable difficulties with feeding from birth onwards, with a deep posterior tongue tie. By two months, his mother, Grace, had concerns about his visual fixation and his failure to pass a hearing test. She found it hard to read him, as he only glanced fleetingly for a second with an almost unseeing quality. I said that he was getting himself together and we needed to think about who this baby was here and now, so his parents might include his sensory profile in understanding his behaviour. With his mother's sadness and anxiety, he had been unable to learn about his feelings through his parents' involvement. His mother had not "seen" him and he could not gaze back. I tried to help her pull back, without increasing her sense of feeling criticised, saying that babies wanted most of all to be enjoyed by their parents and she was then able to relax enough to be present for him; he was immediately able to respond with a smile for the first time. She had wondered what it would be like to have a son with visual and auditory difficulties in twenty years' time, although she became quite upset and phoned me several times as part of the mourning and working though. She shared how she wished at times that she had decided to have a termination. But she also did not want to think of that, to concentrate on not missing his cues.

At four months, Grace was tearful saying that things were not going well. I found George well related, and he smiled and vocalised easily but Grace conveyed that she loomed in his face all the time and I talked about how information-rich our faces were and how babies needed to tune out. I observed and shared with his parents, for example, how he looked over my head and only then could bring his gaze down to my eyes and at times like this Grace might think he was not looking at her. His father was pushing the bottle into him and I first suggested George might need a rest and then talking for him I could also share how he wanted the milk back urgently but under his control and as he felt more in control of something more predictable he took more agency in holding the bottle with both hands. His father said "We don't always have a Frances at home helping us make sense."

Grace said a few weeks later the doctor had been unable to find his testes and tearfully said, "I don't love George the way I love his brother—he's hard to cuddle. I'm telling you this because it is confidential. . . . I want a different boy. I do get upset when I see pregnant mothers. I just want to reverse and delete what happened. I lost my mother. She was never very kind to me; she chose this time to disappear; she said, 'I'm not having this, I'm too old for this.' I rang back three times and she ignored me. I want to be happy so we can see past the pain."

Grace indicated she felt suicidal two weeks previously when I was on leave, but said, "I could see that my husband and the children need me—and it would be a worse outcome, although two weeks ago, it was a reasonable option. My father committed suicide. I feel sorry for my husband because he chose me." She asked for regular times to help her understand her son (to stop the build-up of negative projections). She had often asked me why this happened to her and I sometimes conveyed I had no definitive answers because there are none. When he was seven months old, he had been smiling at her and then noticed that she had started crying; his face changed, which she noticed, and he was sad, not knowing how to cheer her up. Although I commented on his emotional sensitivity she wanted signs that he was progressing the way his older brother had done and was angry with me for not being able to say that everything would be all right with her son and felt I was keeping something back. I was being let go of as she felt her mother had done to her.

A mother's relief at being able to share that she does not feel she loves her baby eases her sense of badness at feeling she has failed at motherhood. We also see the importance of understanding a baby's looking away not as rejection but re-regulating.

## *Distilling out a ladder of responses in interactions*

I describe in ascending complexity the levels with which a therapist might interact with an infant and give feedback to infant and parents, applicable in most clinical situations. A therapist might only implement the first intervention and not further levels if intuiting this might lose the family.

### *Describing the infant's behaviour*

A therapist, observing an infant's mood and behaviour, might offer her thoughts to the parents. Observing and describing the infant's behaviour as a process intervention aims to help the parents think more reflectively. It could include offering an observation for comment that the therapist noticed a sequence of behaviour, for example, that after an action the infant was quiet.

### *Playful interaction*

Imitative and reflective play with an infant, where play is an internal process may not need to be directly interpreted. Interaction with a very young baby may function as an interpretation, representing the highest level without needing to be verbalised. A therapist's own thinking may provide a non-verbal interpretation, for example, when a clinician realised she could break a rather fixed gaze with a fragile baby and look back more softly and the baby subsequently became emotionally freer. When a therapist is available for playful engagement and reflective thinking about how the encounter with an infant relates to the problem, the infant often quickly "gets" the playful intervention as embodied reflectiveness, and feels felt. As an infant begins to monitor the attention of others, those others will at times focus on the infant him or herself. To be able to think reflectively requires a relational context that is conducive to exploring your mind in the mind of the other who has you in mind.

### Verbalising affect and intention to the infant

Verbalisation can be viewed as the highest level for a slightly older infant. In the second year, parents verbalise affects for their infants who can talk of their sadness and worry, and a therapist could build on this in imaginative play. Further verbalisation can take place when a therapist triangulates in interaction and verbally and in this way, brings together the parents' and the infant's narrative (see Chapter Seven). Here verbalisation acts as a total transference interpretation to everyone present.

### A spectrum of difficult infant–parent interactions

Several interactions are difficult to process in the countertransference, ranging from not being sensitive to actively insensitive. They may represent a parent's projection of a severe superego, or a mother's depression where an infant faces a climate of continuous negative affect, or at the extreme end hostility and abuse. Some examples include:

- The parents allow no space between their infant and themselves so that it seems difficult to increase the gap.
- The parents are reluctant to discuss the infant or a sibling, or have difficulty seeing a compliant infant, or do not want the therapist to be involved with the infant.
- The parents seem to sabotage every interpretation ("Yes, but . . .") and to need therapy to fail.
- The therapist has difficulty focusing on a mother when an infant is distressed or in mirroring an infant's animation alongside a mother's lack of enjoyment.
- Some parents are either "disengaged" and do not seem interested in the infant as a person and his or her relationship with them as parents, while others have intrusive thoughts about their own experiences as children.
- Some parents seem rough in their handling and comforting in the face of the distress of their infant, whom they view as misbehaving but different cultural norms operate, and they may exert considerable pressure for help with management. A four-month-old infant spent the whole session following the therapist with

her eyes and the mother feeling jealous said, "Girls are manipulative, I'll cut off your fingers, cook and feed them to gypsies". With the therapist gently saying that they would not, the following session the infant when playing with the therapist turned to include her mother.

- Parents talk very critically of their projections on to their infant who "withers", such as a father saying to his one-week-old son, "You're a wimp!". A mother said as her two and a half-month-old infant's hand reached out lovingly towards her: "You want to slap my face, I hate you when you make that face, you're ugly and will need Botox; you're really very beautiful, it's just because you're my baby, I just want to squash your face, throw you away, you're stubborn, a guts"—the alternating splits are clear.

\* \* \*

Some ways of working with a parent's anger include appropriate use of humour if this seems feasible, listening to it without deflecting it or eventually being able to interpret it directly, and through play. A therapist would aim to change the projections early on if possible, taking them up when they can, for example, "My baby doesn't like me/is not affectionate/tries to irritate me by crying or being difficult". Much of this may be driven by anxiety about being a failure as a mother, so that when one mother told her infant it was "rude to stare" at the therapist, the therapist was able to reinterpret this behaviour, mindful that the mother may have felt excluded from the connection with the therapist. A therapist would try not to be viewed as taking the infant's side too soon, to point out some positives or connections, to find the "ghost" if possible. Some parents want to talk about how awful their life is so that it is difficult to talk about how it is hard for the infant, and a therapist might make more headway interacting with the infant. A therapist may have to work with the infant "on the side", that is quietly and unobtrusively, if a parent blocks the therapist's intervention or is not interested. Some therapists feeling under pressure from the parents might say they are drawing a line at a certain point in the session to facilitate their interaction with the infant.

The pull towards working with the parents can be very strong, if, for example, a mother speaks sharply to her infant who freezes, to find a way to talk to the infant about being stopped in their tracks that relieves them and does not humiliate their mother may seem much more difficult than gently talking to the mother about the effect of her talking sharply.

A therapist might arrange separate sessions if joint ones seem toxic for any family member. If the parents have had very damaging life experiences, including the infant may at times make things worse. A therapist may need to say a clear "no" at times, for example, with parents with lived borderline experiences, to not ignore unacceptable behaviour, but nevertheless conveying ongoing involvement

Parents for whom the rate of change may be extremely slow or up-and-down need to be distinguished from those who are resistant to engage in therapy or to change. While intervention may be slower or more limited with parents who are very negative, it may be possible to do it by asking to hold the infant briefly. Or by videoing and then reviewing the interaction together (on the parents' mobile may be less threatening). Enabling a parent to work with hateful feelings in their infant's presence may offer a greater chance of developing self-compassion.

These situations are very difficult in the countertransference, especially when a therapist feels that they are not getting anywhere, trying to soften defences and promote an openness to reflection is taking too long, the infant is suffering unnecessarily, and that protective services and those with more capacity to offer a wrap-around service need to be involved.

### *Infants who "grow up" in therapy*

Sometimes there is a clinical need to accompany infant and parent for a considerable time, and I continue if possible to see parents and infants for a couple of years or so, at less frequent intervals. Sometimes an older infant who has almost "grown up" in therapy gains a considerable amount from accompanying their parents.

### *Ms R and her infants*

Ms R, a forty-year-old woman, was referred to a London clinic for extreme anxiety in her first pregnancy, after deciding to continue with the pregnancy. She was extremely anxious when flooded with memories of an unhappy, unpredictable childhood, with a father with a drinking problem, abusive friends, and a mother who was unavailable and needed Ms R to parent her. Ms R hated hearing crying infants. Her first baby, Rachel, had several minor illnesses with the potential to complicate attachment security and her second baby, Rosemary, was conceived as she felt it was the right thing to do for the first child. The older daughter became more available in interaction with me, and seemed happier and robustly defiant in a session that I felt was transformational not long before Rosemary was born. Rosemary was robust, one effect of feeling accompanied by me through this pregnancy. When breastfeeding Rosemary, Ms R could tell me for the first time about the memories of childhood abuse flooding back, when no one had backed her up, trusting that it was safe enough in therapy to put them into words. I do not think she could tell me sooner, unconsciously feeling that I had not helped her enough.

With her third baby, Ms R hoped for a boy and was again depressed but volunteered early that she remembered some things I had said before and they were helpful, having internalised something of me. When she asked me if she should accept that it could get no better and stop coming to see me, I fought for her therapy and her future and said I thought she could be happier and I did not want her to stop coming, and she was in tears. I withstood her attempts to terminate the therapy, helped her identify future goals supporting academic studies training, and encouraged her in "playful" activities, always holding out the potential of being kind to herself and having enjoyment (Shahar & Schiller, 2016).

She was sad if she thought she was like her mother, having always feared becoming a mother in case she was a bad mother, and I said we all had aspects of our mothers and that she had given the children a different childhood from hers when she had not been looked after and felt hurt. When she was critical of herself and wondered if they would be better off without her, I said no. Holding out hope I said that she had three children virtually under three years of age, which is the hardest time and it would get easier. I offered an appointment to her husband to involve him and she said he made her come that day, implying that she did not think she was worthwhile and I said I knew she had wanted to back out.

When I saw her ten days later with all the children, three-month old Raelene smiled at me and when Ms R asked her if she wanted to come, she mouthed a "yes"; I commented in amazement and her mother said she had actually waved that morning. Raelene had helped her mother feel she was a good mother towards undoing the projections because she smiled so easily, making her mother feel she was a good mother with a loving daughter. Ms R found the idea that a brain may have assaults a helpful idea, that she was not a bad person or just a permanently miserable one, but an assault needs time to heal. I felt she had achieved a degree of reflective function. When she said that Rachel had been having bad dreams, I read *Where the Wild Things Are* (Sendak, 1963) with animation, to convey to Rachel and her mother that anger is manageable, and I enjoyed being with Rachel. I asked Rachel about her dreams and she said they were "good". When the two older girls wanted to take toys from each other and I said that infants were born with moral feelings and mothers helped sort out these differences, I think she found it helpful that her girls were not innately bad and she was not therefore bad. She felt sad about having been angry with Rachel. Rosemary came to Ms R and hugged her warmly at the end twice saying, "I love you". She was the gentlest mother I have seen.

Within three months Ms R had said that she was in love with Raelene in a different way. She seemed to have an acceptance of who she was and who her unavailable mother was, she had done some mourning, but as I felt she punished herself enormously we needed to work towards her being less vulnerable to becoming depressed, as she still thought of suicide every day, while saying she would not act on it. She did not want medication. When offered more frequent appointments to deal with this, Ms R would say that she did not want to waste my time and not accepting these projections, I said, "You never are".

At the end of a session, she said she felt bad and I was not to take it the wrong way but she used to wonder whether she was coming for my needs. She said she now knew she needed a village to raise children, that is, she needed support. My up-and-down countertransference of feeling better, then feeling despairing pointed to her experience as a child. Every time she had something positive she seemed to fear the negative so that she undermined herself. She brought the children to sessions and I found simple ways to talk, after all they knew their mother's state, but they might all have come because she felt they should be given something, too. She asked that I would not suddenly stop her appointments, and tell her it was the last time.

She now accepted appointments without demurring. I asked the clinic to reconsider their policy of discharging outpatients after a set time, so as not continue the cycle of abandonment. When Raelene was nine months old, Ms R was sad realising how hard it had been for her eldest daughter and had talked to her mother about her mother's difficulties as a child and felt more compassionate to her. Ms R also felt better, like she used to feel. She was depressed after each baby was born but gradually her reflective thinking returned. I (the relationship) had to be there to sustain her until her third child could take over.

At ten months Raelene had marked stranger anxiety with me and Rosemary told her mother, "She's crying because she's scared". Ms R's reflective parenting had raised a child who had empathy for a baby and I thought that Ms R had helped her begin to develop the capacity to mentalize. She told me for the first time what a relief it was that I had said that some children do not sleep much when everybody else had been telling her they ought to sleep a certain amount; I had also said that bright babies learn while they are awake, which helps mothers who feel they have failed if their infant is a wakeful one. She had also remembered I said children can manage on thirty per cent response from their parents to the signals they give. When I talked about her being there for her girls, unlike how her mother had been with her, and that she had not had the help that she should have had, as her mother had not either, she said, "Apart from you", the first recognition of this. She said she had found what I said about the plastic brain helpful as the literature mostly talks of the brain's rigid fixity. When Rosemary asked her at this point why she was crying she said she thought she had not been a good mother. Rosemary, by now nearly three years old, spontaneously said "You *are* a good mother". I learned that before Ms R's mother was born a baby had died, so that her mother may never been seen for who she was and she in her pain in a transgenerational trauma had perhaps passed on to her daughter the feeling of not being seen. Her father recently said that he always saw her as a good baby.

### Mothers with high standards

Several mothers in infant–parent therapy who have high standards have found it hard to let themselves develop a more realistic self-evaluation of themselves. If they deny my importance, they could deny the grief of loss. If they saw coming to see me as to meet my needs, it meant they did not have to acknowledge their dependency on me, just as they did not have to acknowledge their baby's dependency on them when feeding. I do not deny I have a need (my wish to succeed) but they could experience that I was not meeting them with narcissistic demands of my own. When a mother's negative representation of her own mother that interferes with forming a close relationship with her infant is interpreted, the relationship can develop—when a mother fears becoming like her own mother in so many ways she may protect her children by staying away emotionally from them. Her transference had been one in which she was accepting of what I offered but kept part of herself away—I offered a new figure for identification and only gradually could she use it to undo the effects of her own mother who had been remembered as an anti-developmental object.

*Queenie and Quentin*

Occasionally an infant whom I have first seen in a maternity hospital has been re-referred to me in a paediatric hospital. The infant's need for his own intervention is clear in this vignette. With Queenie and Quentin, I initially felt I failed. In London, a psychiatry registrar asked me on a Friday afternoon to see Queenie, a mother with a professional background, three days after the birth of her son with whom she was not connecting, while the registrar considered admission to a mother–baby unit. I was only able to see them for half an hour. The mother had found the Caesarean section birth traumatic and was worried that she would not be able to look after her infant. She had had a psychiatric admission as an adolescent. She looked extremely thin, spoke very little, incredibly quietly and looked down with no eye contact. I asked about support apart from her husband, and she was tearful that her mother was not coming for two weeks but said it was okay. I made hardly any inroads on her extremely inhibited gaze and avoidant presentation. She agreed to an outpatient appointment and came with her husband who, however, was the only partner who has declined to join a session when invited, as most parents, when I say that I am there about the relationship with their infant, welcome such help. The infant looked so little I wondered if she was having difficulty feeding him. While she looked a bit better, she was quiet and hardly looked at me. She was close to tears at the thought of not getting it right talking to her son.

When I saw her two weeks later, she was very quiet and hardly looked at me but eventually said that she was angry about the complications of pregnancy and the birth. I could not get her to talk more about her anger. She carried her three and a half-month-old son curled up in a sling that hid him completely, as though she did not have to look at him, as if in projective identification with his mother he had consented to be *invisible*, and I wondered if this was a child protection issue. He looked a little unfocused, with developmental difficulties—his head wobbled and he looked a little odd. He was distressed when he looked at his mother's closed eyes, as his wish to relate to open eyes was disavowed. I wondered if this might lead to a hostile/intrusive attachment. I tried hard to interact with him but he gave little response and only the hint of a smile. It acted as confirmation of my early countertransference feeling of being a total failure. He was not seen in the same way that Queenie had felt not seen by her abusive father and unavailable mother, creating in him feelings of helplessness and absence. Queenie's difficulty in managing difficult feelings had left her unable to be an adequate container for him. I continued to try to make contact in the next two sessions, however, a mother–baby unit admission was arranged and admission to the unit meant that I did not have to examine my countertransference for a wish to avoid.

She had two long admissions with a severe depressive episode. The consultant psychiatrist said her relationship with her son had started to suffer because of her avoidance as she could not bear to look at him; unusually they considered sending him home to his father, because she found it so hard to care for him. At eight months, he was beginning to avoid her gaze, in which he would have seen anger and would feel that there was no one with an internal intention to know him. The unit was extremely concerned about her phobic avoidance, wondering whether to refer to protective services. The unit thought the diagnosis was likely to be borderline personality disorder and on discharge arranged cover so that she would never be alone, including outpatient psychiatry and psychology follow up, but she started to withdraw from these services. I had thought he might have a disorganised attachment and by the end of the first year it looked that way.

However, they were referred for infant–parent therapy when he was thirteen months old and I saw them for eight months. At the start when his mother was asked to do a Reflective Function Questionnaire, she was unable to speak, her eyes closed, wincing in pain, waving for me to go away. He played with the play cooker at the far end of the room but did look back to keep in touch; she hardly talked or played but tidied. I interacted with him, joining in his play and verbalising his affects, and with her I tried to stay with the experience in the room. Whenever I asked her something, her most common response was "I don't know", whether it was about what he liked or felt or something factual about herself. She once told me she had bad dreams of people she knew and she felt bad in them but she could not tell me more. After two months, her son seemed to fall in love with her. She immediately brought how she sometimes got very angry with him (as if confessing) and I tried exploring this, but it was very difficult to do so.

Two months later, as soon as I felt that a disorganised attachment had been prevented, she asked to stop seeing me, probably to avoid exploring further. By eighteen months he had only three words and I began to feel there was nothing in his eyes. I have never known so little for this long about a parent I saw—a decision I made to try to join with her, *consenting to not know*. It was hard for Queenie to bring the childhood experiences that would have contributed to such dissociative experiences. My impression was her mother was cool and felt to be unavailable, and her father was likely to be more abusive than she ever said. She wanted to have another child and reduced her antipsychotic medication. She seemed in agony not knowing why she had not talked to Quentin early on. Speech therapy was recommended but she felt too guilty to arrange this.

In desperation, I "amped up" up my interaction with him. With this marked mirroring, we turned a corner from one session to the next. She told me tearfully that ECT (electroconvulsive therapy) in the unit had not helped, I thought it had revived the trauma memories, and when her son looked at her crying, I said to him that she was sad and that I would help. He was ecstatic when at the end of the session he and I did a high five. On the phone, he said, "Hello, who's there, Dad? Bye."

## Discussion

I did interpret a link between fear of her father's temper as a child and her angry feelings towards her son but I do not think that alone helped the transformation. Her infant could not initially be seen, just as she had not felt seen by her parents—nor by her husband—until I insisted on finding a way to stay in their lives, if only to being used by being there. There was a change in the representations with a relationship-based intervention. Research suggests that playfulness is intrinsic to the intersubjective attunement that is the foundation for secure attachment and theory of mind. I think that in my playfulness with Quentin there were "pivotal" moments when his mother realised that he had his own thoughts, feelings, and memories and had attributed meanings to their relationship. This would allow her to begin to reflect on his internal world as his own and separate from hers. He was also a most dedicated therapist to her.

She came regularly because I structured it that way, while I consented to not (fully) know so that I did not push with the intrusiveness that she would have felt as a child. I think what helped most was my surviving her criticism of me and re-presenting her infant as functioning well.

She is one of several mothers where the signs they give are missed or there is insufficient time to intervene decisively around the birth. A fuller earlier intervention might have meant they did not have to struggle for the length of time that they did. Her husband was very available around the delivery of their next infant.

## Conclusion

Including the infant in the intervention is likely to contribute most to increased reflectiveness. In hospitals, the tilt is towards viewing what an infant presents with as primarily a medical disturbance whereas a therapist includes the contribution that feelings that are difficult to manage may have made. As the therapist becomes important, the parent and infant can extrapolate the "rules" of this relationship, modifying implicit relational knowing towards more secure relationships. Reflective interaction with the infant seems likely to restore the infant to the parents as, above all, more meaningful.

CHAPTER SEVEN

# Infants and their parents in therapy groups

I describe first a long-term therapy group for mothers and infants that created an environment that maximised the potential for infant-centred interactions. As co-leaders, Campbell Paul and I were interested in exploring how mothers and infants negotiated these processes as they came to understand themselves better. Infants can engage with each other soon after birth and they contributed enormously to the group in which the therapists responded to the infants as entitled to a therapeutic intervention in their own right. I discuss some powerful interactions that occurred, and that seem likely to contribute to change particularly between the infants: infant–infant interaction and the infant as therapist, which may constitute moments of meeting for infants and their mothers. I illustrate with a vignette of a depressed seven-month-old boy and his mother, and then describe some short-term groups.

## A long-term therapy group

We explored what happens in a group for both mothers and their infants, combining principles of psychodynamic group therapy with infant–parent therapy. This mother–baby therapy group model included engaging with the infant in the mother's presence. We provided a space for the mothers to project their internal world, which was also a physical space where they could watch the play of their infants together unfolding, and offered ourselves as responding in a different way to their infants. We verbalised what we thought was the infants' experience, and interpreted group themes and processes and, sparingly, the mothers' negative transferences towards the infants.

Being a co-therapist in a therapy group for mothers and infants in their first year consolidated the view of the infant as an equal member of the group, and, as a *therapist with other infants*. The aim of the group was to provide a space for mothers to explore ambivalent feelings, to start separating past conflicts and anxieties from their view of their infant to see the infant more realistically, and to offer the infants their own space.

While interventions might seem slower or at less depth than was needed, this came to seem essential. The infants attending the group could make rapid changes, and follow-up of mothers and infants suggested positive outcomes for them, suggesting that attendance in the group facilitated the infants to have a longer period of relatively trouble-free development.

Responding to the infants as equal members of the group seemed often to enable rapid change. The infants, having an equal "voice", benefited by direct interaction and often quickly confirmed our verbalisations. Once when I said I thought a toddler would know his mother was pregnant, which she denied, his first action the following week was to place a doll on my lap. As the infants felt their experience was understood as meaningful, they responded to their mothers, and other infants and adults in more readable and caring ways. They seemed to take something they had found helpful quickly back into the relationship with their mothers and were therapeutic in engaging with parents and other adults.

### *Rationale, selection, and composition of the group*

The rationale for the group was to offer the mothers the possibility of a more long-term exploration of these issues and a place where they could share what for them had been an overwhelming experience and begin the process of redefining their sense of self to include the concept of "mother". Some mothers seemed cut off and might be difficult to access in individual therapy; they might, however, use a group, and be more ready to accept confrontation by other mothers, with a greater possibility of a therapeutic identification with their infant and other mothers. Some mothers who had difficulties with their anger might also feel more held in a group and their experience of guilt and feelings of blame would be less persecutory. The therapist's countertransference might also be more available.

The selection criterion was that infants had a psychosomatic symptom, and the infants presented with disturbances of sleep, feeding, and other problems of routine, as well as more serious concerns such as profound gaze aversion or failure to thrive. The provision of a therapeutic setting may offer an infant, who may feel as though he is dead with a depressed mother, the chance of a space in which to catch up (a "dead baby" complex of not feeling present in his own body with unconscious defences of avoidance).

The organisation of a group reflects the setting in the therapist's mind. The group ran weekly for one and quarter hours, with up to five mothers and their infants. It was a slow-open group, available for as long as they felt it would be helpful, six months being an average length of stay. We met mother and infant jointly to prepare for entry into the group.

We said they should feel free to say what came into their mind, and we asked for a reasonable period of notice when they wanted to terminate. We asked permission to video the group to help them and others, and they could review the tapes if they wished. We made the videoing arrangements unobtrusive. We provided a small selection of toys, and were interested in seeing how the infants' use of them changed over time.

Mothers mostly began the group with a positive transference to the therapists, and a hot negative transference only appeared fleetingly. It seemed to be positive to have a male and female co-therapist, as a thinking parental couple, different from one another. We tried to catch hold of the main themes relevant for most group members and we also used the infants' activity as a basis for interpretation. Our interventions followed a core principle of infant–parent therapy, of *being with* the infant.

While psychosomatic symptoms or a mother's depression often improved rapidly, underlying anxieties and conflicts continued and understanding them more fully was important. Parallel therapy for the mothers and fathers was not provided in a formal way, and the question of what help fathers needed was addressed with the couple.

*Guidelines for interpreting*

1. We tried to create a space by not providing direct guidance, aiming for the mothers to feel there was no single "right" way to parent, and to feel comfortable with their individual style.
2. We tried to be mindful of, and to interpret, group process as a whole, balancing between interpreting this and relating to individuals. We tried to use the infants' activity as a basis for an interpretation to the group as a whole, and for example might say, "All the children seem to be cross today".
3. We tried to keep the focus on the infant's communication and the mother–child interactions as much as on mothers' experience of becoming mothers.
4. We saw the infants as of equal standing in the group and part of the group process, and addressed interventions to them.

The lack of structure was not always accepted. One mother said, "There's a very long lead time to get into saying something or whether because there's such a short time that we have, there needs to be more confrontation here, which isn't the stance here. It's very difficult to make the first move."

*Containing*

An apparent lack of transference interpretations and why we had not more vigorously taken up what could look like attacks on the setting, such as lateness, we did not think was only collusion. Certainly, the transference may not always be so clear with so much happening, physically and verbally. The infants ranged in age from three months to about a year, which meant that practical aspects of infant care could often take a considerable amount of time. Diapers might be changed, infants fed, they could be tired or vomit, cry a lot—all this often gave sessions a chaotic feel. Paradoxically at times there was a languid feel that may parallel the feelings that some mothers had that they were going to be stuck with this infant forever, and it sometimes seemed mothers dealt with that by exchanging practical tips.

The mothers also functioned in a split way, partly very regressed in a way that has adaptive elements enabling them to be empathic to their infant's needs. While within the session there might be regression, and aggression towards their infant, the mothers could not abdicate being mothers because their infant needed them to function as a mother.

As therapists, the ability to contain the chaos in the mothers and the infants, and the splitting, projection, denial, regression, and even illness in the mothers, were likely to have helped them to integrate towards the depressive position. In being permeable to the infants' demands, to the chaos, and to bear this in the countertransference, we provided a containment that seemed to act as a good-enough verbal interpretation, contributing to the apparent absence of transference interpretation. We held the infant in the mother and the real infant, and thought about them in a way that allowed the mothers to "find the answers" within them. The mothers, who frequently seemed to feel that they had lost a good internal mother, were initially anxious that we thought the answers were in them because it meant working through the loss of the wishful fantasy that we would "re-parent" them. One mother shared that she thought we were re-parenting her, expressing horror that we should think that the answers were in her, because she did not feel she had any answers and she felt what was inside was so bad; when she left the group she no longer felt the mother of a bad child and felt there were no right answers.

A subsidiary reason for not emphasising the verbal interpretive side was that to interpret if there were only two or three mothers in a session meant there were fewer members for it to be dispersed among so that it could feel more persecutory. We came to trust the group process even when it did not seem to be cohesive.

*Interaction acting as interpretation to the infant*

We related to the infants not only through containing or speaking to the group or to them, but also in the language of gesture, action, and play as a form of communication and interpretation. Initially we wondered whether to intervene if a mother had a blank face, or was negative, or plugged her infant with a bottle and we followed some guidelines from infant observation, for example, only to act if the infant was in danger, or in exceptional circumstances such as when a mother of twins had a bad back.

The presence of the infants in their own right meant we had to consider whether guidelines had to be adapted in view of their developmental status. If an infant came to one of the therapists for them to initiate something, would it be rejecting to not respond as infants ask for and should have an affirming response? We came to view the times when we responded physically to the infants, particularly when we initiated a gesture or an action, as a form of communication to the infant and the group that we were commenting on the infant's experience or ours, and offering our thoughts to the whole group. So that the responses that an infant asked from us, we came to view as something that enabled us to communicate our understanding to the infant and to let them know that we viewed that some answers were in them too. Here we had found our way to embodied communication in advance of much of the published literature.

## Infant response patterns to mothers

The infants' activity was linked with the mothers' themes. They could be responsive, reaching out to mothers other than their own, often empathic to them, gazing sympathetically at them before looking at their own mothers (Liddle et al., 2015). Infants showed concern for their mothers, often very aware of what they were talking about and their activities seemed to echo this: they sometimes elaborated what their mother was talking about. They were often particularly sensitive to their mothers' sadness and distress. One infant, aware that his mother was crying, stopped playing and stared with intent concern at her, startled, and seemed relieved that she was helped by talking. Infants also worked out developmental concerns. A toddler, whom I thought had concerns about his aggressive conflicts, was the one who after I had raised with his mother about her not talking to him about her pregnancy, laid a doll in the centre of the floor and began the group the following week laying a doll on my lap.

Themes included:

1. To highlight, that is, *illustrate mothers' conflicts/anxieties.*
2. To *enact* for mother(s), for example, when they were talking about their difficulties expressing anger and the infants behaved aggressively.

3. To help in joint *defensive manoeuvres*, for example, initially when mothers found a topic anxiety-provoking, the infants would raise a hullabaloo that prevented us exploring material. Sometimes an infant cut across what the mothers said, which was often used defensively, although less so as we became better at linking infant activity with what their mothers were saying. They often seemed to know exactly when to become distracting in a way that provided their mothers with an excuse to avoid painful thoughts and feelings.
4. To *counterpoint* that their mothers were talking about sad things but their infants could have fun.

## Infant–infant interaction: the infant as therapist

Infants have pleasure in interacting with other infants from a very early age, and activities and games are increasingly elaborated with them. As part of maturation they are involved very early in triadic relationships and communication. They actively and pleasurably reach out to touch and engage other infants from two weeks onwards (Goldschmied & Selleck, 1986). The other infants in the group quickly became important. They often reached out to them in an active way with care and concern, which was a very potent therapeutic force. In this way, the *infant acts as a therapist*. Very young infants showed empathy, and pleasure in interaction, with the other infants. They have an inbuilt template to reach out and draw in the other infant, with the expectation that the other infant will respond in an alive way. When an infant does not do so, other infants respond with puzzlement and disappointment (Selby & Bradley, 2003). Even older infants were rarely aggressive.

From very early in the therapy they gave clues that they missed the other infants if they were absent, looking round for them, being low key for a time and repeating the activities they had shared with them. Peer-interaction is more possible when the group is functioning at a depressive position level, less than in a split way.

When parents see their infants engage with each other, powerful effects may be set in train. Once infants engaged with one another, they often engaged with other parents and then tried to make eye contact with their own mothers if they were previously unable to.

*The mothers' themes*

The main themes were the mothers' difficulties as mothers and the changes they had experienced—in themselves, the loss of the ideal of themselves as good mothers, their relationship with their partner, and the loss of a good mother–internal object. Feeling safe in this group, it might not be so hard to see an infant who was healthier than their own because the mothers knew that they were all depressed. These themes were elaborated over time but some aspect might be present in every session.

*Changes in the mothers' sense of self*

The mothers explored how they felt their bodies, minds, and identity had been unreliable since childbirth, and their bodies had in particular felt used and abused. One sequence was feeling out-of-control, their husbands were not perceptive and the mothers felt they might be going mad. The birth story was always told with any resulting physical difficulties. Mothers might label themselves as hopeless. They brought their pathology as mothers, and omitted other symptoms before they had babies. One mother said, "The birth is a shock and you mightn't know what hit you especially if feeding doesn't go well and all this can be swamping." Another said: "The whole doubts about yourself and ability to care for a baby is just lack of sleep. The birth takes so much out of you. I haven't been the same—I've had the test for early menopause. It still doesn't feel right inside—it feels like stitches. I have to do back strengthening exercises. I think there's a lot that happens that's physical and hormonal and you combine that with lack of sleep and then I think you can really get down."

*Changes in their relationship with their partner*

There was usually a sequence of saying first that they felt that their partners were very tolerant, followed by expressing that they felt unsupported by them and were envious of them. "I'm angry with my husband for not helping more. I'm supposed to be Superwoman." One mother said she would not know if there were international wars going on because, as I interpreted, they paled into insignificance with the domestic warfare. Relationships, the couple, and sexuality were recurrent, if muted, group topics. They might wish the infant could repair the couple relationship.

*Loss of the fantasy of the ideal infant*

With the myth of blissful motherhood, the mothers felt they were supposed to be "happy ever after", yet often felt they were in a nightmare, and deskilled. They felt that they were more liable to have difficulties if they were professional women. They felt they lost their self-confidence and could not be in touch with what their baby needed. With loss of the fantasy of the ideal infant they became anxious about having damaged their infant, who would only remember bad things and they wondered, "Did I make my baby worse?", "Have I raised a monster?" One mother who had had one mild disagreement with her husband in the seven years before her infant was born found herself furious with her infant, and my interpreting she felt she was going mad as the projection of her anger was coming undone brought relief. Mothers were competitive with their infants and if they felt we "gave" them too much, they might miss a session. Negative feelings towards their infants could often be acknowledged and interpreted within the group. The mothers often said that they did not want another child.

*Loss of the internal good-mother object*

Above all, they seemed to want support from a mother who just "knew" that her daughter needed support without being told, that is, the wish for perfect attunement by their own mothers. They touched on their difficulty in getting their own nurturing needs met, and felt they received little help from their own mothers. "The surprise with the new baby is at how much you have to go outside the family for assistance and a lot of assistance from the family can be pretty damn useless."

*Transference and countertransference*

Many of these themes were projected in the transference. There was usually an overriding positive transference to the male leader as a combined good mother and father. I was protected to some extent from what would probably be greater negative feelings in the transference, so that a wise father transference may have muted the stronger tendency to activate a negative maternal transference (Jackson & Garner, 2011), although there was some material that the mothers gave while looking at me for support. We were at times seen as laissez-faire because, for example, we did not say that if they picked up a crying infant, they would spoil the infant, or as having conflicting approaches to other professionals, or as busy parents rushing off, or as critical of them if they were late. They were at times envious of us.

Intervening psychodynamically with the infant present affected how we as therapists might need to respond physically to the infant, and to manage our own feelings about this. A second issue is that not only are there multiple countertransferences to infants and mothers but there is also the question of which co-leader's countertransference to privilege (Thomson-Salo, 1997) and both these issues can be seen in the following vignette.

*Eric and his mother*

The first time that seven-month-old Eric and his severely depressed mother attended the group he presented in a concerning way. He was unresponsive with flaccid body tone, could not sit up, and looked depressed. His mother thought that every time he looked at her she had to smile so that he did not feel abandoned: this led to rather fixed smiling on her part so that he got a response he would not feel was genuine. His father thought he was slow to follow with his eyes and wanted this investigated. However, from the start of the second session Eric sat upright, and was more engaged with the group leaders and a girl the same age. His mother saw an individual therapist, so that she did have other therapeutic input but it seemed that, because the change in Eric took place from one week to the next, most of the change could be attributed to the group as it was the only new experience for him that week. This would be an example of an infant's plasticity and resilience if the environment begins to approximate to a good enough one. It also came about because of his mother's wish to get it right for her baby: at one level Eric's mother very much wanted help for him and her desperation for help was such that, viewing the group as being for Eric, she asked if he could come on his own if she were unable to accompany him.

When Eric and his mother first arrived, she sat him on the floor where he could not see her and he balanced precariously. She quickly left the room without telling him she was going. For forty-five seconds, he sat with his eyes locked on to mine, which is so long a time for a depressed infant that another mother commented on it.

*The surprise is how often even a two-month old or younger may do this within seconds of meeting the therapist for the first time.* It would be quite powerful for him to feel that he had succeeded in capturing the gaze of another person, particularly as his mother found it difficult to be genuinely present, and he would gain some relief. In knowing that I should not be the one to break the gaze but try to feel my way into it, I provided something new. Eric needed to hold on to gaze as he had nothing else to hold him.

Gradually as his wrists could no longer support his weight he sank slowly to the floor. My countertransference feelings were of concern about an infant who made a strikingly odd and cut-off impression, and concern that his mother's disturbance might overwhelm the group. It was almost unbearable to watch when he sank to the ground, bearing via projective identification very difficult feelings that he and his mother could hardly bear to know about.

Eight-month-old Marcia gave him a very warm response, with vivacious overtures. As soon as she saw him she reacted with pleasure, wriggling and repeatedly trying to touch him and make contact with him but he seemed unaware of her overtures; later she rolled over towards him and tried to hang on to him. When he collapsed, Marcia slid a toy mirror under his face as if to say, "Look at this". We talked to him at times about what we thought his experience was. We interacted directly with him when he seemed to ask for a response from us, so that, for example, we offered a toy thoughtfully rather than in a way that overwhelmed him, which was often his experience with his mother.

He did not look very much at the other infants but he could not fail to be aware almost immediately of their response. Marcia persisted in reaching out to touch him and vocalise. She seemed upset by his lack of responsiveness and expressed her concern about it, and kept looking at us, as if asking, "Why isn't he responding?" Gradually he could look a little at her and another infant.

The other mothers were quietly supportive of Eric and his mother and gradually they put into words her angry depression about the changes involved in having an infant (see later in this chapter). They conveyed the importance the group had for them. They were unobtrusively caring of their infants: Marcia's mother gently folded her daughter's fingers round her bottle without seeming to make the connection with how Eric's mother was feeding him lying on the floor with her arm fully extended.

### Interactions between infant and therapist: transference and therapists as developmental objects

How Eric was generally with us seemed to be transferred from how he was with his mother. He did not look at us much unless we were active in eliciting his gaze, often withdrawing into mouthing a toy and this did not seem to be accompanied by much fantasy. This seemed to be the transference to a mother who could not hold him or read his cues and who treated him in a strikingly mechanical way, pushed toys towards him or put a bottle beside him that he could not hold, or fed him rigidly at arm's length. His protest to his mother was eventually transferred directly to the therapists; he was interested the first time we rolled a ball at him; the next time it touched his hand, he cried.

We tried to respond from a position of having the infant and his mother at the centre of our thinking. Holding the infant's gaze while we thought about him and responded to him was, we thought, one of our most significant interventions, as gaze in the first year is usually a most exciting stimulus for an infant. Eric's mother's first action was to place him on the floor looking away from her and in my direction. (Here we see the opposite to her fixed gaze, perhaps enacting a sadness that she might lose him.) I held his gaze for about forty-five seconds while one mother commented on his looking. Quite early the other therapist and I had reflected together about what we thought was Eric's experience, and later, I said to Eric as he lost tone and swayed forwards, "It's not quite right, is it?" and one mother elaborating this, commented that Eric looked uncomfortable. At this point, however, his mother could not hear what we were saying and asked Eric, "Did you want to get a bit closer?" before moving him closer to some toys but further away from her. He looked up but his cue was not picked up. My response came out of an alive playfulness that is mindful of the infant and the parents, and was an attunement to the dyad. We offered toys when Eric seemed to have communicated something of his readiness for a new experience, which was different from his mother either pushing toys round him or jiggling a rattle in his face. To leave space for her to ease his physical discomfort, we minimised our interventions, but at one point as he had virtually collapsed to the floor and his mother was unable to act, we both did. She could not look in his eyes and "be with him" when he just looked.

We interacted more directly, initiating play, rolling a ball towards Eric and at times vocalising and talking to him. At the end when Eric's mother held him standing and bouncing up and down with pleasure, I reflected his pleasure and said directly to him, catching his gaze, "Is that nice?", smiled at him and commented, "You're doing big jumps". I unconsciously mirrored this slightly with my own body and when he stopped I commented, "Taking a rest", as in affect attunement, for instance, when an infant feels, "You've got what I am feeling", with a deep sense of meaningful understanding that is infused with feeling.

While the infants usually interacted with us as adults who offered the possibility of a new relationship, aspects of their relationships with their parents were also transferred to us. When a therapist responds to an infant with his or her own playfulness attuned to the quality of the infant's experience, the maturational process of attunement is recruited for therapeutic purposes. The attunement in a playful gaze, in which a therapist allows their gaze to be captured, results in the infant feeling affirmed. Our intuitive non-verbal responses we reflected on afterwards. They came from a capacity in Winnicott's (1971) words to be "free to be playful", to trust the playfulness especially when unconsciously attuned to the infant. For example, I had instinctively moved my body mirroring the jumps that Eric made with his body when I said in an emphasising way, "Big jumps!"

We talked straightforwardly to the infants about their feelings or the feelings the mothers were talking about. With an older toddler who was aggressive to another infant, I said to him that I was not going to let him hurt the other infant because, "We might go bad for you and then you might not want to come back next week". As the transference view of us faded, Eric seemed to use us more as developmental objects to meet age-appropriate needs, perhaps with gender preference for a male co-therapist as a father figure.

*Interactions between mothers*

Towards the end of Eric's first session there was an important intervention that took up Eric's mother's feeling of being swamped and helpless in a hating angry depression, and accepting her initial denial until she could own it. One mother had referred to having had a difficult week and another talked of being totally swamped having a new infant and not knowing what has hit you. I said to Eric's mother, who had so far said nothing of her own difficulties, that the other two were saying something about their knowing how swamping it is to have a new infant. Eric's mother immediately said, "It didn't do that to me" and jiggled a toy in front of Eric, who cried, and continued to do so as she said, "I'm just doing what I have to do". One mother identified with her but added that at the same time, "There is the shock of what is actually there". Eric's mother continued to cut across that saying, "I had expected that, it's my responsibility", and finding it too hard to be more sensitive, pushed toys towards Eric. I took up there was something about her being angry about feeling depressed with a new infant and she was able to say, "Oh yes. I think so." Eric protested and his mother shook a rattle at him, and she asked, "What's the matter, Grumpy?" and rolled him over. Campbell interpreted how hard it was when mothers try to get it right and the infants were still grumpy. Eric's mother agreed, and said, "You learn to switch off" and again shook a rattle at him.

As Marcia yawned the tension was relieved. Eric now looked at Campbell who said, "Is that right?" and gestured with his hands towards him while two mothers expressed their gratitude for the help they got from a parenting centre, which Eric's mother did not feel she had. He cried and his mother fed him with her arm fully extended. After five seconds, he cried again and his mother took him on her lap. Marcia's mother then talked about the self-doubts that come with childbirth and how the birth physically took so much out of her and she was too frightened to have a physical check-up. She denied there being something on her mind but when her daughter to whom she had given some juice choked, she could accept the link about how things on one's mind get in the way. Eric's mother did not take part verbally in this link-making but seemed to be involved. When the group finished shortly afterwards she was the last to leave and thanked us.

At the start of their second session I offered to help her in with her stuff. Instead she gave me Eric to carry in, which seemed symbolic of feeling that we had "held" the real infant as well as her internal infant the previous week, allowing them to come closer. There was a transformation in Eric, sitting more erectly in his mother's arms, with good body tone, and he smiled quickly, and was more interactive, with gaze and body-pleasure. He was more engaged with Marcia and us, moved and vocalised with pleasure throughout, and communicated what he wanted. For the depressed infant, the experience of attuned interactive play with a therapist would be a very different experience from the one he or she usually has with the parents, both of enjoying and being enjoyed. It could impact on the still relatively fluid representations of self and other, however subtly or temporarily.

In the third session, Eric's mother sat beside him and tearfully made a link with the death of her beloved grandmother shortly before he was born and her fear of being attacked. She had a bipolar illness following her loss, and was aware of the effects that parental mental illness could have on infants. She felt she had to interact with Eric but her interactions were very non-attuned, she was either "in his face" in a non-contingent way or positioned him in a marooned way, with his back to her. The group helped her relinquish her despair that overwhelmed Eric and to integrate more.

*Gains*

Change could happen relatively quickly. One mother came into the group with an infant who was almost completely gaze avoidant, with severe reflux, and a cry that was almost unbearable to listen to. She had found the birth experience horrific and said she did not know what it meant to feel bonded to her child. Several months later, after she felt the group was a safe enough place to share her negative feelings, she said insightfully that perhaps she was so out of her mind when her daughter was born that her daughter could only turn away from her, and she now felt bonded with her. Her daughter in the meantime had begun to use her gaze to stay in touch with her mother, had lost her piercing cry, and become an engaging infant.

In the initial stage the members sized up one another. Then with development of cohesiveness, in which there was an increase in trust and self-disclosure, they worked on their relationships with each other. One mother said it was painful when we brought new people in.

One mother, announcing she was leaving the group said:

> I've reached somewhat of an equilibrium in my journey. I've come to the conclusion there are no hard and fast answers to all these things. I've changed quite a lot just in the way I see things, although it's quite subtle ... It's mixed feelings. It's never an easy cut-and-dried thing. I feel I've

moved along the journey as far as I can at the moment. I can see links between experiences I've had and behaviours that I exhibit and I haven't resolved those behaviours but at least I understand why they're there. And I can see things differently with my son and the way he responds, and my attitudes and responses very much relate to how he responds to things, and I suppose that's a very valuable thing I've learnt. It's not that you get so that you say, "I know the answer" and you stop. The group doesn't stay the same even if we don't do a lot of talking in a week, there's still things going on between people and between the kids [an infant made a noise here] so it's changing all the time. Each of us have a lot to give the group and we have given the group a lot and we make the group what it is. I've had the luxury of coming for nearly eight months and that's a long time.

Another mother said:

What you get here is what you don't get in a mothers' group, where you can say certain things and you can talk if another mother is going down the track I went down. I find I do need to come and it's been very much an anchor, even if nothing was happening and I'd get really frustrated [she growled this word], it was an anchor and maybe that's just my personality, but it does carry on. I think what I see this group would be doing is to get the hurt and the anger and everything out without having to be responded to in a certain way as friends would. We feel terrible because we come in here and use it as a whinge session, it's very much a safety valve.

Some mothers and infants with complex difficulties needed a longer period in the group to consolidate. One mother leaving the group said,

Twelve months ago, I didn't have any love for my daughter, it was like a duty. This was the only place I felt I got help. A lot of the time I felt terrible, I wanted to die, I wished she was dead, and I didn't feel courageous enough to say it. Sometimes everything seems so bad like you're drowning in the midst of chaos.

For the mothers, a central theme was the search to find the good internal mother whom they felt they had lost. It was noticeable how, after sessions that seemed chaotic but where we had provided a sense of containment, they felt safe enough to share deep anxieties such as that they had felt like abusing their infant.

## Some short-term group models

Some aspects of the long-term group model were operationalised and an intervention group contrasted with a control group, and run for an eight-week period (Figon, 2000). The mothers in the intervention group demonstrated a statistically significant reduction in the depression scores on the Edinburgh Postnatal Depression Scale, whereas the mothers in the control group did not. The intervention group also showed a trend towards becoming more sensitive in parent–infant interactions. With a time-limited group there can be an invigorated sense of mission in that there is a certain amount of time to face issues confronting them.

This group model was modified in the following ways:

- A six to nine session group for mothers, fathers, and toddlers with difficulties.
- A group for infants in contact with protective services or in care for the first time.
- Time-limited groups for mothers and infants experiencing family violence (Chapter Eight).

## Short-term groups for toddlers and their parents in the second year

We developed a short-term group model for toddlers who were experiencing difficulties around separation or anger, and their parents who had their own mental health problems so that being a member of the group gave validation in terms of therapy for their own problems and anxieties. One rationale for seeing the parents and older infants together is that the group process and playful interaction with the infants is therapeutic for all.

The main port of entry was the infant's imaginative world. We often interpreted to infants and parents in a "soft" way, hoping to shape their representations, for example, talking of making friends with the playful hungry dinosaur who invaded the picnic, "subversively" building on their play. We would *triangulate* between infant and parent—for example, "Did you see him do that? Shall we show your mother, she may not have seen, shall we tell her?" Or we built on unexpected situations or responses. This "sloppiness" (Stern, 2004) may constitute a transformational moment in which representations are dramatically altered. As leaders, we played with feelings in the play, as infants can from five months. One leader might also comment on the other leader's actions in play with another infant, for example, commenting with magnified affect that the other leader was being cheeky, if we thought that this would help the toddler play with potentially conflictual aspects in his mind without having to act on them.

We might interact individually or offer a play activity they could all take part in together, such as joining a railway line. We tried to stay with the infant's experience so that, for example, when a toddler coughed, we might say "Cough, cough" to magnify this and recruit it into meaningfulness. We might initiate play, or imaginatively extend it; even joining in pouring tea can delight an infant because, just as with imitation in the first months, an infant knows he cannot make the adult join in so that the adult must be freely doing it.

What was communicated and played with is the idea that there are additional ways of viewing experiences and internal values. It is a further layer of complexity that toddlers can play with and decode. This play may have worked towards change partly as a special kind of therapist misattunement that toddlers may be very responsive to recognising the adults joining in companionship.

We might comment on what was happening to infants in the group or echo in our own words something that the parent had just told us of the infant's experience that week. So, for example when a nearly two-year-old infant arrived white-faced with distress because her father had brought her late to the group I said, "You're sad because your dad was a bit late." The infant has the potential to feel more helped if the therapist can triangulate between infant and parents as in the following example. Pointing out to a toddler that while her father had talked about her being angry with her brother, he had also just told us he was angry with the hospital security guard, I was "interpreting" that it was acceptable to talk about these angry feelings, and they had a meaning. The intervention had a bi-directional effect in that her father could mute his own anger, and this helped his daughter manage her own anger more appropriately. A verbalisation, acting as a total transference interpretation to everyone, might have gone like this: "The cross crocodile has bitey feelings and your dad has just told us about you being angry with your baby brother and how your dad was angry with the parking man."

Thinking of an infant's therapeutic alliance and shared decision-making changes the lens—in a three-girl group (we had to consider whether, thinking of adding a fourth child after the group had started), the toddlers, who had consolidated as a group, had given consent. From the first session, the group became very important to them: one eighteen-month-old talked about it throughout the week.

If a parent is very negative to their child, having the leaders hear and think reflectively before responding may be a new experience for parent, child, and other group members. Second, when parents have impinged too much on a child who has become frozen, experience shows that, given time, such "frozen" children can reach out warmly in their relating.

We asked the parents to complete the Brief Infant–Toddler Social and Emotional Assessment (BITSEA) (Briggs-Gowan & Carter, 2006) and to rate the following three questions at the beginning and end: what was the problem, how much concern did they have, and how much did it impact their life? The toddlers' pre- and post-test scores improved, sometimes by several bands, on the parent–infant relationship assessment scale of the Diagnostic Classification 0–3 (PIRGAS, 2005). Examples of positive outcomes were parents relating more positively to children (self-report and the leaders' observations, for example, play and initiating activities in group and home), and the parents reporting improvements. We also observed increased effective peer interaction. The children learned to speak in a conversation they had never previously been part of.

*Fay, Grace, and Helen*

Eighteen-month-old Fay's anxious mother was concerned Fay did not interact with the other toddlers and had withdrawn her from childcare after her first two hours because she had cried; her mother was also working on her own ambivalence ("This is my daughter whom I want to be independent but I also want to be dependent"). Grace's mother was worried her daughter was autistic. Helen's father had complained that his daughter was not social and did not share with peers; this was also a reflection of his difficulties and he tried to encourage her not to go down the same path, and the other parents helped him soften this approach.

If there are not enough toys, how do the infants work it out? Grace conveyed, "I want the other koala as well" and asked, "Where's the other one?" Fay moved closer to her mother, pulled a koala to herself and was pleased that she had hidden it. There was a process between the three infants, with Grace not going to get the second koala. Grace and the therapist knew that a koala was in Fay's hands and they pretended to look for it; the therapist made a playful gesture touching Grace—perhaps pretending to be the koala running away and therefore unconsciously mirroring how Fay had moved the koala against her body. Fay argued, "It's my toy and you're not going to play with it" and they had to work out a solution. Fay put the koala in the post box and was quite pleased about that. While Fay's mother did not have a liveliness in herself to join in, Grace's mother could see the joke in the play, contributing that for Fay. Helen's father very considerately returned the koala to Fay.

A therapist's communication should be an actual communication. Once, when Fay, who was often frightened of me, tripped I thought she cried angrily as if blaming me. She then sat facing Campbell Paul, with tears running down her face; he delicately wiped away a tear with his little finger and commented to her that he was wiping a tear and followed her lead respectfully; she then drew his attention to another tear welling up, indicating for him to wipe it away. This seemed enactive communication, "being with" the infant in such a way that it confirms "I can be with you as you are". The following week her mother disclosed for the first time the father's verbal abuse, his yelling so angrily that Fay found this hard, as if the experience with Campbell had "spoken" to the dyad that their distress could be heard and a new representation be co-constructed that strangers could be safe. We considered that here interaction with a young infant functioned as an interpretation. The parents could talk about important issues with their children present, such as this and Helen's father's anger, and did not have to talk in code or avoid the subject.

As the toddlers became more securely attached to the group they generalised these improvements to their individual relationships outside therapy.

## *Group for parents and their infants in contact with protective services*

In a further adaptation, we offered a group for infants and their parents who had been referred to protective services, to explore this experience and help parents understand their infant's mind (through observation), and reach them through pleasurable interaction with their infant, and also to be helpful to the infants. It was set up to offer vulnerable parents and their infants a short-term therapeutic space while waiting for other services to be implemented. The letter to the parents outlined that the group was for parents and infants in their first year where an infant is or has been in care, and stated,

> The group is separate from any assessment. We are interested in how the babies relate to and communicate with each other. We think they can be quite helpful in this way. Their parents would have the opportunity to explore how their own experience has been like that of other parents' and how it has been different. While the group will not be a parent education group we would try to help with some of the issues which arise in looking after small children.

The theoretical framework had been consolidated in the long-term therapy group. We aimed to increase the parent's understanding of their infant's mind through our experience of it. While acknowledging for ourselves the severity of issues the parents faced, such as the lived experience of schizophrenia, and parents with de facto partners who could have abused their infants, we decided that rather than taking a formal history we would accept whatever information the parents volunteered, aiming to achieve a balance with our need for internal freedom.

It was important to consider what factors facilitated parents attending—whether providing light refreshments was helpful when parents feel very deprived, and our sitting on the floor reduced psychic distance. If parents dropped out of the group, we considered whether this expressed their autonomy or whether to follow up vigorously. While this group was set up as an interim intervention, some infants showed an immediate therapeutic effect, as in the following vignette.

## An infant with fractures

An eight-month-old infant and her mother attended this group, after the infant had come to the attention of protective services when it was discovered that by eight weeks of age she had had eight broken bones, for which her single mother and her de facto partner were unable to give an explanation. I found her a pudding-type infant in her first session and while I tried to talk and play with her as part of what we offered the parents and infants, she did not get very much one-on-one time. The next week it was hard to believe the difference—she craned forward in her pushchair when she saw me and babbled alertly, responsively and non-stop for ages. Largely this was because—as there was nothing else that was new in the week for her and her mother—she sensed that her mother could feel supported and there was a playfulness about what we offered to infants and parents.

## Conclusion

The powerful interactions in a long-term therapy group particularly between the infants seemed to have a mutative effect. The attachment of infant and parent to the group was associated with symptom improvement, gains in self-esteem, and resolving conflict. This was the theoretical approach I took into short-term group models when the model was extended to reach parents and infants experiencing different kinds of difficulties, particularly a group for mothers and infants in the context of family violence (Chapter Eight).

CHAPTER EIGHT

# Relating to infant and parent in the context of family violence

Here the needs of infants who have witnessed family violence are explored in therapeutic encounters with them and their families: experience of the effects of violence exposure depend on factors such as the infant's age, proximity of the violence, and relationship with the perpetrator. The vignettes are of infants who have experienced violence towards their mother by her partner as that reflects the presenting population (while recognising that some infants experience violence from their mother to her partner). What I describe refers more to infants exposed to family violence rather than suffering extreme violence themselves, although some have witnessed such extreme levels of violence that they may be challenged in managing their own emotional responses to their parents' violence. A therapist would tune into the terrified world of a very young infant who is surviving in the best way he or she knows how, by freezing. The infant being present when his mother's issues around family violence are appropriately explored seems to help both mother and infant move forward rather than becoming marooned.

It is possible in the context of family violence to offer something even if it is only a single encounter, although it takes longer if an infant has felt helpless for a long time. Sensitive periods of development pass quickly. An attitude of playfulness, without overwhelming an infant in a fragile state, conveys hope; a relationship experience helps resilience increase.

## Some effects of trauma and violence

Witnessing family violence, either acute violence or in cumulatively small doses, may cause as much distress and suffering as experiencing physical abuse, and lead to depressive features. Some infants seem to remember traces of traumatic events from the earliest months and young infants can show in play what they have experienced. A twenty-two-month-old girl enacted in her play how the car she was in as a nine-month-old rolled down a hill with her mother and herself in it (Drell et al., 1993). Infants witnessing family violence have carers who are frightening and frightened. In this situation infants usually develop a disorganised attachment, as those whom they need to help them feel safe are those who make them frightened. When the infant's anxiety is raised by abuse or the threat of it, the infant needs to cling to the attachment figure even if that person also frightens them; it becomes unending fear.

In the first year, infants are hyper-alert to the sounds and sight of the violence (Perry et al., 1995). Infants with exposure to violence may be more likely to use dissociation more than hypervigilance, contributing to developmental delay. If infants cannot use fight or flight they can only freeze (looking warily at what is happening, sometimes with an attempt to be charming), or dissociate, or become quite disorganised, which may be used more by infants who find it difficult to self-regulate. For many, violence may be too much to cope with, disabling the coping systems and flooding the infant so they become dysregulated. Behaviourally an infant may have a motionless face, can become passive, uninterested in anything, hard to know, and does not vocalise much or see the funny side of events. Or an infant might give a social smile of politeness, or be very smiley although they are more likely to be gaze avoidant of those of whom they are frightened.

Feeling that a parent is powerless to protect them results in a traumatic shattering of safety. What may also be traumatic is how infants feel their mothers view them. Mothers who are depressed may dissociate, blame their infant, be unpredictably moody, or suffer flashbacks. A mother waiting for unpredictable violence may "go" behind her fear so that she is unavailable for her infant. What legacy has the infant collected in the mother's eyes, her mind? If there was violence towards a foetus *in utero*, the infant may be born terrified, making them more difficult to parent. When parenting an infant born as a result of non-consensual sex or rape in the couple relationship, mothers experience a continuum of states of mind from acceptance to rejection that impacts their representations of their infant; from the infant's perspective, this affects attachment patterns and representation of the father and impedes development of a positive self-representation (Thomson-Salo, 2010).

Infants who feel it is unsafe to explore may have identified with withdrawn parents and feel that they have done something bad to contribute to this. The shut-down by an infant may be an attempt, as well as trying to be invisible, to stop any contribution to the scene. Trauma in an attachment relationship is the most destructive because the biological basis of attachment is trust and safety (Fonagy, 2005). With trauma, an infant has to cling to her attachment figures but it may be too difficult for the infant to think that the carer intended her harm so that must be split off and not known. As the figures in an infant's mind are likely to be frightening ones, it is hard to feel comforted even when the trauma recedes.

Whenever an infant sees purposive action, her mirror neurons fire in the same way as those of the person who is carrying out the act. In this way, the infant has a sense of the feelings and thoughts that the person intended in the action. The infant watching violence in front of her is then likely to have the violent act in some way mapped in her mind. But if the infant at the same time sees the mother hurt and anxious, the infant has her actions and fear also represented. Infants therefore simultaneously learn about the possibility of being aggressive and being the hurt victim.

The experience of young infants' feelings may feel infinite: when they get stuck in fright and hurt, time seems endless, and development usually slows down. Echoes of violence are present in the following vignette where a mother felt intimidated by her partner and had difficulty thinking reflectively about how the way she fed her baby kept him close to her body rather than her husband.

*Ida and Isaac*

Ida, a forty-one-year-old mother and her husband, Ian, consulted about the sleeping difficulties of their eight-month-old son, Isaac. He gave a very bright smile the moment he saw me, but it froze and disappeared almost immediately so that I wondered how much he had had to learn to warily head off feared situations. At one point Ian triumphantly shouted with his arms raised in the air, thanking me for agreeing with him about his son's crying. His wife immediately said that she did not disagree with me or with him, but was making another point. She breastfed Isaac in the early morning when he, Isaac, was still asleep but found it hard to think with me how this might perpetuate his closeness with her. Isaac was clearly very bright but did not engage with me or the toys. In the light of his father's behaviour, which was subsequently revealed to be more coercive, it seemed that my intuition on meeting their son had pointed to this difficulty and by withdrawing he communicated that it did not feel safe to go further. Ian made a complaint about my professional competence, saying that I had "dead eyes".

## Countertransference

Some infants have been described as the infant whom therapists wanted to save, needy and affectionate infants who often have a profound effect on therapists; others as "emotionally aloof and rejecting" who are much harder to help and do not usually evoke rescue fantasies (Seligman, 1993). They may resemble the depressed infant who sullenly pushes away the therapist—it is harder to respond by persisting. A therapist needs to keep reflecting on how they relate to these infants who may often be nearly invisible.

Many therapists have a background of being touched by some pain that is like that of these infants, revisiting traumas and defences against them or wishing to give the infants what was not given to them; from this a therapist draws on his capacity to put himself in the place of the infant. The sadism and perversion enacted on young infants causes a therapist pain and anger, and he may wonder angrily why parents do not protect their infant, as if blaming them for being a victim.

## The importance of being available for relational encounters

Relational encounters can give an infant a respite from trying to process attachment trauma that feels overwhelming. The brain develops in an experience-dependent way, structured by the experiences it has that forms a template through which all subsequent experience is filtered (Perry et al., 1995). The infant repeats what he or she has learned about being in relationships until new patterns get learned sufficiently well to start taking over from the old ones—that instead of people being hurtful or destructive, they respond with reciprocity.

As a young infant cannot tell her story in words, her psychosomatic symptoms convey when she does not feel soothed or feels sad. Infants may feel sick as if to vomit up the bad feelings. Blood on the mother's body may be particularly distressing because infants know that blood is not usually present. An infant's facial expressions usually have meaning, even if this never becomes known. An infant needs to be met in whatever she is feeling—in irritability, depression, or despair. In that way, she feels that someone understands and if she senses her feelings are recognised is often enlivened quickly. With a young child, if the feelings evoked with the trauma return during play, the therapist could say, "That was then, it is not now."

The therapist having the infant at the centre of his thinking while intervening with the mother, can begin to change the way the infant views the world, which the infant then takes into the relationship with the mother. While a therapist may only, in the brief window of opportunity that is sometimes all that is available, be able to offer the infant an experience of being understood and communicated within their own right, that can be very powerful.

## *A group for mothers and infants who have experienced family violence*

Supporting traumatised parents to help their own infants in a safe environment is most important, so that overwhelming traumatic feelings can be integrated. Group support is particularly important while a woman consolidates her identity as the mother of her infant. I designed a model of a time-limited group for mothers and infants who had experienced violence in the first year of life to help them to connect over their experience, to reflect what it meant if the mother had stayed with the abuser, and what was going on in their infant's mind about the violence (Bunston et al., 1999).

### Activities for infants and their mothers

Even very time-limited groups of six sessions seemed to be effective in making a difference to the infants and their mothers: infants with developmental delay usually sponged up the enjoyment and made rapid forward moves even from the first session and their mothers' depression usually improved significantly in pre- and post-test scores. The intervention aimed to increase infants' sense of trust, reducing their anxiety and offering some positive experience to set against experiences of loss.

Activities for the infants were chosen not just because they were intrinsically pleasurable such as play with mirrors or bubbles, but because they arose organically and seemed right for when the infants needed either soothing or livening up. An infant may need activities that help with what they feel is their mother's withdrawal or re-exposure to being immersed in traumatic memories. Sometimes an infant who has felt overwhelmed by previous contact with people needs the space to just be and recover. Although it is unlikely that specific memories of a trauma would be evoked it may happen, which gives a way to talk very simply about then and now being different. For example, action songs that were frightening the first time they were played can be talked about as, "We did that too fast and it was scary and now we'll do it slower", promoting self-regulation skills. Recognising and repairing a rupture in connection is a crucial factor in therapeutic intervention.

Even *young* infants may refuse to be reassured by false promises. As their mothers become stronger in the group process, infants intuit this. Making it possible for the mothers and infants to have experiences of joy gives the infant the surprise of something good as well as helping mothers see their infants in a way that they may not have done before. When *older* infants have experiences of emotional reliving, what is needed is to make the connection with the trauma— such as saying, "You're scared because you're remembering what happened." A therapist can encourage them to play, with—"What happened?" or to draw. Many infants do not need much encouragement to draw, as when a two-year-old child, trying to symbolise, drew red marks for blood when her father stabbed her mother.

## Talking with infants

When talking to young infants about events, something gets communicated. The earlier an infant has opportunities to start connecting words with what happened, the more helpful. A therapist can talk to them about how they were scared: for the twelve-month-old boy who said in a group, "Daddy hit mummy", or the twelve-month-old girl who said, "You scared me", to think of how to talk about what the father did was very wrong, and should not have happened. An infant tries to find ways to have a coherent narrative about past events to begin to fit him- or herself into it. Clinical experience suggests that when this narrative can develop, the infant's mental health is likely to be stronger: an infant whose parents separated when he was two was able to say, "My dad made my mum cry. He didn't leave because of me". It asks a lot for mothers to think about what is in their infant's mind, so that a therapist could affirm their courage in considering this, and then wonder about it being hard to find ways to *talk* about the infant's wish to have a relationship with the father.

Some mothers, responsive to the possibility of their infant wanting this relationship, could say that they do not understand why they were attached to their partner, why he did what he did, or why they stayed when they found out how he was. What can be conveyed is what the father lost by his actions in the rupture to his relationship with his infant. It is about trying to open a space for thinking to help a mother explore several issues, including the identity of the person she is, and her sense of guilt.

The aim is to return autonomy to the infant to have a sense that he can be active and effective in his world, and restore a crucial aspect of the sense of self—that it is an active one. For example, when a one-year-old was too frightened to play with the toys but the following week could allow himself to be interested for the first time—to say, "You're interested in the toys" could be an interpretative comment about noticing something the infant feels about himself. An eight-month-old who was so severely traumatised by the violence he had seen that, apart from whimpering in distress, he was totally frozen and unable to eat, needed to have a sense of autonomy restored to him by respecting his cues: this would be to not impinge on him, not to unthinkingly give him his dummy but place it near his lips where he could take it when he liked, and above all, respect the relationship that he had had from three months onwards with his foster mother, trying to privilege her care over that of others.

A therapist could assist with continuing a dialogue in an infant's language and evolving understanding of the world. One mother was shocked when her twelve-month-old son said, "Daddy hit mummy". She said, "I didn't realise he could know it or say it". Infants "know" what they are not supposed to know (Bowlby, 1988). If infants are told that their father was naughty and he had to go away, this could have implications they might worry about when they are naughty. If infants are told that they are bad, they could develop difficulties with impulse control. One developmental task facing infants is to learn that their "aggression" is not intrinsically bad and how to manage it. A therapist might differentiate that a father was *very, very* angry to discriminate this from ordinary anger (adding that, "You shouldn't hit people"). A space to think with a therapist can be very important—when a boy looks preoccupied, which his mother may interpret him as being violent like his father, the therapist can wonder with the mother about this being different. To an infant who may be distressed that the father is not present, a therapist could say, "You're upset about your dad doing those things and you're also upset about his not being here". A therapist needs to balance what information the infant is asking for and can handle. A three-year-old whose mother was convicted of manslaughter for the death of his sister confronted her saying that she killed his sister, and the therapist could talk with him, explaining that his mother did not get the help she needed. These interventions may provide enough relief and safety, so that development can move forward.

### Talking with their mothers

A space for mothers who have experienced violence, along with ground rules about keeping themselves safe in the group, is important. In considering whether in talking about the violence in the presence of their infants they would be re-traumatised hearing their stories, much of what their mothers feel about the partner is probably already known at some level by the infants. It is important for the mothers' feelings with their infants not to be inauthentic or masked, to explore what mothers feel is safe to voice in the group, and find ways for them to retell their story around their infants so that the pain from the past and present is lessened. Infants find it very hard when they sense that there are secrets that are not spoken about, as if something is so terrible that even their parents, who should protect them, are too frightened.

As the mothers feel their stories when told were "heard" while simultaneously implicit relational knowing in which they felt that they deserved to be hurt was challenged (both verbally and through their experiences of pleasure in group activities), their sense of self can change. It is often possible to help a mother begin the process of thinking insightfully about her infant as a person in her own right, different from images projected on to the infant, of which she had until then been unaware. Once when a mother said she deserved the violence her own father inflicted on her, the therapist disclosed a feeling of anger on her behalf and asked if the mother thought that her three-month-old infant lying beside her would deserve to be hurt. The mother said no, and that she would protect her (when that protection had been non-existent for her). She had felt accepted in the group so that her wish to protect her daughter was strengthened instead of continuing with a disorganising response.

Intervention aims to reduce the intensity of the overwhelming feelings, partly by helping to develop a coherent narrative that is therapeutic in itself (Coates & Gaensbauer, 2009) and to gain a sense of mastery of events. Communication between parents and infant around the traumatic experience is a precondition for integration by the infant. A therapist's capacity to hear the story non-judgmentally, and to be receptive to the trauma in the past of the adult who was violent, without condoning the violence, may help the mother find a way of talking to the infant about how sometimes the things the father did were because he was troubled and had not received the help he needed. It seems helpful for infants to process this early.

An important factor in recovering from trauma is that of a parent gaining a sense of doing well. As a therapeutic factor, a therapist engaging with the infants in the presence of their mothers contributes to their mothers feeling better about themselves and about their infants in a way that quickly bring results. When mothers view their infants being engaged with, understood, and above all enjoyed, they generally see them differently. Infants in turn feel their mothers are less distant and depressed, they feel less blamed, and have less need to stick like glue. Lieberman and her colleagues' (2005) randomised controlled trial in San Francisco of seventy-five traumatised pre-schoolers exposed to marital violence, supports the importance of intervening with the infant in the presence of the parent. The intervention group mothers showed strong trends towards more improvement in post-traumatic stress disorder (PTSD) symptoms and global psychiatric distress who may, by speaking about the trauma in the joint sessions, have found effective ways of processing their own traumas.

## *Conclusion*

Engaging with infants in groups to counter the effects of family violence contributed to their mothers feeling better about themselves and their infants in a way that brought quick and significant results without extensive deep interpretations. This intervention speaks to the infant-in-the-mother with a message that they too are enjoyed and valued, which confirms their self-esteem and could act as a protection against violence. Just as the effects of trauma contribute to developmental delays in infants, treating the self as intentional, which they particularly need when there has been violence, may have a cascade effect in helping parents and infants. As they see the therapist holding their story in their mind, making sense of it, they can move forward.

# PART IV
# TOWARDS UNDERSTANDING SUCCESSFUL OUTCOMES

CHAPTER NINE

# Countertransference in infant–parent therapy

Here I explore in particular, difficult countertransference feelings such as anxiety, guilt, and shame as well as those cases where I felt I may have missed something, or felt I failed. Countertransference phenomena illuminate how unconscious processes may enhance or interfere with the therapeutic relationships between infant, parent, and therapist, as containing in the countertransference transmutes the transference. Use of countertransference is widely seen as the single most important guide to the therapeutic experience, as possibly the most significant source for understanding. This includes the feelings and associated insights of therapists, as well as attunement to the emotional and psychological needs of infants and their parents. Countertransference shapes the therapy in that increased awareness of it shapes the therapists' stance and their interpretive comments.

I touch on the experience of rupture and repair (Benjamin, 2009). Currently a major model for thinking about countertransference is one of co-creation by therapist and those with whom a therapist engages. Feelings evoked in therapists are a major way of understanding others. Therapists need to be thoughtful about the feelings triggered in them, particularly those they are resistant to, and continuously process a tendency to be critical and disapproving. To understand an infant involves looking at oneself.

When the therapist enters the therapeutic space in the earliest weeks and months of a baby's life, some of the projections the parents place on their baby may be freed up, but they may also turn in a negative transference to the therapist. A therapist using countertransference to guide understanding of ambivalence may be able to offer an intervention early enough before the projections have had time to rigidify, which they might by, say, three years of age, increasing parents' despair and hostility. (See also Chapters Six and Eight.)

## *Countertransference with infants*

Therapists need to work at continuously processing their countertransference (and on their feelings about themselves as infants); increasing interest in the use of countertransference emotional responses has helped deepen assessment of an infant's emotional state. By two months of age or earlier an infant may be amazed at meeting a therapist who tries to make sense of what is happening for him and his parents. If the infant (or parent) puts the therapist in touch with his or her own longings, he or she might be put in touch with his or her own. It is striking how often therapists working with mothers and infants describe physical responses, such as feeling panicky in identification with the infant. Yet it is also sometimes striking how little an infant features in reports, although there is usually an infant in the room; a difficult countertransference may take up a lot of observing space.

Interacting with an infant may, however, feel overwhelming in considerable identification with the infant; a therapist may feel confronted and helpless observing the pain of the infant. A therapist may respond out of his personal history, personality, and attachment style with more anxiety or distress to the infant's cry, particularly if the parent is abusive. If a therapist behaves defensively, breakdowns in communication may be more likely. A therapist may wonder if he has overlooked the infant when he is to be there as a voice for the infant. What is evoked in this way may parallel the way that an infant feels. A therapist may ask a parent what she thinks the infant is taking from the conversation, which she may in considering it for the first time receive better than expected.

Therapists are more aware of how much the body does the feeling and thinking in interaction with the infant. What infants bring of their gender in relating to female or male therapists as well as differences in gendered countertransference responses may have been under-theorised (Thomson-Salo, 2002, 2003). From birth, girl infants are generally more self-contained and boys tend to be more dependent on their mothers for managing their feelings of joy and anger; when they have depressed mothers, they feel more angry and deprived. How they relate differently may affect a therapist's response to them and we need to ask about gender differences in a therapist's experiences of these affects.

While it is helpful to separate countertransference to an infant from that to his parent, it can also be difficult, engaging with an infant to "rescue" her, yet feeling reproach and anger on her behalf at the same time as having to understand his mother's feelings of deprivation and pain before she will trust the therapist.

Attending to countertransference with traumatised infants is important. While an infant may arouse sympathy, he may have also aroused dislike, which is often diagnostic of the infant being hated. Disorganised infants have probably at some level felt rejected. When there is a difficult countertransference with a parent, a therapist can ask why she is this way—if, for example, an infant feels hateful, has he felt hated?

## Countertransference with parents

Countertransference is a most helpful guide to what is occurring and we need over a lifetime to increasingly develop receptiveness in the countertransference to projections of infant and parent. We also need to not only continuously work on our conscious intention not to be critical of parents for issues we find ourselves not in agreement with, but also that we are not being so self-conscious of ourselves that we miss what infant and parent feel in coming to see us. Countertransferential issues may be particularly complex and layered, for example, thinking of an infant conceived in more technical circumstances rather than in joyful sexuality, where the parents have used reproductive therapy.

Traumatised parents may evoke maladaptive interactions offering the potential for repair of the traumatic experience in the therapeutic relationship. Monitoring the countertransference is most necessary when a parent misses an infant's cues. Other stresses are the urgency for an infant, as well as time pressures. Therapists find it painful when parents seem rejecting and cold, or when parents struggle to connect with their infant who is like a sack of potatoes, or is failing to thrive and emaciated. A therapist may feel overwhelmed by parents' unmet needs. He may feel guilty when intervening with some parents, for example, if he does not like the parent because progress is slower. An intimate contact occurs between minds and bodies that are maltreated psychologically, and the minds and bodies that maltreat psychologically, as well as the mind that must hear and see, and put into a personal language and then into a professionally acceptable language what was observed (Nesic, 2014). It was striking, thinking about how the internal world and emotional needs of *fathers* can be forgotten when there were strong countertransference difficulties, they may not take up the offer to join or absent themselves physically or in my countertransference, which seems further evidence of a relationship difficulty.

Wondering whether countertransference may feel stronger with infant–parent dyads than with individuals, I reflected on experiences I found difficult, or at times ashamed of. They formed four clusters, and I then thought that these might alert us to the inner world of infants at risk, their sadness at cruelties in relationships, and how as therapists we enter the sadness but also defend against it. For clinicians who work in child protection, my examples may seem mild. But early warning signs may be easily overlooked and without a greater awareness of difficulties in the countertransference as a warning, the risk may remain unrecognised. I did not categorise the responses according to difficulties with which parents present, but according to my experiencing some anxiety about engaging, or feeling no traction in engaging, or feeling anger, for example, in response to a parent's negativity to her infant, and finally a feeling I had failed with some families. It can be hard to think about the negative in us. These responses would link in some way with insecure attachment styles. These all represent ways of trying to parse different kinds of countertransference.

### Anxiety in the countertransference

I am not so much thinking about the fear of known violence (such as when a mother's partner is threatening, or is known to carry a bag of knives) but the effect on a therapist in the initial encounter with parents and infant—an "affect storm" of feelings when a therapist becomes anxious without being fully aware of what it may expose him to his own conflicts. We may unconsciously avoid the fullest engagement in a therapeutic contact because of the pain. It may be hard to keep parents in mind if they are depressed, traumatised, or deprived, particularly if they are defended against it, and to listen empathically and be used as parents need to use us. The moment I walked into the NICU ward, one father used to walk away from his infant and wife—as an eight-year-old boy he was rejected by his mother and just as she was unavailable he was unavailable for me, with his feelings evacuated. Twice I told referring staff I had not been able to connect; the third time I just sat down beside the cot, finding a "home". Countertransference anxiety and distress would be present in every meeting with a dyad, if we can recognise it, as well as guilt.

At times, we may feel it is too soon to explore a parent's mixed feelings: a very commanding health professional mother in a same-sex relationship whom the first time I met her in a busy NICU ward within seconds called her infant "hammerhead" (like a shark) and I was initially lost for words. She said that he was out to get her and called him "stinky". My "internal supervisor" (Casement, 1985) urged me that I *had* to say something, because I knew the research. (Projections in the first month if unaddressed can contribute to insecure attachment decades later, and a mother in a relationship with higher conflict is more likely to have distorted and negative views of her infant before and after birth (Huth-Bocks & Hughes, 2008). Parents' inconsistent messages and negative attributions from the first month onwards negatively affect the attachment process and contribute to the development of an incoherent sense of self and need to be reframed, so that the pathological link with the past is lessened and does not contribute to insecure attachment.)

What I managed eventually to say, looking back and forth between her infant and her, was that she needed him not to hear what she was saying. (I could have said, "I wonder what it's like for him to hear you say that, let's reframe it.") She then told me, "I don't *say* it to him". I added how sensitive babies were. (I could have said that babies do not have the brain development to get at us.) On follow-up after discharge she told me that although she was tired, things were going well as though she had after all been able to let something of what I said penetrate her. My intervention seemed more of the maternal "no" in a care-taking function. She may have wanted to see if I was intimidated and when I survived, was reassured that she had something good to give her son.

Sometimes our anxiety may be linked with a mother's fear about a partner's potential violence. We may sometimes out of anxiety shy away from asking the hard questions about abuse and rape, to avoid awareness of family violence. A mother may tiptoe around a partner who is violent, with his closed fists resting on the carpet beside his son it crosses my mind might he punch us. A mother, frightened that violence between them may start again, may "tell" without telling me, with unfinished sentences, and with her eyes and body language, and a feeling in my body. We may try to justify not fully disclosing our concerns in case we may lose the mother if we act. If the relationship is precious to a mother as she feels it is all she possesses, we may fear to rock the boat, joining with her fear—fearing the family may not come back and it is better to continue with our hands tied (as hers are) in the hope of doing something, however little.

### *Countertransference feelings of no traction, even indifference*

With parents who were dismissing, therapists tended to have predominantly negative feelings of boredom, irritation, and indifference (Daniel et al., 2015). With some parents and infants, I did not get to first base—either the session was question-and-answer, or like pulling teeth. A mother may seem to think concretely, for example, to want extra help in the home, and I did not seem to be able to move to becoming curious about why she is in the predicament she is in. I might find myself giving up too easily or "drifting", feeling that *she* is not communicating when it is I who do not understand. If I have a feeling of boredom has there been such denial of affect that mother and I (and the baby) are left with an empty, bland (boring) experience? In not being able to reflect on it I may have enacted an experience that she and her infant share. Two of an infant's most painful experiences would be being left alone and being with someone who is depressed—and this is what may be repeated with parents who do not seem interested to think with me.

A mother may try to get a therapist to feel that she is okay, and to let her go, perhaps trying to soothe a struggle in the countertransference, and feeling that he has done what the mother wanted.

One mother who nearly died of a heart attack in childbirth came to see me without her baby, and this acts as a red flag: she kept saying everything was fine and I nearly ended the session after thirty minutes when usually I see new referrals for at least an hour. It was only the internal supervisor saying I needed to keep going that I continued with. She could then bring her intense shame that in nearly dying she had abandoned her infant, so that I could say she had had no conscious control when her heart arrested in labour. While a mother may blame herself for a whole spectrum of reasons and her feeling of being a failure can be explored it may be important at some point to be clear she is not to blame as in this example.

When parents feel in considerable *despair* about themselves, they may subtly discourage the therapist from asking important questions that need to be asked, so that the therapist thinks everything is satisfactory. A parent may both want us to hear her anxiety and not want this, so that difficult ghosts can remain undisturbed.

A therapist may bump up against parents' defences of dismissiveness and feel that he is being treated contemptuously. Parents may seem indifferent with a strong pull to make us indifferent or we may experience it as a refusal to experience the affect. How do we stay with that, and find the feelings behind what may feel like a blank screen of nothingness, to try and imaginatively resonate with what may be shame, horror, disgust, or despair? A parent's difficulty in talking with me and her infant may, behind indifference, conceal anger with the infant. A mother may not be able to think about her own parents' minds if, when she was a child, they did intend to harm her so that this knowledge must be split off and initially her mind may seem emptied of content.

Even when emotional cruelty is not marked, a therapist may still find it difficult to think. Lack of emotional availability on a mother's part *can* be emotional abuse. This may be more damaging than an infant's body being hurt, if it is felt as a rejection of the total self as worthless and hopeless, and may need a long term therapeutic relationship to alter it.

### *Experiencing feelings of anger and hate in the countertransference*

In reflecting on negative feelings and ambivalence in the countertransference, Winnicott's (1949) therapeutic notions of surviving hateful feelings in the countertransference are crucial to bear in mind. In short-term interventions in a maternity hospital there may be less space for exploring hateful feelings than in longer-term interventions, and interpreting ambivalence and the negative may not be as straightforward soon after a baby's birth because of the fragility of a new mother's self-esteem.

We might not like how parents conduct themselves and meet resistance in ourselves—we do not want to like them even though we know we probably need to understand them for any chance of being effective. When in the countertransference we feel dismissed, this points to the therapeutic alliance being under severe strain. I may feel anger that nothing has succeeded in helping infant and family, or because of a parent's hostility that may be actively evoked because of trauma. The strongest negative reactions of fear, hate, and splitting are evoked by hateful and verbally abusive parents. We need to recognise hate in the countertransference before deciding the most therapeutic way to act.

I now touch on some links between a parent sensing hateful feelings in us and sensing us face them, and how this might translate to infants, to consider further about what may be transformational. A therapist's misunderstandings and failures are inevitable and may open the door to the experience of rupture and repair as a healing one. Parents need to feel their anger and hate is accepted through being understood. In intersubjectivity, parents are likely to become aware of the therapist processing hateful feelings to them at times. Wilma Bucci (1997) drawing on both neuroscience and infant research, argued that everything the other person feels is felt and known in the other's body and mind, that it is inescapable that what infant and parent feel is felt and known in the therapist's mind and body, and in turn experienced by infant and parent. A therapist finding a way of accepting hateful feelings towards a parent, and a parent's courage in facing this may lead most to transformational moments. Parents have described how the most transformative moments are when they felt their *hateful* parts were accepted non-judgmentally, and the therapist continued engaging with them. A parent sees countertransference feelings are not rejected and feels the therapist has faced his own hateful feelings. The therapist refuses to be provoked into acting on hating, trying to understand why a parent needs to be this way, with the belief that an empathic interest in others will eventually find meaning in feelings and thoughts that seem relatively non-understandable, and even destructive.

While it is a therapeutic challenge to both *feel* the negative and not lose working towards positive feelings about the parent–infant dyad, a therapist needs to face undertaking this for the ambivalence or hate to be integrated.

*Joanna and Joe*

Joanna, and her son, Joe, a six-month-old infant with the most beautiful eyes, were referred as he was a whingy, unsettled infant, whose mother always seemed angry with him. I suggested meeting with them weekly, which soon became very much less frequent although the sessions still seemed very important to Joanna. I found it difficult to get past her anger and whatever I would comment on she would rebut forcibly. Joe found it difficult to manage transitions and he sometimes needed to be calmed before slowly trying to repeat the transition; suggesting this did not seem to have an effect for Joanna. When I suggested that he might hear her being angry with other people as something he might misconstrue as her being angry with him, she interrupted me to disagree strongly that she was not angry with him. I felt I had to move carefully around her representations in trying to make a comment that could land gently without evoking a defensive stance. I once got the details wrong at the beginning of a session and thought that they would feel they were wrong for each other. He was not conceived when she wanted to conceive him and she had to wait two years for this and had become resigned to having a boy instead of the girl she would have preferred. She projected her anger into him, seeing him as having cycles of negativity and it was easy to see how all professionals who had encountered her might go along with her view. She occasionally brought her seven-year-old son to the session and he said that she yelled at Joe, whom she called her little devil. She then seemed better while saying that Joe was no better—and I began to wonder whether she was despairing that things would ever change and it came over as anger with him. It was like he felt that crying was the way to be, or perhaps he was responding to her lack of pleasure in him, or was angry at being miserable. Joanna had been told by her own mother, who was depressed, that she would just have to wait till he grew out of it, which left her with nowhere to go. Joanna could then bring how her depression might have affected him and he became a delightful baby with his mother becoming more and more insistent how difficult he was. But the interpretation that he did not see the mother who loved him, only the mother who was cross, seemed transformative in helping her see a different infant. Perhaps she needed to feel she would get help for herself although I wondered whether she was aiming to be the best at being the worst, fulfilling the grandmother's prophecy and Joanna knocked back every intervention I offered unless it was to do with a baby who needed to be fixed. I had to carry the hope entirely.

*The struggle to find a place of liking*

It was with Ken's parents in the next vignette that I particularly had to struggle to find a place of liking, a valuable clinical learning to take into all subsequent clinical interventions. The struggle to find a place of liking itself indicates how difficult countertransference processing may be, and as the vignette below will show, a therapist might want to respond in a tit-for-tat way: "I don't want to make the effort".

*Ken and his parents*

With Ken's parents, I had to struggle in the countertransference *to find a place of liking for them*. Eighteen-month-old Ken and his parents were referred because they were very anxious as he would only breastfeed in the dark between 8 p.m. and 9 p.m.

At birth Ken stopped breathing on the breast, went blue and had to be resuscitated. This linked him with the losses the parents had already suffered of their homeland and family. Ken vomited his first breastfeed and always vomited a dozen times a day, which confirmed what his mother felt was his rejection of her—getting food into Ken was a life and death issue, and he was a source of endless despair. His parents could not just be with him and enjoy him, so that he met alternating solicitousness and intrusion, and detached withdrawal with masked hostility. From his point of view refusal asserted some autonomy, whether of gaze, food, or speech. On formal assessment, he would have been assessed as autistic. An early sentence was "I fright" and he was a very frightened child.

In the first session, as Ken looked towards his mother, her eyes shut and she looked away, refusal of gaze being felt to be life threatening for many infants. Her arms hung down, not enfolding. She offered a blackened banana to a boy with severe eating difficulties. We did some family sessions. Once when the parents had asked their usual question of what they should do and we had suggested that they try and have fun, his father had asked, "What, all the time?"

We arranged sessions for Ken, while I saw the parents in the room opposite. I felt I was given very little room for movement by them. They would report physical symptoms and ask me for strategies. His mother was so anxious that sometimes she would say "no" before I had finished speaking, or she would give contradictory information. I found it hard to get a clear picture of the facts of Ken's life and his parents' history. It was not easy to look at the emotional meaning of experiences for him; when I suggested something, his parents seemed unconvinced. Above all, there was no playfulness and a deadening quality. I did not learn of any childhood trauma that affected Ken's mother, although it seemed likely she had had an eating disorder and felt her own mother to be very critical. (She conveyed it would be intrusive to discuss whether she had a current eating disorder. Could Ken's feeding disorder memory include an implicit memory about his mother's face of anxiety or disgust?)

A predominant feature was of undermining her husband. He would say something, she would disagree and he would agree with her even if it meant denying his own perception. He said, "The mother is always right." The sessions were the hardest in the week, and I thought if I felt stuck in the face of Ken's mother's negativism, what would it be like for Ken? I thought my feeling critical of her would have something to do with the critical grandmother transference–countertransference; feeling despairing about my capacity to intervene effectively would be the mother's despair; feeling there was no space for me would be how Ken felt. Ken's father always attended sessions, partly to buttress his fragile wife and in being aware of their fragility I seemed to lose some of my autonomy, like what Ken did in the threat to his self. Trying to explore with his mother whether she had been anorexic she volunteered nothing. I struggled with why I could not find a way to take up difficulties in the session.

After six sessions, I thought that I *must* find a way of liking this mother or I would lose the case. I may have wanted to reject something projectively identified with in the countertransference and I felt rebellious, (as perhaps Ken was), although my internal object was offering me something that could sustain me. This led to an internal change in me so I found a way to effortlessly take up their difficulty in functioning as a parental couple.

The next session the parents disagreed with each other more than before, with his father saying he had seen Ken trying to take his toys back when other children snatched them and his mother categorically denying he did this. I wondered aloud why when they described the same thing it felt as though I was hearing two different stories. This opened a space. His father wondered whether Ken would eat more if he went hungry for two days and his mother said that he would starve. When I tried to explore, using her words, her fear he would starve to death she said sharply that I had put it too strongly, the first overt expression of criticism towards me. I said I thought she was angry with me, and his father said, "Perhaps you two therapists need to consult with some people experienced in working with children with eating disorders". (My putting her fear back to her in words lessened its fear, particularly as she could also attack me and I survived.)

When Ken joined us at the end, he was very lively. He had fallen off a wall and got a black eye, and his father joked that they had bashed Ken. I said that sometimes they felt like bashing him and his father agreed and said, "It's all right if kept in this realm." But the anger between everyone was now in the realm of words and therefore less dangerous than when it had to be carried in the body, as well as the anxiety behind what I had felt as the parents' contempt. Processing my experience of being viewed as a critical parent figure and having to struggle not to feel like one led to the intervention about them seeing things differently, which addressed the anger Ken's mother had not expressed towards her husband, and which was now allowed a space where it could be felt not to kill off any of us. In the transference–countertransference I had moved from being the frightening critical mother.

I then heard about many firsts. The parents came to the next session saying that Ken had moved from his cot to his bed and stayed there, and that for the first time this child who was so restricted at kindergarten was told off for being naughty. The parents were slightly warmer with each other and more relaxed than previously. After describing something Ken had eaten his father made his first joke, "You can bet money on whether my wife will agree with me". She did not. He felt Ken had eaten a lot of banana and his wife said that he had taken an inch in three mouse-like bites. She good humouredly joined in and they described how much sausage Ken ate and they sat there with their fingers pointing, the father's length twice as long as that of his wife's. I looked from one to the other with a smile and they laughed; the father said his length was before the sausage was cut and the mother said, "I'm agreeing with him this time." When his mother cuddled Ken, it was *en face* for the first time. His father said, "As you said last week, he's using words with the intention to communicate" and he described the expectant look in Ken's eyes and on his face as he waited for them to communicate. This was the first time the parents let me know they had taken in anything from me, having previously seemed to choke on what was offered. Ken's attachment to his mother changed to emerging secure.

*Being used as needed*

Being used as needed ranges along a spectrum of no longer being needed like a discarded teddy, to agreeing to not know/ask, to agreeing to work within a very narrow register often in the face of continual negativity and complaining, to accept being a passive receptacle for whatever parents bring, to appear to give up therapeutic hopefulness about aims—although I try to never give up hope. I try not to accept defeat even while there are some families where I feel that nothing I do seems therapeutically helpful and I therefore feel hopeless, mainly with parents with the lived experience of borderline difficulties (see Queenie and Quentin, Chapter Six).

I am sometimes used with some characteristics of a transitional object when a parent seems to shape how I am in sessions. I would see this as a very early pre-stage of a therapeutic alliance, an aspect of being used as the family needs. (This links with "Criteria for ending", Chapter One.) In the following vignette, I could avoid projecting my own feeling of rejection by deciding to accept a mother's complaints, that is, accept the rejection.

*Lola and Luis*

Lola and her second boy, nine-month-old Luis, born prematurely, were referred in London to process the traumatic experience of NICU. At one point in therapy she transferred to me her experience of being little and abused and I had to withstand something relatively minor that, I think, could feel unconsciously cruel. I think she would have been depressed with her baby in the NICU, with his low birth weight and developmental difficulties. I found her extremely complaining of everything, and she seemed castrating of her partner: much of the time I could hear an angry bitterness, and a narcissistic quality of entitlement. She described her biological mother as crazy and had been adopted at four years of age. She said her adoptive father was insensitive and it seemed unlikely her adoptive family could provide much protection from her four older adoptive brothers who bullied her. Her adoptive parents had died five years previously, just before her first child was born.

Nothing I verbalised seemed to help much. I probably carried the anger, rage, hurt, and loneliness of her childhood. I tried to help her understand the meaning of her infant's communication—but I felt despairing because nothing seemed to make a difference. She expected him to play by himself and not impinge on her time with me. She seemed tough with her children as part of the family style. Within about three months I came to feel that all I could do was just listen to her. Maybe this was a therapeutic despair (Durban, 2014), which may paradoxically allow the therapist some freedom. I decided to *be in her world as she wanted me to be*. Occasionally I could see small changes as when, after months, she cried in a session. In another session, when all I could do was try to stay in emotional contact, she found some warmth towards her partner. But after six months, I thought that she was more negative towards her son and her partner, and she might not be able to change, and would complain all her life. I did not see her as loving and scaffolding for her son as much as could be possible. An image came to mind of a mother who while she could not be demonstratively affectionate would fight for her infants passionately like a tigress. She was stressed having to protect her infant from getting a respiratory infection around other children. I came to think she had no option but to complain—like a child who feels something is not right and is not heard.

When Luis was two years old, there was a turning point. She unexpectedly brought both boys; Luis still walked with a wobbly gait, was not well co-ordinated, and had delays in speech and relating, and was thought to be gaze avoidant and possibly autistic. At one point, I felt quite chilled when the older boy, Luigi, pressed his hand down on Luis' hand. Luis looked at me, his eyes brimmed with tears but he did not protest. It was the longest few seconds. His mother, who was pregnant again, laughed at him and did nothing—she thought he should sort it out by himself.

I felt shocked, speechless, and hated what was being done to him, in total identification with him and rooted to the spot. I could not speak or act as I have done with other children where I have felt hurt and angry. It was all I could do in the session to remain emotionally regulated and to manage myself to try to stay in emotional contact with them.

Luis looked at me and would see me fail. His mother had let me see an internal object externalised and acted out. She eventually told the older boy to mind his brother's hands. Yet my surviving the moment helped her become slightly kinder to her son. Things immediately improved with her partner and with the only mother figure in her life, her mother-in-law whom she had hated.

She had, I think, underneath felt hopeless, unlikeable, angry, and hating. With this incident, I was "invited" in the countertransference to dismiss feelings, as hers had not been validated and reflected on, so that I might know how she had felt invalidated. In this difficult enactment, countertransference–transference dominated the therapeutic situation to ensure that we overcame, for example, rage.

The difficulty in bearing strong emotional experiences in the therapy and the shame that these feelings can bring when recounting them probably point to her shame and whether what I was doing was psychodynamic witnessing as a prerequisite to therapy as a way of approaching trauma, when traumatic memories are still raw. My face would probably have looked helpless and powerless. I had to live with my guilt, feeling that I was not good enough as a therapist. Luis could not name the feeling that was perhaps induced in me as an affective mirror. His mother subsequently seemed to have a livelier sense of her own subjectivity. Feeling "known" by me and having her negative feelings accepted seemed to have contributed to a capacity for loving. She was no longer angry after this incident. I did not do "nothing", but it was not in words or action. My implicit communication, expressed through behaviour in surviving the episode, was "before" interpretation, and its impact seemed to go "beyond" verbal interpretation in terms of its transformative effect.

She made no further complaints and asked if she could go on seeing me. She became kinder in helping her finicky son eat. She said,

"I'm tickling him to trick him to eat—it's better than forcing him." He continued to make slow progress.

*Countertransference in enactment*

Thinking about Luigi's action, it seemed to be a brother's hostile feelings and a mirroring of a parent's unconscious going along with it. Could this be "accepted" by me as the months of complaining had been, so she could feel known in a different way? Had I become a maternal object who was not crazy and did not give her up for adoption, or die? I felt I had to be there and to feel the hurt to the infant's hand. Did his looking at me and not at her point to his feeling of abuse because of her unconscious negative feelings towards him as a premature infant? Was he enacting behaviourally an implicit memory—the body "keeps the score"—through his hand being hurt, by me gazing at it with pain; was something trying to be repaired through our bodies? Until then she may not have been sure I could bear to be in contact with very negative feelings and survive. I stayed without overt condemnation.

Countertransference processing results in a space for a mother to process hateful feelings. The mother–infant relationship showed me what they could not put into words about early trauma. Perhaps his mother could not gaze at his body empathically just as she could not in the session and perhaps had not been able to in the NICU? A countertransference enactment is an important element in understanding the clinical process. My difficulty mobilising myself to intervene may have mirrored the infant's frozen immobility in the face of hostility and could be understood as projective identification. Enactments induce powerful countertransference responses, especially when the therapist finds him- or herself standing in the place of an abusive parent or hurt child; the more traumatised the parent or infant, the more highly charged and affectively potent these are likely to be. These dynamics arouse deep conflicts in all those taking part in therapy but when what cannot be told can be *shown on the body*, it offers a chance to re-work the outcome.

\* \* \*

It is much more accepted that all therapists struggle with hostile reactions to hostile parents or react in more negative ways to parents who are severely impaired—and we need to understand what is communicated, for example, that our emotional reactions may help elucidate personality disorders (Colli et al., 2015). Anger in the countertransference might signal disorganisation if parents and infants do not receive a timely intervention.

## Feelings of failure in the countertransference

With those cases in which the therapist felt they had not done enough or had failed, this may signal hateful feelings that are not integrated, with the therapist split off from the family, as in the following vignette.

### Maggie and Magnus

A pregnant mother, Maggie, with her elfin-looking two-year-old boy, Magnus, were referred as she felt that she had never enjoyed him since his difficult birth after which he was said not to feed for six weeks. I thought that his aggression was not too far away in his throwing balls in my direction and wanting to bite a ball and to take toys. I verbalised that I knew that he had these big boy feelings but set some limits. At the end, she said it was a revelation that he was smiling with me because she had never had any enjoyment with him. I think his smiling was because the little attention I gave him was genuine and meaningful for him. It was agreed I would ring the following week to see how things were, which I did. She said she was exhausted, it was her first day off work, Magnus was sick, and she was on antibiotics. She said she appreciated my calling but she wanted to stop running around and she would be in touch. Here the negative transference kicked in before we had enough of an actual good relationship to withstand it. She had withdrawn in a therapeutic impasse. I felt she was angry, although she could not confront me with it, in the same way that she may have often felt her communication went unrecognised. Here I was too "successful" with the infant and not with the parent. This interaction seemed beyond repair, and led to an early ending of therapy. I had offered an intervention that was felt as bad and I did not get a chance to work back from that. Mothers of disorganised infants are unempathic, if not rejecting, and the infant does not feel seen and known in the mother's gaze, as the mothers probably were not with their own mothers. I wondered if this was so for him.

## The role of countertransference

I want now to conceptualise the role of the countertransference in becoming aware of the perceptions inside their mind, both therapist and also parent and infant. I try to endure for the length of time that it takes to recognise the early warning signs, and to link the specific qualities of the feelings, such as what they communicate about a mother's experience of her infant, of her own mother and partner, and the infant's experience. Tuckett's (2005) three key competencies for assessing analytic work are relevant for reflecting on countertransference.

### Protecting a participant–observational frame

Maintaining a participant–observational frame can refer to the therapist's capacity to "identify instances in which we are able to reflect on the therapeutic process rather than 'act in' " (Diener & Mesrie, 2014, p. 161). Therapists need to keep monitoring themselves: "Whether our attitudes fall within the range of despondency, sadness, or guilt over the life circumstances of parent and infant, or are on a spectrum of puzzlement, fear, ethnic prejudice, or dislike, they will be detectable" (Lijtmaer, 2001, p. 73) by parent (and infant) and can be a critical point of contact with the parent's (and infant's) transference or conflicts. We can wonder what it might be like to be with this parent and what the infant does when the parent is like this. Countertransference patterns are systematically related to the personality pathology of the parents, suggesting that therapists can make therapeutic use of their own responses (Betan et al., 2005). A parent may feel very ashamed and evoke something in us to not see this.

### Conceptualising

Being able to think through a countertransference rather than only respond to the affects is crucial. We need to reflect on how unconscious countertransference phenomena may enhance or interfere with the relationship between therapist, parent, and infant. I considered whether there was likely to be a link between the four groups and the main attachment categories, for example, the infant who "disappeared" in the perinatal period (Quentin, Chapter Six), and was becoming disorganised.

Supervision is crucial in maintaining a reflective space to maintain the capacity to think, to address hopelessness, indifference, and anger in us, and become more aware of what may trip us up, and when appropriate to challenge us.

*Containing and interpreting*

In containing, a psychological shift in a therapist often facilitates a shift in a parent, as for example, with Ken's parents. Countertransference processing includes moving from a personal response to a professional language, to be able to use it. I might use countertransference to interpret, without disclosing my own feelings but, for example, talking of a sense of a small child feeling abandoned, or of an image. When I interpreted from my feeling bored with a little girl cutting holes in paper to wonder if she felt deadened, she vehemently agreed that no one cared if she lived or died. The containment a therapist offers has a transforming effect, in turn increasing the therapist's capacity for containment, as is so clearly seen in infant observation. It can also be seen in how often one is asked in some referrals to carry anxiety when it has been difficult for the referrer to think what is needed.

## *Conclusion*

Therapists need to process their negative countertransference evoked by negative transference or the therapy suffers (Carsky, 2013). The anxiety that they experience in the countertransference when meeting the unknown and how they meet this, is the main knowledge tool they possess. When a therapeutic intervention is apparently stuck, breakthroughs emerge through strong countertransference experiences in which feelings such as rage or fear are faced, as with Ken's parents and Lola. Extreme hostility and psychotic process may prevent a therapist from thinking and acting as he ordinarily would as a therapists. But it is crucial to being open to being affected in this way. The journey back towards good-enough therapeutic functioning gradually restores the integrative functions of the parent.

With a rapid turnover of referrals, there will be some parents and infants with whom a therapist seems unable to make much difference. This may be where there is severe early disturbance and/or the parents have a vested interest in maintaining the status quo or react to the external world in a blaming way. It is hard if the infant appears to benefit from any attention received but the parents cannot change with what is offered, or withdraw from intervention. It may mean that some parents, however hard they try, will not succeed in being able to take their infant home and the therapist needs to accept internally the inevitable limitations of what it is possible to achieve with those who are disadvantaged, vulnerable, or destructive. While even if it seems that little change is possible with a parent and infant, a therapist should never at the back of his mind give up believing that it is possible, as Zeanah (2010) suggested—which may contribute to what can be done even in seemingly inauspicious circumstances.

CHAPTER TEN

# The therapeutic alliance, the presence of the therapist, and transformational moments

*Therapeutic alliance: in infants*

The quality of the therapeutic alliance is a robust predictor of therapy outcome and includes variables such as the life histories, personalities, and attachment styles of infant, parents, and therapist (Barber et al., 2012). What does a collaborative therapeutic alliance look like in an infant? Infant research highlights that in the early stages of the infant–mother interaction the infant is the initiator and the primary architect of reciprocity while the mother (and the therapist) is the follower (Call, 1980). An infant may, more than we realise, initiate the therapeutic encounter and the therapist follows, which may turn out to be a transformational moment. Yet it could be so subtle, it may be hard to justify as therapeutic alliance. This would be so in the vignette illustrating transformational moments (Natalie, this chapter), when I thought I made the move but the infant had already signalled to me. Therapists who communicate their intentions clearly and empathically to frightened infants, by, for example, tone and touch, contribute to the infants developing trust in the therapeutic alliance.

We can see a working alliance in older infants, for example, the three-year-old who came immediately with me and quickly and spontaneously talked of the "work" he and I did, or another three-year-old, who when his mother got the session time wrong and wondered whether to postpone, said he wanted to "see Frances" to talk to me about the dinosaur (angry feelings). He then in the session drew a dinosaur and a crocodile. He wanted help with his angry anxiety and sexual swearing at his mother for being an "f. . .g horse" (whore) after access visits with his father who was violent. When his mother started to discuss this with me by allusion, I asked her if we could talk with him about it, and I said to him that his mother wanted us to talk about what he said and did to her after the visits. I talked of his mixed-up feelings, and talked to them both about the anxiety behind the angry feelings, and his wish to protect her from his anger. I also suggested that she could say, "Don't hit me, it hurts."

A positive reaching out could form the basis of an alliance in a younger infant: a six-month-old infant whose mother had just become depressed lay on his back on the floor staring at his hands clasped together above his face. He started making an "Errrh, errh" sound and the therapist repeated the noises in a similar tone. He looked over at her. She made the noise again in a slightly higher tone. His eyes widened and his hands stilled. He then moved his clasped hands and made the sound himself, gazed at her intently, then abruptly rolled to his side away from her. She remained quiet. He rolled back, looked at her, waved his arms and kicked his feet on the ground. He started to babble as if telling her a long story. She felt relief that he was interacting in such an engaged manner and thought he might be feeling a similar relief that someone was listening and engaging with him. Within two weeks his mother's mood improved.

Parents with less serious difficulties often spontaneously turn their infant round to see me, or hold their infant out to me or say, "Here's Frances, you've come to see her" or, "This is your time with her". They see it as positive and it underlines their unconscious understanding of the therapeutic effect of playful interaction.

Infant, parent, and therapist co-construct a therapeutic alliance that is an integral part of the therapeutic relationship.

### Parents' therapeutic alliance

In psychotherapy research, one of the most consistent findings for the success of therapy and more positive therapy outcomes is the quality of the alliance, particularly if parents have strong experiences of a developing positive alliance in the first session or soon after. "Exquisite" sensitivity to how a family wishes to heal is needed to guide how the alliance is shaped (Wampold, 2006). Most parents want this kind of intervention, which underpins a therapeutic alliance. Knowing when to be silent and appropriate use of transference interpretation and countertransference contribute to a strong alliance (Barber et al., 2012); being able to facilitate expression of affect in short-term interventions is also linked with good outcomes.

Involving a father in therapeutic intervention co-opts him further into an alliance and usually deepens engagement with more enduring results (Wright, 2015). There is likely to be a better outcome for an infant in feeling more contained and surrounded by the mirroring gaze of his parent(s) and the therapist, with the therapist's wish to help and appropriate playfulness, and whose input is amplified in the eyes of the mother and father.

A mother who came for sessions with her husband and two children talked of being rough with one infant whom she did not get on with and said, "It makes me feel guilty. I should be patient." I said gently, "So many 'should's, the pleasure doesn't seem to be there, the 'should' gets in the way." Given the time and space for containment, she was then able to talk about feelings that were almost never said to anyone else. "It's the things you say at 2 a.m. when you want to . . .", and here she shook her fists, implying "(kill them), that you can't tell anyone". I said simply that I thought these feelings were shared by other mothers. Once acknowledged, her thoughts became bearable. Two sessions later the infant whom she had rejected tried to get two adult ducks going the same way as the baby ducks in a jigsaw puzzle. Her mother and I laughed and her mother said, "Usually we're going in the one direction and the children in the other direction". Here I think we see the intermeshing of the parents' therapeutic alliance with the infant's.

Much of what brings lasting therapeutic effect results from changes in the intersubjective relational procedural domain (Stern et al., 1998). This comprises intersubjective moments that can reorganise a parent's implicit relational knowing with others, and powerful therapeutic action occurs within implicit relational knowledge. Parents may have complex transferences and therapeutic alliances, for example, Joanna would rebut everything I suggested but always made herself available to attend whatever time I offered. And the good result was, I think, mainly because I could persist.

With those who make weaker alliances, there is a risk of less optimal therapy responses and an early termination. A mother with a personality disorder may have the most difficulty maintaining a therapeutic alliance. Attending to an impairment in the alliance is likely to be a major way that therapy works.

### *Therapist factors when interacting with infants: attunement in body language and empathy*

Relationship variables emerge as the most important common factors in therapeutic outcome, such as warmth, consistency, being boundaried, and having a capacity to manage countertransference. Recent understandings of the importance of empathy, attunement, and the role of the therapist's subjectivity in intersubjective communication need to be set alongside any discussion of interpretation. Empathy as the ability to understand and share another's emotions, partly through body channels, develops early in infants, as do reciprocity and kindness, so that the basis for a therapeutic alliance exists very early. Non-verbal communication is a central aspect of empathy, of interpersonal attunement, and of therapeutic change. A mother said, "You think it's the things you say—but it's you being there." With an infant, a therapist would have not only empathic gaze but also gestures—as part of infant "language", to play and imitate. With relationally traumatised infants and their parents, empathy and sensitive responsiveness are of central importance.

### *Authenticity*

I turn now to some aspects of the therapist's presence and, in particular, authenticity and a playful approach. In some ways, it is artificial to separate attunement from authenticity when an infant feels himself to be with an attuned person who responds authentically.

An authentic response includes interacting and talking about the present moment, about the infant's affect and experience with the therapist, about the experience of being *that* infant, bringing relational enrichment. When a therapist interacts with an infant, in that infant's pleasure he also experiences safety and hope. Differences in qualities of being attuned to the infant and response depend on styles of engaging, personality, and gender.

Infants sense authenticity when others communicate to them, including the therapist. When making an interpretation to the infant that is really about the parent but is addressed to the infant to soften the effect on the parent, communication may be confusing. A delight in a process slowly unfolding may be part of an authentic interchange. As the therapist becomes important to the parent and infant, they begin to observe how the therapist functions and regains emotional balance; one way that what we have to do to matter enough to be watched by the infant may be to be "emotionally open, transparent and readable so that patients become interested in what they learn from how we tick" (Buechler, 2008, p. 36). Being authentic is partially surrendering to the process, not knowing what will happen. We use countertransference as a guide to what feels real and authentic. What they will see on my face may at times be pain, sadness, and frustration about what they have had to face and in this way, may be put more in touch with themselves and in the encounter, acquire their own space. A parent's sense of shame may be most relieved when parent and infant sense the therapist's authentic respect for them.

Recognising there are difficult clinical moments when a parent is very negative to infant or therapist, or a therapist risks making a parent too jealous so that she may withdraw from therapy, a therapist would engage less with the infant, or modify his approach.

## Spontaneity

Infants love the element of surprise that may promote the alliance. Parents and infants respond better if a therapist is experienced as someone alive. A therapist who is emotionally expressive facilitates infants and parents being more empathically in touch with thoughts and feelings. With non-verbal communication, it is impossible not to be seen; if the body gives away secrets, infants will read this too, such as genuineness (*vs.*, for example, a forced smile). There is an action language in how a therapist says things and the frequency of her comments.

When a therapist takes a risk about spontaneousness in play this is usually therapeutic and carries a conviction for parents. For example, a therapist, with an eighteen-month-old infant who was very traumatised and depressed after many surgeries for his illness, risked making a fool of herself in front of colleagues and popped a ball on her head, which rolled off. He responded with a smile from ear to ear which his mother could see. The therapist had conveyed to the infant, "I see you and I think you might be up for a humorous interaction."

When a therapist is looking for meaning, she is open to trusting her intuitions to find a way of connecting with even the most shutdown infant. How I respond to infants is always unique for them.

### *Playfulness, humour, and teasing*

Play creates the possibility for the parent to see the infant differently. Parents often smile with pleasure even with a premature infant. If an infant feels met, he feels he is not alone but valued, and change at a procedural level is possible.

In engaging in play with the infant a therapist opens a space for engagement in thinking and hope. Enjoyment puts the child in touch with the self, and scaffolds new possibilities. However, if an infant is taken too quickly out of a depressed state into a positive one, the therapist may have missed an opportunity to understand the sadness.

Reaching embodied integration—fine-tuning how a therapist manages the clinical interaction through the lens of embodied subjectivity, the approach is characterised by tuning into the moment-by-moment emotional interaction with parent and infant via signals from a therapist's own body.

Even with a sick or traumatised infant, play can form part of an intervention, as in the peek-a-boo game; humour and teasing can become part of a therapeutic relationship. Infants' capacity for humour, if treated respectfully, is a most powerful way of intervening with them and their families. Infants can disrupt adults' intentions in their own humorous way. Gentle teasing, for example, when the therapist offers an infant a toy, hides it, offers it again but lets the infant win, as well as sharing the joke, implies an intersubjective belief that an infant understands playful intentions. Other examples include playing with gaze aversion, voice, and other facial expressions such as a therapist cheekily imitating a pretend coughing game. With a toddler, whose mother was anxious that she was autistic, the therapist took the teapot lid off, which she did not want him to, and popped something inside that did not belong. But she coped, smiled at him, made eye contact for the first time and engaged in a game. If parents participate they may see a different aspect of their troubled infant. They may see in the infant's play with the therapist something they never were aware of before, including that the infant was affected by the mood in the home.

If there is a freedom in the therapist's activity this can surprise and evoke relational curiosity. When an infant experiences fun, there is the potential for humour and for seeing things in a new way. Infant therapists may always have unconsciously aimed for humour—appropriately—in interventions. An infant in using humour is letting the other know he or she is resilient. Humour may be transformational in allowing hope to continue.

Laughter may be part of transformational moments and might occur when a therapist responds to an infant, before the parent has changed. Humour is usually a sign of progress and early humorous engagement may indicate that this infant capacity is a major therapeutic pathway, and far more than a technique for engagement, but a means of communication. Seligman (2014) in a conference panel suggested that humour is,

> ... a certain kind of shining moment: when something happens that a baby finds funny. This kind of joy, which reaches into the edges of surprise, of things not being quite what was expected and yet turning out well—is often followed by the people around the baby getting it, and showing through their own laughter or joy that they get that the baby gets it.

Amusement between parents and infant may open a capacity for thirdness, to see the infant as different from them. Infants love the surprise that lies at the core of humour: a slight violation of expectation is a strong stimulus for laughing. Infants' perception of humour is clear from three months onwards when they laugh at the absurd behaviour of others—and clown around themselves. Many infants make others laugh by deliberately repeating actions to elicit laughter again. Infants can see the funny side of things very early—the capacity for humour may be present from birth, and as infants from birth onwards may seek humorous engagement because it is playful and hopeful, it can be part of a therapeutic encounter.

## Transformational moments

Transformational moments have sometimes been viewed in the child psychotherapy field as heralding major positive change. Are they linked with the therapeutic alliance and the presence of the therapist, and is such a moment enough for substantial change?

Many of the examples throughout this book have been about transformative encounters. One mother described a light bulb moment when I asked to hold an unsettled baby who then stopped grizzling and vocalised with me: she said it was a revelation because she thought she had to walk for two hours to settle her baby and now saw her differently as someone with whom she could have a conversation. The example of the therapist letting a ball roll off her head in the "Spontaneity" section earlier in this chapter is another one. I'll now give a vignette in which there was a transformational moment on the back drop of containment, exploration, and interpretive comments.

### Nadia and Natalie

Nadia and her newborn, Natalie, were referred as she was thought to be at risk of an adolescent depression recurring. Nadia lacked support from the maternal grandmother, was doing a home renovation, had had an unexpected caesarean section birth, and was upset that her baby had to go to the special care nursery after a seizure. She did not feel bonded and found Natalie difficult, as she cried a lot and arced away from her. Nadia had difficulty in making enough milk and found breastfeeding painful and a nightmare; she hated that Natalie could not breastfeed well and felt such shame about breastfeeding in front of her husband that she had to feed alone in a separate room. More emerged—a poor relationship with her mother, who sounded narcissistic and needy, and a marital relationship that was about to break up at the point that Natalie was conceived.

I saw them weekly from when Natalie was two weeks old, and after two months, I was concerned as she had such marked gaze aversion that she would turn her head frantically from side to side to avoid her mother's eyes, to avoid shared relational fear, anger, and sadness. I commented about what I thought Natalie's experience was—a bright, passionate infant who would suddenly "crash". But this did not seem to help Nadia develop a capacity to think reflectively. One day when Natalie was crying I talked to her about how hard it was for them both, and she stopped rapidly and looked at me. I carried on talking to her, and her mother was interested and pleased that I could still see her infant as potentially reachable. Natalie started to grizzle and I think she would have started crying because her mother did not speak to her to help her regulate; when I spoke to her, she stopped grizzling almost immediately and looked at me with eyes that were fully "there". The following week Nadia said Natalie had been good, was feeding and sleeping better and Nadia was talking with her much more lovingly and warmly and said that they felt more connected.

But Natalie became unsettled and pushed away from her mother towards me and while consciously trying not to disempower Nadia, to my surprise I found the words coming out of my mouth, asking her if I could hold her for a few seconds and I asked Natalie if I could hold her (enacting the rights of an infant). Her mother gave her to me. I soon turned around so that she could face her mother saying, "I'm turning you round so you can see your mum." After talking with her a little, like, "It's hard … that's your mum … you're interested in looking around" I soon after gave her back. Not long after, they had about twenty minutes of the most responsive interaction I had ever seen with coos, smiles, and turn-taking. Her mother began looking forward to having fun with her.

They had been mirroring each other's distress. The infant initiating the move to me brought the change, the serve for my return. She remembered from the earlier session and wanted a safe enlivening to take back into the relationship with her mother. Taking and finding the infant and turning her round so that she could see her mother pulls the infant out of despair. In turning her to face her mother, I was "saying" to the infant, "It is OK to face your mother", unconsciously interpreting their shared projection that it felt difficult to look. And I was also "saying" to the mother, "You have a right to expect your daughter to face you". I was "joining" with the infant, then joining them together, triangulating like a "third". In this way, I offered the mother a different representation of her infant. Most of this was unsaid. Asking to hold the infant was responding to her as she initiated it and could be viewed as not taking over doing things that the mother felt that she could not, as I soon gave her back to her mother. That I returned her to Nadia enabled her to feel confident.

The infant avoiding her mother sends a message and the mother feels that she is bad. The infant looking at her mother helped her see her infant differently as well as making her a mother. She could see that the infant was not criticising her and therefore neither was filled with "badness". Nadia's shame could indicate her intense wish to be connected to the world, helping her find loving mothering in herself. The infant *heals* the mother, particularly the shame. Did Natalie need me to connect her to her mother, because they were stuck, and I looked at her without angry eyes? At the time, I was only aware of deciding to trust an intuition.

Nadia had become a mother looking at her daughter with loving eyes: a mother who does this presents not only her claim and willingness to engage with her infant, but also her desire to look after and protect the infant, creating a moment in which being seen by the other becomes transformational. The look is an active function by a good-enough mother who "looks after" her infant (Wright, 1991), a containing mother whose look transforms the experience of the self.

With her next infant, Nadia was the relaxed mother of a relaxed infant whom she could breastfeed with pleasure. Having a second infant may substantially repair the relationship not only with the first, but also a mother's view of herself as unsuccessful.

## Conclusion

I have explored some factors in what infants and their parents may bring to a therapeutic alliance as well as some therapist qualities as part of conceptualising "ways-of-being", as therapists' ways of intervening owe a considerable amount to their personality and experience, in a psychodynamic approach. Clinical experience suggests it is likely that the first meeting is crucial when perceptions of the therapist's level of knowledge, expertise, and interest are communicated both verbally and non-verbally to infant and parent, and may suggest why it is possible to work relatively quickly in maternity and paediatric settings. An infant's actions are often unnoticed, (even disavowed), yet interaction with the infant seems to modify implicit relational knowing faster than at other times and to speed therapeutic action.

Therapists may act in ways that are unexpected to infant, parent, or themselves. Engaging the infant and his or her family in communicative play and reverie contributes to developing reflectiveness through therapeutic action that can be conceptualised in the chaotic "subversiveness" of play, as in what happens when the hungry dinosaur joins the doll in her tea party, and "overturns" everything. Infant, parent, and therapist need to remain open to the influence of the other in the creation of what does not yet exist, a way of *being* with another. Therapists generate the "two most protective experiences human beings can produce: hope and meaning" (Allen et al., 2003, p. 3). Parent, infant, and therapist all need to be open to being transformed in the therapy process.

Transformational moments would be predicated on a positive therapeutic alliance and therapist factors such as intuitiveness to reach out to an infant, with the infant entering the transitional moment and the therapist following. Talking to an infant and turning her round to face her parent may bring quick change because the parent is so convinced by the therapist's action as with Nadia and Peter (Chapter Eleven). But a transforming encounter is more usually part of a process and builds towards change. A parent often needs to see the infant change before she can change. Very occasionally, I need to struggle to find a way to like the parent (as with Mariah and Ken's parents), which takes longer for change to happen.

CHAPTER ELEVEN

# Responding to infants and interpreting transference

I now consider interpreting infants' transferences, with vignettes illustrating moments of affective communication and shift, when intervening at the level of emotional connectedness with the infant. I will first outline some ways when a therapist may respond and talk indirectly to the infant, in which I wonder if this subtly makes the infant an object, and then discuss engaging with infants. While play is not the same as a verbal interpretation in not revealing what is "behind" whereas interpretation does, for infant and parent it may nevertheless usher them into a transformative process.

### Aims and ways of engaging infants

The aim of engaging infants and their parents is not primarily about improving parent–infant interaction but to communicate with the infant to understand the meaning of the symptom so as to relieve distress. However, in several different kinds of responses, the therapist may not truly be talking *with* the infant. If the quality of engagement with which a therapist interacts with an infant is not always contingent, appropriately attuned mirroring, it may matter less if a therapist speaks with sincerity, when it is not authentically to the infant, especially if, as in "speaking for the baby", this intervention is often effective in having an almost immediate effect on the mother and then on the baby who improves rapidly. When a therapist comments to parents about his observations of the infant's behaviour and mood in the session, even young infants have a sense that he is talking about them. Lieberman and van Horn (2009) report a therapist saying to an infant whose mother was at that point hostile towards him, that he had tried to help her when labour started but was too little to do so, and she softened immediately in response to this and able to bring that she felt a failure. Such comments are undoubtedly containing for both parent and infant. Sometimes an interpretation directed to the infant is a way of talking to the parent in a gentle way, although it seems more truthful if a therapist could find a way of saying it directly to the parent. However, in making a more adult and sometimes long type of verbal interpretation to the infant, it is hard to be clear what sense the infant makes of it (apart from the sustained attention), in that current views of an infant's cognitive functioning do not support a view of an infant understanding such interpretations, and it cannot therefore be interpreting *to* the infant.

As an infant communicates and understand others using body, voice, and looking, in a kind of primary empathy, the therapist responds with embodied attentiveness (Bloom, 2009), in affective communication with sensitivity, authenticity, and vitality. That is, therapists are available for affective resonance, modulating their responses according to an infant's developmental age:

- gaze and the musical prosody of voice with a newborn
- the communicative gestures of interaction (mirroring, imitation) with an infant
- and vocalisation as well as gestural language with an older infant.

There is a spectrum of authentic ways of responding to an infant. An intervention in developmentally appropriate affective communication in which the infant's pain is received and understood may most effectively ease symptoms carried in the transference. Embodied communication responding to an infant's affective communication is more likely to be transformatively effective because the infant feels safe and above all understood.

A containing, communicating, and empathic gaze in interaction conveys the sense of a therapist's mind on an infant, "being" with her, like embodied parental reflectiveness. An attuned therapist would unselfconsciously mirror an infant's expressions of affect, perhaps ramping it up a little. Infants read the play of facial and hand gestures and the "unseen" intentions in a therapist's engagement. The space of silence also allows time for watching, for an infant to digest, for her response to be heard, for taking turns. Intuitively emotionally engaging an infant may appear sloppy yet neuroscience research suggests that more emotions than previously thought—such as sympathy or negative feelings—can be communicated in brief expressive behaviours (Matsumoto et al., 2008).

An infant needs time for her response to be listened to. For contingent reciprocating behaviours, it is important that a therapist, like the parents, uses language that is appropriate and allows adequate silences between interactions. If a four-month-old starts to talk, a therapist needs to respond with the timing and space that makes it possible for the infant to truly communicate. It is not only that a therapist speaks out of respectful engagement with an infant, where the port of entry is likely to be the infant's representations. It is not only the unconscious processing but it is also the non-verbal signs, language, and the silences that convey that a therapist is accepting and non-judgemental. "Talking with" an infant is enhanced with a way-of-being that takes time (to take turns). Engagement consists of talking, vocalising, and gestural language while giving an infant enough time to digest.

With an older infant, the emphasis would be more on words but always in a matrix in which playfulness is available. Communicating responsive thinking through interactive playfulness about feelings that have until then felt too hard to bear can be immediately effective. This approach aims for "embodiment" rather than explanation.

### *The therapeutic nature of a contingently playful approach to an infant's transference*

Communicative playful interaction can convey understanding of an infant transference that contributes to obstructing development and ease it. Receptive playful availability creates a transitional space in which the infant can let go of fear, and the need for a symptom and related transferences. Age-appropriate contingent playfulness shaped by the therapist's thinking about the infant is transformational because an infant knows it is for her (that is, a felt connection) and feels accepted, affirmed, and freer, as transformational as a verbal interpretation.

## *Communicating transference insights to infants*

Here my focus is on interpreting in the transference in the first year of life, discussing non-verbal interventions, which frequently ease the transference. We watch and listen to acknowledge how hard it has been for infant and parent. We interact to understand the infant, and communicate that her distress can be accepted and understood. An infant's transference expectations may directly arise in the infant's relationship with the therapist or are indirect, patterned on her parents' expectations of the therapist.

An infant can be in a relationship with a therapist that is in part different to those with other people. Therapeutic engagement can occur as an engagement that is beyond interpretation and speaks to the affective language of the infant, acknowledging the infant's innate drive towards relatedness. The infant as an active subject brings her own specific language of emotional connectedness.

In considering the transferences of infants primarily in the first year, I'll start with Freud's (1910a) noting that "Transference arises in all human relationships" (p. 51), and draw on a current view that in the first year the therapist is a transference object on whom the infant projects fears and hopes (Halberstadt-Freud, 2013). As infants seek to engage with others from birth, this shapes what they bring to the therapeutic encounter.

I'll make five points before giving some vignettes:

1. What is transference in a very young infant when there are less memories of interaction from an earlier relationship to be "transferred" on to the therapist?
   An infant relates to the therapist based on hundreds of interactions with the parents, meeting the therapist in the present. While for infants in the first year the past is not so very past, it is

nevertheless a profound past that drives them to make a particular relationship with the therapist.
2. Is the encounter with the therapist "contaminated" by other encounters as an infant expects what has happened before?
The encounter could also be seen as a novel one as an infant seeks "the new" as a positive nutrient. An infant can see a therapist in a different sort of relationship to that which he has with other people because of the expectations that his parents bring to the therapeutic encounter and what the therapist brings of herself to engage therapeutically.
3. While an infant may develop a strong relationship to a therapist, is this basically independent of the mother's relationship to the therapist?
It could be embedded in a few seconds of experience, which is independent of the mother.
4. In urgent intervention with infants and parents should a therapist be in a more real here-and-now relationship to enable the infant to feel connected and contained rather than feeling isolated, withdrawn, and heavily defended?
Rather than being a "should", the way the therapist uses her presence would arise out of what the therapist thought that this infant and family needed.
5. Does a therapist need to facilitate a positive transference between infant and therapist?
A positive transference is likely to develop, driven by developmental forces. The generative possibilities of the positive feelings for the therapist may facilitate a "profound reordering of the inner experience of self and others" (Tessman, 1999, p. 39).

I'll outline three kinds of relationships an infant in the first year could make with a therapist:

1. Infants transfer a current positive relationship with a parent.
If infants have a *positive relationship with their mother*, they easily see the potential of the new person in the therapist, and clinical experience suggests that they are ready to engage with the therapist—as someone different and available for a therapeutic encounter.
2. With negative aspects in the relationship with the parent, an infant may be able to *split* and relate positively to a therapist.

3. With *negative aspects in the relationship with their mother*, infants might use a therapist for a positive experience.

For example, infants of mothers who with postnatal depression, and who showed a rather flat response to her, respond in a different, less depressed way to others who are not depressed. As Tronick (2015) has shown, infants are shocked and hurt when their mothers' positive regard is withdrawn in the still face experience. A therapist talked of how she was aware of the transference of an infant who had been removed from a very deprived background and who needed to hold her gaze to be contained and organised, and the countertransference of her own internal conflict of needing to meet and sustain the infant's gaze to give her an experience of being seen for herself.

Infants in the first two groupings usually remember their positive experience with the therapist at their next meeting. But with negative aspects in the relationship with a parent, it may take longer to bring about change.

Infants may transfer an aspect of a *masked* negative relationship with a parent in the past. Some infants may look at a therapist for a few moments conveying "Go away!"

### Example from infant observation

For the first eight months of a weekly infant observation, an infant seemed to be acting out his mother's unconscious hostility to the observer (she would at times forget the observer's visits). It was not until well into the eight months' observation visit that he made eye contact with the observer. As a splitting off in enacting what his mother felt—something negative for the observer to contain—perhaps it was not entirely the infant's transference to the mother of the past who was negative towards him because he was born following her beloved daughter. She had been the first child in her family of origin followed by a second child with cerebral palsy. Unusually, she never told the observer the infant's birth story but the observer knew she had had a caesarean section birth, which she thought the mother had chosen, and she wondered whether the mother could have been depressed in her pregnancy and the infant "sensed" hostility *in utero*.

## Ollie, a depressed infant, and his mother, Oona

A mother, Oona, and her eight-month-old infant, Ollie, were referred as while she appeared to have recovered from depressive feelings, he seemed still affected. He seemed to hang on to these feelings in connecting with me. He seemed flat and to look at me in a sullen way, and I had to work very hard in the countertransference to feel sympathetic. He seemed to have a negative transference, relating to me as if I was the mother of the past. A temperamental characteristic reflecting negative emotionality associated with insecure attachment may have contributed to his seeming to need to maintain the negativity, but it conveyed considerable disturbance, perhaps conveying he wished to end it all (to be dead).

Transference implications include the countertransference processing required to sense the infant's internal state beneath the presenting facade, in a process like that of parental embodied reflectiveness, to be able to respond appropriately to both layers. They also include the importance of recognising when the infant is potentially open to a change in engagement, and titrating this to the needs of infant and parent. A therapist needs to intervene with the last two as these are more likely to affect the trajectory of development. It might need considerable time and attention to the infant's needs if a parent felt challenged by the intervention.

## Peter: Interpreting in the transference with an "unseen" infant

In this detailed vignette, I attend to the detail of how a therapist might communicate beyond language. A seven-month-old boy, Peter, and his mother had attended the long-term mother–infant therapy group (Chapter Seven). He was an unsmiling, passive, frozen boy, who had been referred for various psychosomatic symptoms and constantly held out his arms rigidly at right angles to his body like scaffolding, self-protectively, bracing himself, sensing his mother's anger, and glancing quickly at times at her with subliminally fearful looks. The previous year his one-year-old sister had died from Sudden Infant Death Syndrome. This was a psychological catastrophe for him as his mother's anger interfered with mourning her daughter; when she looked at this boy she had always seen her daughter's face superimposed on his. Her relationship with him was conflictual; she had never been able to play with him and said she did not like him. They had attended for five weeks, with no symptom improvement for either of them, and she indicated some anger with us, believing that we had no experience of bereavement: "No one who hasn't lost a child can understand". His self was not fully autonomous—with outstretched arms he could not master his environment, needing to extensively reference his mother for safety, and he had little enjoyment. My countertransference was of feeling helpless and despairing (as they both felt), and with an impending long break from therapy, the situation was urgent.

### Intervening with his mother's transference

His mother's anger about her daughter's death precluded her seeing Peter for himself; she saw us as unhelpful—partly defensively against getting hurt again in a close relationship. We had attempted to alleviate the angry projection on to Peter for not being his sister, and to share our understanding of the infant's experience from interactive experiences with his parents.

Her *transference* to the therapists and to Peter was worked on as appropriate: her anger (perhaps even hating) us for, she thought, not having suffered a death, and hating her son—Peter being alive confirmed that his sister was dead. Being looked at by another who wants to understand the truth, that is facing the hate, is containing. But exploring the pain, and accepting her anger and negative transference had brought no change for either of them.

### Intervening with the infant's transference

With us, Peter was initially as hesitant as he was with his mother and only related to us in a blank, anxious, shut down way; he had never related in a positive way.

In the last session before a holiday, she put him down face down on the floor—as though dead—and watched him cry for a seemingly interminable fifteen seconds while she left him as if abandoned (enacting the dead sibling), and told him to lift his head up. When with her support, he stood, he watched with quiet enjoyment as Campbell Paul attuned to his almost imperceptible hand movements with playful gestures of his own fingers. Campbell asked him, "What's going on?"

Peter seemed to feel rescued. He overcame his inhibition and by shimmying, "invited" the therapist to engage.

His mother said that all Peter did was whinge, and I talked with her about her experience of this. Campbell wiggled his fingers and Peter again shimmied with pleasure. His hands went to his mouth with pleasure and then dropped down as his mother began to differentiate Peter from his sister saying that his round face was not that similar to hers.

Campbell and Peter continued their game. Campbell began gently clapping.

When Peter responded with pleasure, he said "It's very exciting." Peter imitated him and moved one hand.

Campbell said encouragingly, "Do you think you can do it? ... Yeah, that's one hand, isn't it?", paused to follow Peter's lead and Peter vocalised, urging him to continue.

"He's going for the other one at the same time". Peter shimmied and I spoke for Peter saying, "Don't stop" and his mother said, "You're mean if you stop, isn't he?"

Campbell gave a breathy sigh, waited then said, "Yes, you do it".

Having waited, giving the infant time, he now moved to the infant to touch his hands and talk to him, following his actions.

"It's a bit hard. That's it, both at the same time". And gradually Peter, holding Campbell's hands, brought his hands to his mouth and mouthed Campbell's thumb.

His mother said, of Campbell's hands, "They're big fat fingers, aren't they, compared with dad's". With the support of Campbell's hands, Peter could relax his arms; Campbell gently brought his arms together in a playful way, and then turned him to face his mother. Holding Campbell's hands, he could playfully bite his fingers.

As Peter and he mirrored chuckles, Campbell said, "I think you're enjoying this, aren't you?"

His mother said she probably would not get pregnant just yet (which would make a space for Peter not to be blotted out by a replacement child). She acknowledged, "He's had a hard life, I admit it".

Once Campbell had responded to an "invitation" by the infant shimmying in pleasurable anticipation that he might engage Campbell, and in the safe space of ten minutes playing with him in the presence of his mother, he could bring his arms in, mouth Campbell's hand, and then relax. Campbell turned him round to face his mother as if saying, "He should face you".

With the changes in the representations of both mother and infant simultaneously she smiled at Peter for the first time and he relaxed and also smiled for the first time. In response, she smiled again, tossed him in the air, kissing him, and laughing and playing with him for the first time, grooming him in a bonding way, and he began vocalising. She, seeing him in a different way, claimed him immediately, which was what he wanted above all else. He had read that the anger in her eyes, his being denied recognition, had disappeared. Less anxiously inhibited, he no longer needed to hold his arms out and began exploring. At follow up four years later he had continued to develop well.

*Discussion*

Peter did not feel himself to be an infant who was alive for his mother but an anxiously attached one. His positive, loving feelings for her were split off and unconscious. What seemed to be most transformational for her was seeing Peter change and become an engaged infant as Campbell engaged him. His intervention addressed the mother's unconscious hate, he "spoke" to them both about this, that he felt that Peter felt hated and frightened, and to his mother that while she had hated Peter she also did not want him dead.

This intervention was with the transference as the infant had his own anxious transference relationship with us separate from his mother's transference of masked anger with us. Peter's fearful transference was addressed in affective communication. I imagine it might feel like, "When he talks to me in my language, I feel he's understood that I feel frightened and bad (I am hated and hateful and I should be dead), and he still accepts me as okay. He plays with me, just for me—and because of that I can let go my protection. He holds me containingly when I face my frightening mother. I can bite him—my aggression is not dangerous."

The therapist waiting when Peter cried was feeling his way into the internal landscape of infant and mother rather than rushing into action. His mother welcomed the intervention rather than feeling that her role was usurped. Peter was able in playful interaction to mouth Campbell's fingers, which meant he could relax his arms. Campbell had built on a tiny positive action that the infant could do with his own hands so that his mother could see him in a different light. He was ascribing affect and thinking to Peter.

Campbell tracked Peter's behaviour seeing meaning in it and responded playfully in a way that elaborated Peter's actions. He began clapping, unconsciously showing Peter something that he could mirror in his mind, if he were free to have fun: it is possible to bring hands together without hurting someone. Campbell had responded to the infant's gesture, offered by him as an invitation to join an interaction and be playful. We had enjoyed his enjoyment—I laughed *with* Peter. Campbell built on the infant's body movement, and responded with attuned playfulness, which fostered the infant's autonomy conveying that what he did was important. Nearly half of what Campbell said was gentle questioning and I think this may unconsciously have matched Peter's unspoken puzzlement.

Embodied mentalizing is a "capacity to (a) implicitly conceive, comprehend, and extrapolate the infant's mental states (such as wishes, desires, or preferences) from the infant's whole-body kinesthetic expressions and (b) adjust one's own kinesthetic patterns accordingly" moving towards "the infant's realm of experience—that of quality of movement, rhythms, space, time, sensations, and touch. Implicit mentalizing is nonconscious, nonverbal" (Shai & Belsky, 2011, p. 187) in interpreting the infant's movement as manifestations of mental states or in determining a therapist's embodied responses.

Peter's mother could not interpret changes in his movements and rhythms as expressive meaningful signals or respond in an embodied manner, and this compromised his ability to feel—*at an embodied level*—that he was the owner of his body, an active agent able to influence other people. She had not been able to transform his movements into meaningful and intentional mental states.

This interaction helped Peter be less frightened and with this change of feelings his mother could change. Peter was now free to use his arms to find her: we came to understand that he braced himself feeling frightened.

The infant reads some of what a therapist is feeling, thinking, and intending and this is carried through embodied reflectiveness, where the therapist uses his own self and body to engage the infant. Playful interaction that is unique and co-created (Tronick, 2003) helps an infant elaborate "a conversation", an interaction in which both people are equal but different in which the infant "finds" an experience that is co-created. The therapist did this with gentleness, and his embodied responses followed the infant's need for pauses and modulated responses. The infant was responding from a position of being in the presence of another who used embodied reflectiveness to communicate an understanding of the predicament in which the infant had found himself.

## Conclusion

A therapist builds on body movement, and identifies through *countertransference* with attuned play. This approach is effective, not only with infants who have eating or sleeping difficulties or are irritable, but those who are severely injured, very disabled, dysregulated with mothers with the lived experience of borderline difficulties, failing to thrive, dying, or on their own—such as an orphan, a refugee infant, or an infant with a substance-using mother who is about to be adopted. As with Dee in her mother's absence, if with Peter we had only used containment and verbal interpretation the change would not have been as instant.

Interpretive play in the relationship with a therapist offers the chance to free an infant from ongoing relationship difficulties by "speaking" to these difficulties, as playing carries a communication by a therapist of his understanding of what is impeding development. A young infant does not have the full capacity to process language but is organising experience around moments of emotional connectedness with the other. A therapist tries to feel his way into the anxiety and conveys that together they will face it and transform it so that the infant can take the risk of being herself and facing the parent and in play symbolise it. Contingently sensitive playfulness conveys embodied reflectiveness very powerfully, communicating meaning. This is likely to be a main mechanism of change with young infants and bring greater change for them than an adult interpretation, and when parents see a therapist intervening with the infant they have a "shift of empathy" (Cassidy, 2013).

In summary, many factors might ease symptoms carried in a transference. While transference links made in a therapist's mind are, even if not verbalised, known at the same time in the other's mind, what may have more therapeutic action for a young infant is non-verbal communication carried in a playfulness that communicates safety, feeling felt, fun, and hope. And this matters at those times when an infant feels particularly alone. As de Ahumada and Ahumada (2015) write, recognising can be considered interpretation in the widest sense, observing an infant play, trying for an attitude of discovery rather than of certainty, and the discovery of meaning should be that of infant and parent.

CHAPTER TWELVE

# Revisiting mechanisms of change in infant–parent therapy

As a result of therapeutic intervention, parents and infant each create a slightly changed self. Here I summarise what has emerged of the therapeutic factors. An infant-focused approach sees the infant as an active participant in the therapeutic process and a therapist using embodied communication intervenes in the infant–parent relationship, where the intervention needs to take place. With an accommodating infant, a therapist would engage to reignite a sense of expectation that the adult world will look after and excite her; with an infant who has less capacity to be accommodating, this would need to be more titrated. The power of enacted reflective moments is impressive. The new relational experiences infants and parents have with a therapist are likely to aid their internalising of the therapeutic relationship and facilitate affective communication as well as enhance their capacity for containment.

Relatively serious pathology can change quickly with the developmental push in infants, in the capacity for self-righting in the first year, as well as the chance that parenthood offers to rework difficulties, and change can also act as a foundation on which a parent with early deficits may risk engaging longer and further. The key to bringing about deep change is mourning for what has been lost or never been, with an often powerful resistance to mourning. With more fragile parents and infants the gain is more developing the capacity for self-reflectiveness.

While a therapist's verbalisations often contribute to developing the capacity to think self-reflectively, parents use aspects of the therapeutic relationship, in particular becoming more containing of painful feelings and identifying with a therapist's less self-critical capacities. As parents usually want to get it right for their infant, a positive transference intensifies the therapeutic relationship, and intervening within this transference can be transformational.

This approach also provides an infant with the experience of someone who can contain him or her, that is, interactional language that speaks to the infant. This creates the possibility of experiencing and communicating emotional truths in a significant relationship as a "present moment", with a possibility to begin to think reflectively.

The therapeutic alliance, infant and parent's, and common therapeutic factors are two most important mechanisms of change. Empathic therapeutic relationships make it possible for parents to hear and use interpretations, and interpretations build therapeutic relationships because infant and parent feel understood.

What do change mechanisms look like in infant and parent? In the intersubjective turn in psychodynamic interventions, we see interactions from the infant and parent's point of view and recognise a therapist's role in these interactions, and in a continuum of interventions of interpretive therapy with supportive elements co-create at a moment in time what an infant and parent would be most responsive to. Their perceptions of a therapist, partly emotional in the therapist's bodily responses and countertransference, are transformed in an internal shift to less persecutory feelings.

It is through relationships that therapists effect the greatest change. This way of working has been known over many years to be effective clinically. The approach described in this book has some elements in common with Lieberman's evidence-based, relationship-based child–parent psychotherapy programme (Lieberman & Van Horn, 2009), although the infants are younger and seen for briefer episodes than in her programme. There are also the emerging results from the toddler and the peekaboo groups (Chapter Seven) but above all from the programme for young mothers described in Chapter Four.

### Therapeutic alliance

The alliance is an agreement between parent, infant, and therapist on the goals of therapy and a strong bond with a therapist building trust and expressing her understanding to infant and parent, to which the infant as therapist also contributes. *Ruptures* as enactments can bring fresh understanding and repair of the past in the relational present (see Chapter Ten). However, those parents with features of self-critical perfectionism may need more time to develop a positive therapeutic alliance (Blatt et al., 2010).

### Therapist factors

The quality of a therapist's relationship with infant and parent is very important and includes genuineness, openness, and a sense of playful humour, as well as being able to process in the countertransference and offer containment, serving as a mind for the other, not to collapse or retaliate. A therapist would be open and attuned to a small, unplanned moment of interaction as potentially therapeutic, with a responsiveness that creates responses for infants and parents that may never be repeated with another.

A therapist offers sustained empathic, aware attentiveness within relatedness to which parents and infants respond with development, if they can (Parsons, 2016). Bowlby thought that it was not interpretation in child psychotherapy that helped a child to get better but that he felt liked, cared about, and in the mind of someone who thought about him (Hopkins, 2011). The child psychotherapist, Juliet Hopkins (2011), noted that therapists, with greater awareness of attachment needs across the life cycle, have over the years become kinder to their patients who can allow themselves to believe that they are likeable enough to be liked by their therapist. In these encounters, each person brings her subjective sense of herself while remaining open to the influence of the other in creating something that until then has not existed, so that the uniqueness of every encounter shapes how the relationship evolves.

### Embodied communication as a vital mechanism

Play "has the effect of drawing the child's attention to communication itself" (Bruner, 1975, p. 10). A therapist offers playfulness recruited for understanding, which the infants "get", and can use this new freedom in relationship to the therapist to improve their relationships with their parents.

If infants can join a therapist in playfulness it signals that they have entered a relationship in which they can both enjoy and be enjoyed. This links with the idea of the central importance of being a source of joy to the parent, and Bowlby's point that infants are drawn to form attachments with adults who are playful with them, and find pleasure in their company (Hopkins, 2013).

Parents mirror their infant's expression of emotion through facial expressions and vocalisations, and when they have difficulty doing this, a therapist can contribute this.

Infant, parent, and therapist may co-create a countertransference *enactment*, of high communicative importance and often as the only way to convey information. Such an enactment carries the possibility, in offering a new experience, of also being able to communicate meaning to the infant (as with Lola's infants).

Work with an infant alone suggests infant-directed embodied communication is a crucial mechanism. With Dee, where the therapist facilitated a symptom cure in two days, therapeutic action did not include containment of the parents, nor verbal interpretation in adult mode, which would not have achieved the same result as quickly as infant-directed embodied communication.

Tronick and his colleagues (1998), considering the factors that bring about therapeutic change in addition to interpretations suggested that an interpretation would be carried in a moment of authentic person-to-person meeting where the person had an experience of really being "met and known", such as those moments in mother–infant interaction where the infant had a subjective feeling of fulfilment in being "met and known".

## *Seeing the therapist in embodied communication may effect immediate change, with the therapist also recognising their parenthood*

Therapist–infant interaction is likely to more quickly shape parents' representations, and implicit memories of relational knowing and behaviour, than many other interventions. When parents see the therapist intervene and neuronal pathways are activated, they are likely to have available the possibility of parenting differently from old patterns in implicit memories, they can see their infant in a different light when seeing their lively interaction with the therapist while discussing their own inner and relationship problems. When a therapist engages an infant in contingent mirroring, moments of meeting are likely to occur, which could begin shaping the infant's and parents' representations, and increase responsive thinking. For a parent, seeing a therapist relate may not only lessen projective identification between parent, infant, and therapist but, further, by rearranging unconscious links in thoughts may result in a greater freedom to create thoughts. *The change becomes the insight*. Parents may need to see their infant change in a kind of embodied communication before they can be convinced to lessen the projections. The infant uses the safety of the therapist, often having sought it out, to gaze at the parent, who realises the infant is seeking and conferring parenthood, which is transformational.

Interventions with high risk families would be more successful when environmental difficulties as well as infant–parent relations are addressed.

## Developing reflectiveness

As noted in Chapter Six, as infants begin to monitor the attention of others, those other people at times focus on the infant himself. The infant then monitors the attention of the other to him in a way that was not possible previously. The infant's face-to-face interactions with others are then radically transformed. He now knows he is interacting with another intentional agent who intends things toward him. For an infant to think reflectively requires a relational context conducive to exploring his mind in the mind of the other who has his mind in mind; therapists assist in co-constructing new representations (Allen & Fonagy, 2006). The therapist mirroring, as a parent would, provides a stimulus that organises an infant's experience and names what he is feeling so that out of the interaction the ability to think about the mental states of the other grows (Fonagy, 2002).

Parents and infant being in the presence of a therapist who relates differently from how they had expected, allows the possibility of infant and parent to be "re-presented" to each other, which begins to impact on the internal object representations in the implicit memory systems, and to reinforce verbal interventions. The therapist's spontaneity in interaction may be comparable to Stern's present moment, which can be powerful in contributing to the change process.

In changes in ways of being with someone, the change is in the reorganisation of the representational systems, of the parent's inner world view of themselves and significant other people. This alters ways of being with another person in that patterns laid down in procedural memory exert a less powerful pull. The therapist acts as a third when a parent having identified with an infant's distress has difficulty in thinking; the parent then feels that the therapist aids in restoring a good internal object.

A parent who had a depressed mother changes in that the feeling state of being with a depressed mother reduces and is less often unconsciously recreated. In working with vulnerable families, the aim, however difficult to achieve, is towards convincing them of the importance of thinking about their infant's experience. Some infant–mother dyads need longer in therapy because of the enduring pain of their early traumatic histories, communicated consciously and unconsciously. With infants and parents in vulnerable families, increasing the parents' capacity to think reflectively about their infant's mind is therapeutic. Sometimes there may be no more than a single relational encounter (with containment of feelings and thoughts at a time when unconscious meanings distort a parent's relationships with their infant); a therapist gives an infant support in affirming his experience.

A transformational moment may be when parents realise that the infant has his own thoughts, feelings, and memories and had attributed meanings to their relationship. The parents may also start to understand the relevance of their internal world as a child to them in the present.

### *Processing emotions in a countertransference that feel hateful is usually transformational*

While clinical descriptions highlighting single moments of impact are appealing, incremental change seems more likely: a therapist may often feel that they do not have much of an impact on a parent's very ambivalent feelings in a short intervention.

With several parents and infants who needed a long term therapeutic relationship, a process of struggle took place in the countertransference towards accepting being used as they needed and finding a way to like them. Two clinical concepts described in a hierarchy of therapist responsiveness to these feelings, namely achieving *a sense of liking* for some parents (and infants) and *being used* as the parent needed to use the therapist, can be viewed as signs of the impact of the parents' ambivalence and negative feelings. They evoke strong feelings of negativity in response (see Chapter Nine). With parents with considerable early deficits a therapist may have to continuously work to find a place of compassionate, respectful liking. When a family continues to attend sessions it is important that a therapist does not give up hope. With parents who have more difficulty, a therapist has to survive their hateful feelings without acting on them, for there to be any hope of change in implicit memory.

In the intersubjectivity between infant, parents, and therapist, parents are likely to have some awareness of the therapist's hateful feelings at times. The parent, seeing the therapist struggle with this and not reject them, but continue to respect them, is likely to be transformational.

## The infant as therapist

I want to give the last space to this concept. We may, for too long, have underestimated the capacities in infants to early and fully use a therapeutic encounter. An infant, who longs for his parents' happiness, in which he can be reflected, can be extraordinarily powerful in what he adds to the therapeutic process, often reaching out to a therapist before the therapist realises it.

When a therapist interacts with an infant, not only does the infant know the therapist as someone who is genuinely present, the parents see this too, and this interaction may be key. The infant thinking about others' minds can be seen with the adolescent mother, Saphire, telling me about another infant who had empathically understood the crying of Sara, her three-month-old daughter.

When an infant looks at a therapist, his sadness, anger, and pain is known through the intersubjectivity between them, and the infant can also see his acceptance through the wish to understand, her wish that it was not so hard for the infant, with the implicit message of hope. Both infant and therapist have a moment of shared holding of the pain, and the infant has a sense of agency in having generated that moment, which can lead to mutual empathy and comforting that the infant takes back to the parent.

## *Conclusion*

The relationship of infant and parents with a therapist is a decisive factor contributing to the therapeutic action, with other factors such as interpretation of anxiety constellating this. I return to interventions with Helen and Jane to again draw attention to how little intervention it takes for an enduring good result, although rather than turning points we are more likely to see a process of building towards change. It is about clinically refining an answer to the questions of what is going on for the infant in the room. Why are the parents giving this description and can we wonder together about the infant's experience at the time that the parent describes in order to relieve distress and encourage development? The embodied communication with which a therapist connects with infant and parent not only defines the approach described throughout this book, but has relieved distress and brought change for so many families.

# AFTERWORD

The title of the book has a double meaning. While it is about connecting with infants, it is also a recognition that as therapists, free enough to become engaged with infants, we usually find them engaging, and their parents seeing that, usually also connect. The approach of engaging infants assists them and their parents to find self-definition within relatedness, or even, imagining in the words of an infant, "You gave me the space to play with who I am." Infants quickly remember the encounters as highly significant, with a therapist offering as Anne Alvarez said "a more intensive, vitalizing insistence on meaning" (Boulter, 2016, p. 22), they find the new ways of being very influential. Profound levels of connectedness may happen very quickly and they utilise them. Responding to the infant promotes reflectiveness, a way of engaging that may open new moments.

If a moment of meeting can combine a transformational moment of parenting with a transformational moment in the therapeutic relationship, it is extremely powerful. "To become a person someone has to be held and contained and tuned into, these are the things you need to become a person and unfold" a father told me.

The process of change in infant–parent therapy is a complex bi-directional process, with a cascade effect in treating an infant's self as intentional. Infants, in their search for who they are, are subjects doing their own acting upon the other, interpreting and constructing their own meanings.

# REFERENCES

Abrams, S., Field, T., Scafidi, F., & Prodromidis, M. (1995). Newborns of depressed mothers. *Infant Mental Health Journal, 16*: 233–239.

Acquarone, S. (2004). *Infant–Parent Psychotherapy: A Handbook*. London: Karnac.

Alcorn, N. (2008). *To Be Delighted In*! Available from: tobedelightedin@hotmail.com.

Allen, J. G., & Fonagy, P. (Eds.) (2006). *Handbook of Mentalization-Based Treatment*. Chichester: John Wiley.

Allen, J. G., Bleiberg, E., & Haslam-Hopwood, T. (2003). Mentalizing as a compass for treatment. *The Menninger Clinic Article*. Available at: www.menningerclinic.com/education/clinical-resources/mentalizing

Auhagen-Stephanos, U. (2013). Inside the mother's womb: the mother–embryo dialogue. In: I. Moeslein-Teising & F. Thomson-Salo (Eds.), *The Female Body: Inside and Out* (pp. 153–167). London: Karnac.

Barber, J. P., Muran, J. C., McCarthy, K. S., & Keefe, J. R. (2012). Research on dynamic therapies. In: M. Lambert (Ed.), *Bergin and Garfield's Handbook of Psychotherapy and Behavior Change* (pp. 443–494). New York: Wiley.

Barnett, L. (1989). *Sunday's Child*. Concord Video.

Benjamin, J. (2009). A relational psychoanalysis perspective on the necessity of acknowledging failure in order to restore the facilitating and containing features of the intersubjective relationship (the shared third). *International Journal of Psycho-Analysis, 90*: 441–450.

Benoit, D., & Goldberg, S. (1998). *A Simple Gift: Comforting Your Baby*. Toronto: The Hospital for Sick Children.

Berg, A. (2012). When a little means a lot. *The Signal, 20*(2). Available at: http://perspectives.waimh.org/wp-content/uploads/sites/9/2017/05/When-a-little-means-a-lot.pdf

Bergman, J. (2010). *Hold Your Premie*. Cape Town: New Voices.

Betan, E., Heim, A. K., Conklin, C. Z., & Westen, D. (2005). Countertransference phenomena and personality pathology in clinical practice: an empirical investigation. *American Journal of Psychiatry, 162*: 890–898.

Bick, E. (1963). Notes on infant observation in psycho-analytic training. *International Journal of Psycho-Analysis, 45*: 558–566.

Biringen, Z., & Robinson, J. (2008). Emotional availability in mother-child interactions: a reconceptualization for research. *American Journal of Orthopsychiatry, 612*: 258–271.

Blatt, S. J., Zuroff, D. C., Hawley, L. L., & Auerbach, J. S. (2010). Predictors of sustained therapeutic change. *Psychotherapy Research, 20*: 37–54. Available at: http://dx.doi.org/10.1080/10503300903121080

Blick, B., & Warren, B. (2003). *Getting to Know You: Recognising Infant Communication and Social Interaction*. Sydney: Northern Beaches Child and Family Health Services & The New South Wales Institute of Psychiatry.

Bloom, K. (2009). Embodied attentiveness: recognising the language of movement. *Infant Observation Journal, 13*: 175–186.

Boulter, P. (2016). Report on conference. *Bulletin of the Association of Child Psychotherapists, 265*: 22.

Bowlby, J. (1988). *A Secure Base. Clinical Applications of Attachment Theory*. London: Routledge.

Briggs-Gowan, M. J., & Carter, A. S. (2006). *Manual for the Brief Infant–Toddler Social and Emotional Assessment (BITSEA), Version 2*. San Antonio, TX: Psychological Corp and Harcourt Press.

Bruner, J. (1975). The ontogenesis of speech acts. *Journal of Child Language, 2*: 1–19.

Bucci, W. (1997). *Psychoanalysis and Cognitive Science: a Multiple Code Theory*. New York: Guilford Press.

Buechler, S. (2008). *Making a Difference in Patients' Lives: Emotional Experience in the Therapeutic Setting*. New York: Routledge.

Bunston, W., Crean, H., & Thomson-Salo, F. (1999). *Parkas (Parents Accepting Responsibility—Kids Are Safe)*. Melbourne: Federal/State Government—Partnerships Against Violence PADV) Initiative.

Call, J. D. (1980). Some prelinguistic aspects of ego development. *Journal of the American Psychoanalytic Association, 28*: 259–289.

Carsky, M. (2013). Supportive psychoanalytic therapy for personality disorders. *Psychotherapy, 50*: 443–448.

Casement, P. (1985). *On Learning from the Patient*. London: Routledge.

Cassidy, J. (2013). Discussion point. AAIMH conference, November, Canberra, Australia.

Circle of Security (2002). *Shark Music Educational Video*.

Coates, S., & Gaensbauer, T. J. (2009). Event trauma in early childhood: symptoms, assessment, intervention. *Child and Adolescent Psychiatric Clinics of North America, 18*: 611–626.

Colli, A., Tanzilli, A., Dimaggio, G., & Lingiardi, V. (2015). Patient personality and therapist response: an empirical investigation. *American Journal of Psychiatry, 171*: 102–108.

Daniel, S. I. F., Lunn, S., & Poulsen, S. (2015). Client attachment and therapist feelings in the treatment of bulimia nervosa. *Psychotherapy, 52*: 247–257.

Daws, D. (1989). *Through the Night: Helping Parents and Sleepless Infants*. London: Free Association.

de Ahumada, L. C. B., & Ahumada, J. L. (2015). Contacting a 19 month-old mute autistic girl: a clinical narrative. *International Journal of Psychoanalysis, 96*: 11–38.

Diener, M. J., & Mesrie, V. (2014). Supervisory process from a supportive–expressive relational psychodynamic approach. *Psychotherapy, 52*: 158–163.

Drell, M., Siegel, C., & Gaensbauer, T. (1993). Post traumatic stress disorder. In: C. Zeanah, (Ed.). *Handbook of Infant Mental Health* (pp. 291–304). New York: Guilford Press.

Durban, J. (2014). Despair and hope: on some varieties of countertransference and enactment in the psychoanalysis of ASD (autistic spectrum disorder) children. *Journal of Child Psychotherapy, 40*: 187–200.

Eisold, B. (2012). The implications of family expectations, historical trauma, and prejudice in psychoanalytic psychotherapy with naturalized and first-generation Chinese Americans. *Contemporary Psychoanalysis, 48*: 238–266.

Feldman, R. (2012). Discussion point. Joseph Sandler Conference, 3 March 2012, Frankfurt, Germany.

Figon, N. (2000). Evaluation of a mother–infant therapy group. Master of Psychology Thesis, Charles Sturt University.

Flynn, L. (2007). Personal communication.

Fonagy, P. (2002). Understanding of mental states, mother–infant interaction and the development of the self. In: J. M. Maldonaldo-Duran (Ed.), *Infant and Toddler Mental Health, Models of Clinical Interventions*

*With Infants and Their Families* (pp. 57–74). Washington, DC: American Psychiatric Publishing.

Fonagy, P. (2005). Attachment, trauma and psychoanalysis: Where psychoanalysis meets neuroscience. Keynote lecture, IPA 44th Congress on Trauma: New Developments in Psychoanalysis, 28 July 2005, Rio de Janeiro, Brazil.

Fonagy, P. (2008). A genuinely developmental theory of sexual excitement and its implications for psychoanalytic technique. *Journal of the American Psychoanalytic Association, 56*: 11–36.

Fonagy, P., & Target, M. (2007). The rooting of the mind in the body: new links between attachment theory and psychoanalytic thought. *Journal American Psychoanalytic Association, 55*: 411–456. Available at: doi: 10.1177/00030651070550020501

Fraiberg, S. (1975). Ghosts in the nursery: a psychoanalytical approach to the problems of impaired infant–mother relationships. *Journal of the American Academy of Child Psychiatry, 14*: 387–422.

Freud, S. (1910a). Five lectures on psycho-analysis. *S. E., 11*: 1–56. London: Hogarth.

Goldschmied, E., & Selleck, D. (1986). *Communication Between Babies in Their First Year*. (Video) London: National Children's Bureau Enterprises.

Greenacre, P. (2015). Discussion of Chapter One. In: N. L. Thompson. (Ed.), *Play, Gender, Therapy: Selected Papers of Eleanor Galenson* (pp. 35–46). London: Karnac.

Guedeney, A. (1997). From early withdrawal reaction to infant depression: a baby alone does exist. *Infant Mental Health Journal, 18*: 339–349.

Halberstadt-Freud, H. C. (2013). Emotional turmoil around birth. In: E. Quagliati (Ed.), *Becoming Parents and Overcoming Obstacles. Understanding the Experience of Miscarriage, Premature births, Infertility, and Postnatal Depression*. London: Karnac.

Hart, S. (2008). *Brain, Attachment, Personality: An Introduction to Neuroaffective Development*. London: Karnac.

Hilsenroth, M. J., Cromer, T. D., & Ackerman, S. J. (2012). How to make practical use of therapeutic alliance research in your clinical work. In: R. A. Levy, J. S. Ablon, & H. Kachele (Eds.), *Psychodynamic Psychotherapy Research: Evidence-based Practice and Practice-based Evidence* (pp. 361–380). New York: Humana Press.

Hoeg, P. (1993). *Miss Smilla's Feeling for Snow*. London: Harvill.

Hopkins, J. (2011). Personal communication.

Hopkins, J. (2013). Personal communication.

Huth-Bocks, A. C., & Hughes, H. M. (2008). Parenting stress, parenting behavior, and children's adjustment in families experiencing intimate partner violence. *Journal of Family Violence, 23*: 243–251.

Jackson, W. K., & Garner, C. G. (2011). Gender matters. Available at: http://internationalpsychoanalysis.net/2011/12/19/gender-matters-by-wynn-k-jackson-and-charles-g-gardner/

Johnson, A. N. (2008). Engaging fathers in the NICH: taking down the barriers to care to the baby. *Journal of Perinatal and Neonatal Nursing, 22*: 302–306.

Jones, A. (2005). Personal communication.

Kagan, J., & Lewis, M. (1965). Studies in attention in the human infant. *Merrill-Palmer Quarterly of Behaviour and Development, 11*: 95–127.

Karlsson, H. (2011). How psychotherapy changes the brain. Understanding the mechanisms. *Psychiatric Times, 28*(8). Available at: www.psychiatric times.com/display/article/10168/1926705

Kelly, D. J., Quinn, P. C., Slater, A. M., Lee, K., Gibson, G., Smith, M., Ge, L., & Pascalis, O. (2005). Three-month-olds, but not newborns, prefer own-race faces. *Developmental Science, 8*: F31–F36.

Kleeman, J. A. (1971). The establishment of core gender identity in normal girls. II. How meanings are conveyed between parent and child in the first 3 years. *Archives of Sexual Behavior, 1*: 117–129.

Kuschel, C. A. (2014). The forgotten parent. Cool Topics Neonatal Symposium, November, Melbourne, Australia.

Lemma, A. (2012). Keeping envy in mind: the vicissitudes of envy in adolescent motherhood. In: P. Mariotti (Ed.), *The Maternal Lineage, Desire, and Transgenerational Issues*. London: Routledge.

Liddle, M.-J., Bradley, B. S., & McGrath, A. (2015). Baby empathy: infant distress and peer prosocial responses. *Infant Mental Health Journal, 36*: 446–458.

Lieberman, A. F., & Van Horn, P. (2009). Child–parent psychotherapy: a developmental approach to mental health treatment in infancy and early childhood. In: C. H. Zeanah (Ed.), *Handbook of Infant Mental Health* (3rd edn) (pp. 439–449). New York: Guilford Press.

Lieberman, A. F., Van Horn, P., & Ghosh Ippen, C. (2005). Towards evidence-based treatment: child–parent psychotherapy with preschoolers exposed to marital violence. *Journal of American Academy of Child and Adolescent Psychiatry, 44*: 1241–1248.

Lijtmaer, R. M. (2001). Countertransference and ethnicity. *Journal of the American Academy of Psychoanalysis and Dynamic Psychiatry, 29*: 73–83.

Lyons-Ruth, K. (2003). Dissociation and the parent–infant dialogue: a longitudinal perspective from attachment research. *Journal of the American Psychoanalytic Association, 51*: 883–911.

Malone, J. C., & Dayton, C. J. (2015). What is the container/contained when there are ghosts in the nursery?: joining Bion and Fraiberg in dyadic interventions with mother and infant. *Infant Mental Health Journal*, 36: 262–274.

Martinson, F. M. (1973). *Infant and Child Sexuality: A Sociological Perspective*. Saint Peter, MN: The Book Mark.

Maselko, J., Kubzansky L., Lipsitt L., & Buka, S. L. (2011). Mother's affection at 8 months predicts emotional distress in adulthood. *Journal of Epidemiology and Community Health*, 65: 621–625.

Matsumoto, D., Keltner, D., Shiota, M. N., O'Sullivan, M., & Frank, M. (2008). Facial expressions of emotion. In: M. Lewis, J. M. Haviland-Jones & L. F. Barrett (Eds.), *Handbook of Emotions* (3rd edn) (pp. 211–234). New York: Guilford Press.

McCue Horwitz, S., Leibovitz, A., Lilo, E., Booil, J., Debattista, A., St. John, N., & Shaw, R. J. (2015). Does an intervention to reduce maternal anxiety, depression and trauma also improve mothers' perceptions of their preterm infants' vulnerability? *Infant Mental Health Journal*, 36: 42–52.

McWilliams, K. (2013). Personal communication.

Meins, E., Fernyhough, C., Wainwright, R., Das Gupta, M., Fradley, E., & Tuckey, M. (2002). Maternal mind–mindedness and attachment security as predictors of theory of mind understanding. *Child Development*, 73: 1715–1726.

Morgan, A. (2007). Personal communication.

Murphy, S. M., Zweifach, J., & Hoffman, L. (2011). The everyday concerns of mothers of young children and the motivation to seek ongoing parenting support from experts. *Early Child Development and Care*. Available at: DOI:10.1080/03004430.2011.597505.

Murray, L., & Andrews, E. (2002). *The Social Baby*. London: The Children's Project.

Murray, L., Cooper, P. J., Wilson, A., & Romaniuk, H. (2003). Controlled trial of the short- and long-term effect of psychological treatment of post-partum depression. 2. Impact on the mother–child relationship and child outcome. *British Journal of Psychiatry*, 182: 420–427.

Nesic, T. (2014). Thinking the "unthinkable" and seeing the "invisible". *ACP Bulletin*, 253: 4–11.

Newman, L. (2015). Parents with borderline personality disorder—approaches to early intervention. *Australasian Psychiatry*, 23: 696–698.

Newton, N., & Newton, M. (1967). Psychologic aspects of lactation. *The New England Journal of Medicine*, 277: 1179–1188.

O'Brien, K., Bracht, M., Macdonell, K., McBride, T., Robson, K., O'Leary, L., Christie, K., Galarza, M., Dicky, T., Levin, A., & Lee, S. K. (2013). A pilot cohort analytic study of family integrated care in a Canadian neonatal intensive care unit. *BMC Pregnancy and Childbirth*, 13(Suppl 1): S12. Available at: DOI:10.1186/1471-2393-13-S1-S12.

Pally, R. (2005). A neuroscience perspective on forms of intersubjectivity in infant research and adult treatment. In: B. Beebe, S. Knoblauch, J. Rustin, & D. Sorter (Eds.), *Forms of Intersubjectivity in Infant Research and Adult Treatment* (pp. 191–241). New York: Other Press.

Panksepp, J., & Burgdorf, J. (2003). Laughing rats and the evolutionary antecedents of human joy? *Physiology and Behavior, 79*: 533–547.

Parent–Infant Relationship Global Assessment Scale (PIRGAS) (2005). *Diagnostic Classification of Mental Health and Developmental Disorders of Infancy and Early Childhood, Revised (DC: 0–3R)*. Washington, DC: Zero to Three.

Parsons, M. (2007). Raiding the inarticulate: the internal analytic setting and listening beyond countertransference. *International Journal of Psycho-Analysis, 88*: 1441–1456.

Parsons, M. (2016). Faith in psychoanalysis. Paper presented at scientific meeting of the British Psychoanalytical Society. 20 January, London, UK.

Paul, C. (2014). The sick baby in hospital In: C. Paul & F. Thomson-Salo (Eds.), *The Baby as Subject: Clinical Studies in Infant–Parent Therapy*. London: Karnac.

Paul, C., & Thomson-Salo, F. (1997). Infant-led innovations in a mother–baby therapy group. *Journal of Child Psychotherapy, 23*: 219–244.

Perry, B. D., Pollard, R. A., Blakley, T.L., Baker, W. L., & Vigilante, D. (1995). Childhood trauma, the neurobiology of adaptation, and "use-dependent" development of the brain: how "states" become "traits". *Infant Mental Health Journal, 16*: 271–291.

Porges, S. W. (2011). *The Polyvagal Theory. New Physiological Foundations of Emotions, Attachment, Communication, and Self-regulation*. New York: W. W. Norton.

Raphael-Leff, J. (2014). *The Dark Side of the Womb: Pregnancy, Parenting and Persecutory Anxieties*. London: Anna Freud Centre.

Schechter, D. (2012). Discussant. Joseph Sandler Conference, 3 March 2012, Frankfurt, Germany.

Selby, J. M., & Bradley, B. S. (2003). Infants in groups: a paradigm for the study of early social experience. *Human Development, 46*: 197–221.

Seligman, S. (1993). Why how you feel matters: countertransference reactions in intervention relationships. *WAIMH News, 1*: 1–6.

Seligman, S. (2014). Humour in infant–parent work. *Contribution to Panel at WAIMH Meeting*, Edinburgh, June.

Sendak, M. (1963). *Where the Wild Things Are*. New York: Harper & Row.

Shahar, G., & Schiller, M. (2016). Working with the future: a psychodynamic–integrative approach to treatment. In: M. Kyrios, R. Moulding, G. Doron, S. S. Bhar, M. Nedeljkovic & M. Mikulincer

(Eds.), *The Self in Understanding and Treating Psychological Disorders* (pp. 29–39). Cambridge: Cambridge University Press.

Shai, D., & Belsky, J. (2011). Parental embodied mentalizing: let's be explicit about what we mean by implicit. *Child Development Perspectives, 5*: 187–188.

Shedler, J. (2010). The efficacy of psychodynamic psychotherapy. *American Psychologist, 65*: 98–109.

Siegel, D. J. (1999). *The Developing Mind. How Relationships and the Brain Interact to Shape Who We Are*. New York: Guilford Press.

Spitz, R. A., & Wolf, K. M. (1949). Autoerotism; some empirical findings and hypotheses on three of its manifestations in the first year of life. *The Psychoanalytic Study of the Child, 3/4*: 85–120.

Stern, D. N. (1985). *The Interpersonal World of the Child*. New York: Basic Books.

Stern, D. N. (1995). *The Motherhood Constellation: a Unified View of Parent–Infant Psychotherapy*. New York: Basic Books.

Stern, D. N. (2004). *The Present Moment in Psychotherapy and Everyday Life*. New York: W. W. Norton.

Stern, D. N., Sander, L. W., Nahum, J. P., Harrison, A. M., Lyons-Ruth, K., Morgan, A. C., Bruschweiler-Stern, N., & Tronick, E. Z. (1998). Non-interpretive mechanisms in psychoanalytic therapy: the "something more" than interpretation. *International Journal of Psycho-Analysis, 79*: 903–921.

Tang, N. M., & Gardner, J. (1999). Race, culture, and psychotherapy. *Psychoanalytic Quarterly, 68*: 1–20.

Tessman, L. H. (1999). A cry of fire, an old flame, the matter of fireplace. In: D. Bassin (Ed.), *Female Sexuality* (pp. 33–48). Northvale, NJ: Aronson.

Thomson-Salo, F. (1997). Countertransference in a mother–baby therapy group. *ANZAP (Victorian Branch) Bulletin, 23*(Spring): 5–12.

Thomson-Salo, F. (2002). Working psychoanalytically with the infant in the consulting room. In: J. Raphael-Leff (Ed.), *Between Sessions and Beyond the Couch* (pp. 77–79). Colchester: CPS Psychoanalytic Publications.

Thomson-Salo, F. (2003). The woman clinician in infant–parent psychotherapy. In: A. M. Alizade (Ed.), *The Embodied Female*. London: Karnac.

Thomson Salo, F. (2007). Recognizing the infant as subject in infant–parent psychotherapy. *International Journal of Psychoanalysis, 88*: 961–979.

Thomson Salo, F. (2010). Parenting an infant born of rape. In: S. Tyano, M. Keren, H. Herrman, & J. Cox. (Eds.), *Parenthood and Mental Health* (pp. 289–299). Chichester: John Wylie.

Thomson-Salo, F. (2014a). A preventive attachment intervention with adolescent mothers: elaboration of the intervention. In: R. Emde & M. Leuzinger-Bohleber (Eds.), *Early Parenting and the Prevention of Disorder: Psychoanalytic Research at Interdisciplinary Frontiers* (pp. 343–357). London: Karnac.

Thomson-Salo, F. (2014b). *Infant Observation. Creating Transformative Relationships*. London: Karnac.

Thomson-Salo, F. (2014c). Care of the long-stay infant and parents. In: R. J. Martin, A. A. Fanaroff, & M. C. Walsh (Eds.), *Neonatal–Perinatal Medicine, Volume 1* (10th edn) (pp. 642–646). Philadelphia, PA: Elsevier Saunders.

Thomson-Salo, F., & Paul, C. (2001). Some principles of infant–parent psychotherapy. *Australian Journal of Psychotherapy, 20*: 36–59.

Thomson-Salo, F., & Paul, C. (2009). Being there: the "something more" that the baby brings to the therapeutic process. Paper presented at AAIMH & Marce Society Conference, 1 October 2009, Melbourne, Australia.

Thomson-Salo, F., & Paul, C. (2014). Levels of feedback, levels of interaction. *The Australian Association of Infant Mental Health Newsletter, 27*: 6–7.

Thomson-Salo, F., Paul, C., Morgan, A., Jones, S., Jordan, B., Meehan, M., Morse, S., & Walker, A. (1999). "Free to be playful": direct therapeutic work with infants. *Infant Observation Journal. The International Journal of Infant Observation and Its Applications, 3*: 47–62.

Tomasello, M. (2000). *The Cultural Origins of Human Cognition*. Cambridge, MA: Harvard University Press.

Trevarthen, C. (1996). Personal communication.

Trevarthen, C. (1998). The concept and foundations of infant intersubjectivity. In: S. Braten. (Ed.), *Intersubjective Communication and Emotion in Early Ontogeny* (pp. 15–46). Cambridge: Cambridge University Press.

Trevarthen, C. (2001). Intrinsic motives for companionship in understanding: their origin, development, and significance for infant mental health. *Infant Mental Health Journal, 22*: 95–131.

Trevarthen, C. (2011). What young children give to their learning, making education work to sustain a community and its culture. *European Early Childhood Education Research Journal, 19*: 173–193.

Tronick, E. Z. (2003). Of course all relationships are unique: how co-creative processes generate unique mother–infant and patient–therapist relationships and change other relationships. *Psychological Inquiry, 23*: 473–491.

Tronick, E. Z. (2007). *The Neuro-Behavioral and Social-Emotional Development of Infants and Children*. New York, London: W. W. Norton.

Tronick, E. Z. (2015). Workshop presentation, 49th IPA Congress, 25 July 2015, Boston, MA, USA.

Tronick, E. Z., Bruschweiler-Stern, N., Harrison, A., Lyons-Ruth, K., Morgan, A. C., Nahum, J. P., Sander, L., & Stern, D. (1998). Dyadically expanded states of consciousness and the process of therapeutic change. *Infant Mental Health Journal, 19*: 290–299.

Tuckett, D. (2005). Does anything go? Towards a framework for the more transparent assessment of psychoanalytic competence. *International Journal of Psycho-Analysis, 86*: 31–49.

Tzourio-Mazoyer, N., DeSchonen, S., Crivello, F., Reutter, B., Aujard, Y., & Mazoyer, B. (2002). Neural correlates of woman face-processing by 2-month-old infants. *Neuroimage, 15*: 454–461.

Wampold, B. E. (2006). Three ways to improve our psychotherapy effectiveness. Available at: http://societyforpsychotherapy.org/three-ways-to-improve-our-psychotherapy-effectiveness (accessed 6 December, 2014).

Weiss, C. H. (1997). Theory-based evaluation: past, present, and future. *New Directions for Evaluation, 76*: 41–55.

Winnicott, D. W. (1949). Hate in the counter-transference. *International Journal of Psycho-Analysis, 30*: 69–74.

Winnicott, D. W. (1971). *Playing and Reality*. London: Tavistock.

Wright, K. (1991). *Vision and Separation*. London: Free Association.

Wright, P. (2015). Mourning, melancholia, and the mirror. *IJPopen, 2*(90): 1–44 (web based paper).

Zeanah, C. Z. (2010). Conference point. American Academy of Child and Adolescent Psychiatry 57th Annual Meeting, 26–31 October, New York, USA.

Zeanah, P., Stafford, B., & Zeanah, C. (2005). *Clinical Interventions to Enhance Infant Mental Health: a Selective Review*. Los Angeles, CA: National Center for Infant and Early Childhood Health Policy at UCLA.

Zoccolillo, M. (2003). Personal communication.

# INDEX

abandonment, 22, 57, 91, 122, 136, 167, 179, 200
Abrams, S., 51
abuse, 55, 67, 117, 134, 147, 150, 153, 166, 173, 176
   child, 41, 43, 46, 56, 120
   emotional, 167
   experiences of, 6
   father's, 59, 61
   history, 57, 94
   physical, 150
   sexual, 43, 64
   verbal, 146
Ackerman, S. J., 76
Acquarone, S., 36
affect(ive), 26, 32, 36, 55, 92, 107, 163, 167, 178, 202
   attunement, 139
   communication, 193–194, 202, 207
   denial of, 166
   distressing, 47
   expression of, 17, 183, 195
   infant's, 13, 184
   language, 196
   magnified, 144
   mirror, 175
   negative, 51, 84, 117, 165
   positive, 93
   -potent, 176
   predominant, 109
   resonance, 194
   of sadness, 47
   states, 76
   storm, 165
   verbalising, 46, 117, 125
aggression, 55, 64, 96, 131, 133, 139, 151, 156, 177, 202
   behaviour, 82, 132
   conflicts, 132
   hidden, 58
Ahumada, J. L., 205
Alcorn, N., 83
Allen, J. G., 191, 211
Andrews, E., 73, 78
anger, 11, 28, 45–46, 62, 68, 83, 88–89, 93–94, 98, 110, 112, 114, 118, 121,

124, 129, 132, 135, 142–144, 146,
152, 163, 168–169, 172, 174, 177,
179, 182, 189, 200, 202, 213
*see also*: anxiety
concealed, 11, 167
feeling of, 157, 164, 167–168
infant's, 16
management, 94
masked, 202
mother's, 199–200
ordinary, 156
anxiety (*passim*) *see also*:
countertransference
angry, 182
attached, 202
catastrophic, 31
core, 70
deep, 142
-seated, 45
-driven, 34
extreme, 54, 56, 62, 88, 119
face, 13
feelings, 45, 51
increased, 79
infant's, 68, 79, 110, 150
inhibitions, 202
interpretation of, 214
-laden problem, 110
mother, 29, 145, 171
over-, 86
painful, 52
parental, 82
-provoking, 133
separation, 93
severe, 93
shameful, 97
source of, 9
stranger, 122
symptoms, 41
transference relationship, 202
underlying, 129
attachment, 7, 17, 48–49, 81, 87, 91,
151, 155, 173, 210 *see also*: anxiety
ambivalent, 63
bridge, 91
categories, 179

disorganising, 32, 46, 69, 124–125,
150
early, 78
figures, 91, 150–151
hostile, 124
infant, 42, 73, 85, 148
insecure, 25, 113, 164–165, 199
intervention, 72
intrusive, 124
maternal, 93
needs, 209
patterns, 151
process, 74, 82, 165
relationship, 151
secure, 7, 67, 73, 120, 126, 146
style, 162, 181
trauma, 152
Auerbach, J. S., 209
Auhagen-Stephanos, U., 42
Aujard, Y., 15
autism, 6, 106, 112, 145, 170, 174, 187
autonomy, 26, 85, 112, 147, 155,
170–171, 200, 203
avoidant, 11, 59, 63, 90, 123, 141, 150,
174

Baker, W. L., 150, 153
Barber, J. P., 181, 183
Barnett, L., 34
behaviour(al), 6, 18–19, 21, 28, 32, 34,
73, 81, 90, 95, 114, 116, 118, 142,
150, 175–176, 203, 210 *see also*:
aggression
absurd, 187
changes, 12, 20
cues, 85
expressing, 195
externalising, 98
father's, 152
infant's, 6, 12, 19, 72, 74–75, 116, 194
meaning of, 84
nurturing, 82
optimal, 51
parental, 17, 93
rebellious, 67
reciprocating, 195

INDEX     229

relational, 20
sequence of, 116
unacceptable, 119
Belsky, J., xi, 3–5, 203
Benjamin, J., 161
Benoit, D., 73
Berg, A., 17
Bergman, J., 82
Betan, E., 178
Bick, E., 5
Biringen, Z., 72
Blakley, T. L., 150, 153
Blatt, S. J., 209
Bleiberg, E., 191
Blick, B., 73
Bloom, K., 28, 194
Booil, J., 93
Boulter, P., 215
Bowlby, J., 156, 209–210
Bracht, M., 84
Bradley, B. S., 132–133
Brief Infant–Toddler Social and
    Emotional Assessment (BITSEA),
    145
Briggs-Gowan, M. J., 145
Bruner, J., 14, 209
Bruschweiler-Stern, N., xi, 183, 210
Bucci, W., 168
Buechler, S., 185
Buka, S. L., 109
Bunston, W., 153
Burgdorf, J., 27

Call, J. D., 181
Carsky, M., 179
Carter, A. S., 145
Casement, P., 165
Cassidy, J., 204
Christie, K., 84
Circle of Security, 73–74
clinical vignettes
    *A loved twin*, 100–101
    *Aimee*, 6–7
    *An infant with fractures*, 148
    *Anne and her family*, 101
    *Ben and his mother*, 10–11

*Blaze and his mother*, 16, 112
*Cal and his parents*, 106, 112–114
*Candie and Colin*, 18
*Dario*, 30–32
*Dee*, 4, 111–112, 204, 210
*Eric and his mother*, 29, 136–141
*Eva and Erin*, 43–44
*Fay, Grace, and Helen*, 145–146
*Fred*, 45
*Grace and George*, 114–115
*Helen and Hugh*, 22, 49–50
*Ida and Isaac*, 151–152
*Ilene and Iliana*, 52–53
*Jane and Jack*, 54–55, 214
*Joanna and Joe*, 169–170, 183
*Kaye and Kobie*, 55–56
*Ken and his parents*, 170–173, 179,
    191
*Lola and Luis*, 173–174, 179, 210
*Lou and Len*, 56–57
*Maggie and Magnus*, 177–178
*Mariah and Mary*, 55, 58–61, 70, 191
*Ms R and her infants*, 119–122
*Ms T and her infant*, 78–79
*Nadia and Natalie*, 188–191
*Nora and her infants*, 62
*Ollie and Oona*, 199
*Oriana and Olena*, 62–63
*Paulette and Pattie*, 64–65
*Peter*, 191, 199–204
*Queenie and Quentin*, 123–125, 173
*Rosalie and Roxana*, 86–87
*Saphire and Sara*, 68–72, 80, 213
*Ursula and Urwin*, 86
*Vee and Vicky*, 87–88
*Wendy and Wilson*, 93–94
*Xander*, 91
*Yvette and Yves*, 95–98
*Zepha*, 95
*Zoe and Zara*, 98–99
Coates, S., 157
Colli, A., 177
Conklin, C. Z., 178
conscious(ness) 189 *see also*:
    unconscious
    communication, 212

control, 167
intention, 163
non-, 13, 203
self-, 51, 163
un-, 71, 195
containment, 6, 19, 23, 32, 46–47, 57, 61, 107, 131, 142, 179, 183, 188, 204, 207, 209–210, 212
Cooper, P. J., 72
countertransference (*passim*) *see also*: transference, unconscious
anxiety, 164–165
awareness of, 56
bodily, 36
difficult, 57–58, 97, 161–164, 170
enactments, 22, 69, 176
feelings, 69, 124, 137, 166, 168
gendered, 163
multiple, 136
negative, 179
patterns, 178
phenomena, 161, 178
processing, 54, 77, 97, 176, 179, 199
reactions, 34
responses
emotional, 162
powerful, 176
Crean, H., 153
Crivello, F., 15
Cromer, T. D., 76

Daniel, S. I. F., 166
Das Gupta, M., 74–75
Daws, D., 19
Dayton, C. J., 9
de Ahumada, L. C. B., 205
Debattista, A., 93
depression, xii, 18, 27, 29, 41, 50–55, 58–59, 61–62, 67, 71, 76, 80, 91, 96, 105, 110, 113, 120–122, 127, 134, 136, 141, 143, 150, 152–153, 157, 165–166, 169, 174, 182, 186, 188, 198–199
angry, 137, 139
bipolar, 54
extreme, 52
features, 150
feelings, 51, 53, 140, 199
infant, 10
maternal, 7, 10, 43, 51, 117, 129, 154, 163, 212
ongoing, 51
parental, 7
paternal, 51
position, 131, 133
postnatal, 43, 51–52, 72, 198
risk of, 51
severe, 124, 136
symptoms, 51, 73
underlying, 71
DeSchonen, S., 15
development(al), 5, 7, 12, 14, 17, 27–28, 36, 79, 149, 151, 156, 165, 195, 209, 214
age, 194
appropriate, 73, 194
brain, 15, 84, 94, 165
care, 82
challenge, 67
change, 114
check up, 54
child, 93
cognitive, 87, 94
of cohesiveness, 141
concerns, 132
delay, 5, 67, 150, 154, 158
difficulties, 53, 106, 124, 174
early, 91
effective, 111
emotional, 48, 84
factors, 7
forces, 197
impeding, 204
infant, 12, 16, 22, 82
interconnecting, 19
of intersubjectivity, 15
neuro-, 81
objects, 138–139
anti-, 123
ongoing, 11, 71
optimal, 15
perspective, 33

physical, 87
psychomotor, 84
push, 207
of reflectiveness, 47
stages, 19, 85
status, 132
task, 156
trajectory, xii, 91, 199
trouble-free, 128
Dicky, T., 84
Diener, M. J., 178
Dimaggio, G., 177
disorder
   bipolar, 54, 96
   conduct, 67, 73
   eating, 171–172
   personality, 42, 58, 71, 177, 184
      antisocial, 68
      borderline, 61, 71, 124
   post-traumatic
      feeding, 110
      stress, 41, 158
   psychiatric, 12
   psychosexual, 41
   psychotic, 41
Drell, M., 150
Durban, J., 174
dyad(ic), 138, 146, 165
   assessment, 73
   infant–
      mother, 212
      parent, 164, 169
   minority patient, 17

Edinburgh Postnatal Depression Scale, 143
Eisold, B., 17
Emotional Availability Scales, 72
empathy, 7, 9, 15, 37, 57, 67, 71, 78, 112, 122, 131–133, 165, 168, 176–177, 181, 184–185, 194–195, 204, 208–209, 213–214
envy, 10, 22, 57–58, 70, 98, 134, 136

fantasy, 5, 50, 62–63, 107, 131, 135, 138, 152

Feldman, R., 78
Fernyhough, C., 74–75
Field, T., 51
Figon, N., 143
Flynn, L., 36
Fonagy, P., 33–34, 36, 151, 211
Fradley, E., 74–75
Fraiberg, S., 6
Frank, M., 195
Freud, S., 196

Gaensbauer, T. J., 150, 157
Galarza, M., 84
Gardner, J., 17
Garner, C. G., 135
Ge, L., 17
Ghosh Ippen, C., 157
ghosts in the nursery, 6
Gibson, G., 17
Goldberg, S., 73
Goldschmied, E., 133
Greenacre, P., 27
Guedeney, A., 7
guilt, 10, 12, 43, 45, 54, 88, 92–94, 99–100, 109, 125, 129, 161, 164–165, 175, 178, 183
   maternal, 49
   parental, 10
   sense of, 155

Halberstadt-Freud, H. C., 196
Harrison, A. M., xi, 183, 210
Hart, S., 26
Haslam-Hopwood, T., 191
hate(ful), 8–9, 20, 45, 53, 55, 58, 109, 112, 118, 120, 163, 168–169, 175–176, 188, 200, 202 *see also*: unconscious
   feelings, 4, 10, 49, 57, 119, 167–168, 177, 213
Hawley, L. L., 209
Heim, A. K., 178
Hilsenroth, M. J., 76
Hoeg, P., 70
Hoffman, L., 79
Hopkins, J., 209–210

Hughes, H. M., 165
Huth-Bocks, A. C., 165

illness, 16, 43, 105, 186
　bipolar, 141
　infant's, 6
　mental, xii, 7, 16–17, 41, 53, 63, 67,
　　94, 109, 141
　minor, 120
　mother's, 54, 131
　psychotic, 94
intervention (*passim*) *see also*:
　attachment
　antenatal, 80
　brief, xii, 86, 108
　clinical, 4, 32, 170
　culturally appropriate, 16–17
　direct, 82
　early, 45, 48
　group, 72, 76, 79–80, 143, 158
　long-term, 42, 44, 168
　mental health, 87, 105
　multi-directional, 21
　neonatal, 74, 77, 80
　oral, 85
　playful, 27, 116
　post-birth, 65
　psychodynamic, 21, 136, 208
　relational, xii
　short-term, 22, 168, 183
　therapeutic, 3, 10, 42, 44, 81–82,
　　127, 154, 179, 183, 207
　traumatic, 89
　urgent, 197
　verbal, 16, 196, 212

Jackson, W. K., 135
jealousy, 10, 35, 57, 59, 70, 78, 83, 118,
　185
　oedipal, 33
　reactions of, 83
Johnson, A. N., 82
Jones, A., 13

Kagan, J., 36
Karlsson, H., 76

Keefe, J. R., 181, 183
Kelly, D. J., 17
Keltner, D., 195
Kleeman, J. A., 36
Kubzansky, L., 109
Kuschel, C. A., 88

Lee, K., 17
Lee, S. K., 84
Leibovitz, A., 93
Lemma, A., 70
Levin, A., 84
Lewis, M., 36
Liddle, M.-J., 132
Lieberman, A. F., 157, 194, 208
Lijtmaer, R. M., 178
Lilo, E., 93
Lingiardi, V., 177
Lipsitt, L., 109
Lunn, S., 166
Lyons-Ruth, K., xi, 19, 183, 210

Macdonell, K., 84
Malone, J. C., 9
Martinson, F. M., 33
Maselko, J., 109
Matsumoto, D., 195
Mazoyer, B., 15
McBride, T., 84
McCarthy, K. S., 181, 183
McCue Horwitz, S., 93
McGrath, A., 132
Meins, E., 74–75
mentalization, 4, 32, 122, 203
Mesrie, V., 178
Morgan, A. C., xi, 33, 183, 210
mourning, 6, 99, 114, 121, 199,
　207–208
　unresolved, 31
Muran, J. C., 181, 183
Murphy, S. M., 79
Murray, L., 72–73, 78

Nahum, J. P., xi, 183, 210
neonatal intensive care unit (NICU),
　xi–xii, 42, 74, 81, 83, 86–88,

91–93, 95–96, 99, 101, 165, 173–174, 176
Nesic, T., 164
Newman, L., 57
Newton, M., 34–35
Newton, N., 34–35

object, 5, 19, 58, 193 see also: development, transference
  containing, 30
  dead, 63
  external, 32
  good, 12, 14
  -mother, 135
  inanimate, 54
  internal, 10, 19, 47, 134, 171, 175, 212
  maternal, 176
  primary, 50
  -related, 7
  relations, 46
  transitional, 22, 173
  traumatising, 56
O'Brien, K., 84
O'Leary, L., 84
O'Sullivan, M., 195

Pally, R., 21
Panksepp, J., 27
Parent–Infant Relationship Global Assessment Scale (PIRGAS), 145
Parsons, M., 8, 27, 209
Pascalis, O., 17
Paul, C., 4, 25, 105, 127, 146, 200
Perry, B. D., 150, 153
Pollard, R. A., 150, 153
Porges, S. W., 26
Poulsen, S., 166
Prodromidis, M., 51
projection, 6, 19, 45–46, 48, 77, 79, 97, 118, 121, 131, 135, 162–163, 165, 169, 173, 211
  ambivalent, 10
  angry, 200
  collection of, 6
  cycle, 7
  distorting, 6
  intrusive, 6
  negative, 43, 77, 109, 115
  parental, 6, 117–118
  shared, 189
  unhelpful, 6
projective identification, 8, 47–48, 53, 57, 69, 79, 86, 110, 124, 137, 171, 176, 211
psychodynamic see also: intervention
  approach, xii, 8, 190
  exploration, xii
  group therapy, 127
  principles, 17
  thinking, 23
  witnessing, 175

Quinn, P. C., 17

Raphael-Leff, J., 43
Reflective Function Questionnaire, 125
regulation, 65, 76, 189
  dys-, 7, 12, 32, 42, 56, 96, 106, 112, 150, 204
  emotional, 175
  problems, 51
  re-, 116
  self-, 7, 83, 150, 154
Reutter, B., 15
Robinson, J., 72
Robson, K., 84
Romaniuk, H., 72

Sander, L. W., xi, 183, 210
Scafidi, F., 51
Schechter, D., 77, 79
Schiller, M., 120
Selby, J. M., 133
self (passim) see also: conscious, regulation
  agency, 11
  -compassion, 119
  -confidence, 135
  -contained, 163

-critical, 48, 208–209
-definition, 215
-disclosure, 141
-doubts, 140
-esteem, 10, 15, 33–34, 73, 79, 148, 158, 168
-evaluation, 122–123
-fulfilling, 51
-harm, 49
individual, 17
intentional, 3, 7
internal, 17
-introject, 62
loss of, 106
-organised, 12
-protective, 28, 69, 199
-reflective, 208
-report, 145
-representation, 76, 141, 151
-righting, 207
sense of, 3, 5, 15, 27, 106, 128, 134, 155, 157, 165
-stimulation, 37
-understanding, 8
we-, 17
Seligman, S., 152, 187
Selleck, D., 133
Sendak, M., 121
sexual(ity), xii, 26, 32–35, 37, 134
see also: abuse, disorder
base, 33
breast, 70
enjoyable, 33
essential, 33
excitement, 32–34, 36–37
expressions of, 17
feelings, 32
highly, 33
infant, 32, 36–37
intimacy, 85
investment, 37
joyful, 163
parental, 37
relationship, 93
response, 34
swearing, 182

thoughts, 36
Shahar, G., 120
Shai, D., xi, 3–5, 203
Shaw, R. J., 93
Shedler, J., 23
Shiota, M. N., 195
Siegel, C., 150
Siegel, D. J., 29
Slater, A. M., 17
Smith, M., 17
Spitz, R. A., 35
splitting, 57, 87–88, 98, 118, 131, 133, 151, 167–168, 177, 197–198, 202
St. John, N., 93
Stafford, B., xii, 7
Stern, D. N., xi, 3, 20–21, 47, 51, 143, 183, 210, 212
subjectivity, 7, 9, 12, 175, 184, 186, 209–210
inter-, 4–5, 15, 25, 29, 126, 168, 183–184, 186, 208, 213
Sudden Infant Death Syndrome (SIDS), 199

Tang, N. M., 17
Tanzilli, A., 177
Target, M., 33
Tessman, L. H., 197
therapeutic, 22, 42, 47, 57, 88, 108, 128, 143, 157, 178, 180, 186, 197, 212, see also: intervention
action, 18, 20, 111, 183, 190–191, 204, 210, 214
advantages, 77
aims, 22
alliance, xiii, 25, 46, 76, 107, 145, 168, 173, 181–184, 188, 190–191, 208–209
approach, 3
challenge, 169
change, 184, 210
contact, 56, 165
despair, 174
effect, 147, 182–183
encounter, 9, 13, 25–26, 149, 181, 188, 196–197, 213

engagement, 27, 196
experiences, 57, 161
factor, 157, 207–208
force, 133
helpful, 173
hopefulness, 173
identification, 129
impasse, 177
input, 7, 80, 136
  psycho-, 65
mechanism, 5, 23
nature, 195
notions, 167
outcome, 184
partner, 18
pathway, 187
potentially, 209
process, 21, 25, 29, 178, 207, 213
purposes, 139
relationship, 9, 23, 76, 161, 167, 182, 186, 207–208, 213, 215
rupture, 56, 163–164
session, 110
setting, 129
situation, 29, 175
space, 107, 147, 162
way to act, 168
window, 77
Thomson-Salo, F., 4, 13–14, 25, 136, 151, 153, 163
Tomasello, M., 19
transference (*passim*) see also: anxiety, countertransference
  complex, 183
  expectations, 196
  fearful, 202
  interpreting, 8, 17, 117, 130–131, 144, 183
  negative, 8, 10, 47, 49, 56, 64, 108–109, 128–129, 135, 162, 177, 179, 199–200
  object, 196
  observation of, 99
  positive, 22, 48, 129, 135, 197, 208
  view, 139
Trevarthen, C., xi, 14–16, 27

Tronick, E. Z., xi, 51–52, 183, 198, 203, 210
Tuckett, D., 178
Tuckey, M., 74–75
Tzourio-Mazoyer, N., 15

unconscious(ness), 6, 18–19, 56, 61, 69–70, 174, 176, 187, 202–203
  see also: conscious
  attuned, 139
  avoidance, 165
    defences of, 129
  communication, 212
  countertransference, 178
  factors, 8
  feelings, 69, 120
    negative, 176
  hate, 202
  hostility, 198
  interpretation, 189
  level, 62
  links, 211
  meanings, 23, 212
  mirroring, 139, 146
  processes, 9, 161, 195
  recreation, 212
  understanding, 182

Van Horn, P., 157, 194, 208
Vigilante, D., 150, 153
violence, 10, 18, 55–56, 94, 97, 149–151, 153, 155, 156–158, 164, 166, 182
  acute, 150
  attacks, 98
  effects of, 149
  extreme, 97, 149
  family, xii–xiii, 12, 55, 81, 143, 148–150, 153, 158, 166
  father's, 56–57
  history of, 95
  marital, 158
  partner, 41, 55, 69, 95, 98
  past, 96
  potential, 166
  unpredictable, 150

Wainwright, R., 74–75
Wampold, B. E., 183
Warren, B., 73
Weiss, C. H., 79
Westen, D., 178
Wilson, A., 72
Winnicott, D. W., 29, 139, 167
Wolf, K. M., 35
world, 13, 27, 107, 153, 155–156, 174, 190
  adult, 207
  exciting, 57, 180
  imaginative, 143
  infant's, 19
  internal, 9, 22, 99, 126, 128, 164, 212
  outside, 69
  terrified, 149
Wright, K., 183, 190

Zeanah, C., xii, 7, 180
Zeanah, P., xii, 7
Zoccolillo, M., 73
Zuroff, D. C., 209
Zweifach, J., 79

For Product Safety Concerns and Information please contact our EU
representative  GPSR@taylorandfrancis.com
Taylor & Francis Verlag GmbH, Kaufingerstraße 24, 80331 München, Germany

www.ingramcontent.com/pod-product-compliance
Lightning Source LLC
Chambersburg PA
CBHW071825300426
44116CB00009B/1444